T0132653

Automating the Design of Computer Systems

The MICON Project

Automating the Design of Computer Systems

The MICON Project

William P. Birmingham
Department of Electrical Engineering and Computer Science
University of Michigan
Ann Arbor, Michigan

Anurag P. Gupta and Daniel P. Siewiorek
Department of Electrical and Computer Engineering
Carnegie Mellon University
Pittsburgh, Pennsylvania

Jones and Bartlett Publishers

Boston   London

Editorial, Sales, and Customer Service Offices
Jones and Bartlett Publishers
20 Park Plaza
Boston, MA 02116

Library of Congress Cataloging-in-Publication Data

Birmingham, William P.
    Automating the design of computer systems : the MICON Project /
    William P. Birmingham, Anurag P. Gupta, and Daniel P. Siewiorek.
        p.   cm.
    Includes bibliographical references and index.
    ISBN 0-86720-241-6
    1. System design.   2. MICON Project.   3. Computer-aided design.
    I. Gupta, Anurag P.   II. Siewiorek, Daniel P.   III. Title.
    QA76.9.S88B57   1992
    621.39'2'028563--dc20   91-44782
                                                                            CIP

Printed in the United States of America

96   95   94   93   92   10 9 8 7 6 5 4 3 2 1

To our families and parents

Contents

Preface

In the summer of 1982, Dr. Raj Reddy of Carnegie Mellon University's newly formed Robotics Institute posed the following question to us: "Can micro-processor-based, single-board robotic controllers be automatically generated from a high-level specification?" With that question, the MICON project was born. After nearly nine years of research, we can emphatically answer "*yes*". And, while the interest in robotics has waned some, a stronger, and perhaps more profound, boom in workstations and personal computers (PCs) has provided us with additional motivation. Thus, MICON today can do more than just single-board controllers, it can design most of the digital machinary needed for workstations and PCs.

We intend this book to appeal to a broad range of interests, including computer-aided design, artificial intelligence (AI) and concurrent engineering. Those in the fields of electronic computer-aided design (ECAD) and electronic computer-aided engineering (ECAE) will find a unique approach to a challenging ECAE problem. The research described in this book, however, will appeal to those studying design and automated knowledge acquisition in the AI community. MICON is, essentially, a configuration system, with much in common with such systems built for other engineering design disciplines, such as mechanical and civil engineering, with some interesting differences, of course. Because MICON is knowledge-based, it must be programmed with hardware design expertise. Thus, we have developed a knowledge-acquisition tool to support this exercise. Finally, those interested in concurrent engineering will find interest in the multiple expert approach to design used by MICON, where a synthesis expert is advised by a design-for-reliability expert on how to improve a design's reliability. We also overview an interface to a mechanical rapid prototyping system, allowing us to design enclosures for the electronics simultaneously with designing them.

This book is not a text, but we have provided background material for topics with which one of our groups of readers may not be familiar. We have also attempted to provide a broad list of references for background material so that following up on a topic should be easy.

Our objective in writing this book is to explain MICON's operation and to show experimental and anecdotal evidence that it works. Since MICON performs a number of functions, a natural organization for the book was provided. Thus, it is organized into five parts.

Part I introduces the system and provides motivation for our view of design and for the particular problem on which we have chosen to work.

Part II describes the philosophy and implementation of MICON's synthesis engine, M1. We conceptualize design as two related search processes, where function and structure are refined from abstract descriptions into real artifacts. From this conceptual view, an algorithm, called the design cycle, is developed. The design cycle is the heart of the MICON system, and is, we believe, applicable to various engineering design problems.

In Part III, the knowledge-acquisition tool, CGEN, is detailed. This tool allows hardware designers to build large, working knowledge bases without having to write code or learn about knowledge-based systems.

The experiments and anecdotal evidence are given in Part IV.

The book concludes with Part V, where we describe efforts in concurrent engineering and domain-independent design. ASSURE, the design-for-reliability tool, is introduced. We also describe how MICON was modified to design mechanical and software systems.

WPB, APG, & DPS
Ann Arbor & Pittsburgh

Acknowledgements

Over the course of the MICON project, a number of students and researchers have lent us their considerable talents and have helped to create a rich research environment. Without these people, we would not have been able to build MICON. We wish to thank the following people for their contributions:

Dario Giuse and Veerendra Rao built the first MICON Z80 board and provided many helpful ideas to the first two versions of the synthesis tool.

Robert Tremain and Nikhil Balram were instrumental to the development of the second version of the synthesis tool (M0.5).

Ajay Daga developed the FAILURE module for M1, adding redesign ability to MICON.

Audrey Brennan developed the design-for-dependability advisor and added design-for-dependability knowledge to the synthesis tool.

Patrick Edmond developed a second version of the design-for-dependability advisor, and added design knowledge for the Motorola 68010 microprocessor family.

Raj Merchia developed the database, the communication software, and database editing tools.

Joe Najjar added knowledge for the Motorola 68008-based design and developed a program that aids the knowledge-acquisition tool.

Ajai Kapoor added knowledge for an Intel 80386-based design and extended the synthesis and knowledge-acquisition tools to the problem of automatically sequencing tools in a design environment.

Nino Vidovic worked on developing a design environment for the MICON tools.

Drew Anderson, Bob Barker, and Mark Holland (our hardware gurus) built the 68008-based board, added the design knowledge for the 80386-based workstation, and then built it, and provided many helpful suggestions during the development of M1.

Forrest Cavalier and Glenn Schuster developed monitor software for debugging the MICON-generated boards.

Dan Haworth added knowledge for the 80386SX and 8086 processor families and is developing a design-for-testability advisor.

Viju Menon refined the FAILURE module.

Andrea Dusseau, Larry Bach, Antonio Martinez-Eskenasy, and Andy Rosenbaum developed support software and performed data entry.

We would like to thank Jim Rehg and Sarosh Talukdar for their assistance with the mechanical engineering domain.

We would also like to thank Michael Kaelbling from Siemens for reviewing an earlier draft of the book and Nancy Leach for help with some of the drawings.

We gratefully acknowledge funding by the Engineering Design Research Center (a National Science Foundation funded research center), by the NSF grant to the DEMETER project and to contract MIPS 9057981, by the Semiconductor Research Corporation, by the Boeing RAMCAD project, by the Office of Naval Research, by Intel Corporation, and by Siemens Corporation.

Part I

The Process of Design

1

Introduction

Design is an activity that pervades the engineering process. Broadly speaking, the objective of the design task is to transform a specification of a process or artifact into a more detailed description that can either be executed or manufactured, respectively. Design, in some form, is at the root of all industrial enterprises. Thus, design represents a significant intellectual and economic activity.

Design is a major part of all engineering disciplines. Our research concerns one of these disciplines – computer engineering. The lessons learned in our research, however, can be transferred to companion areas. Indeed, there is a growing body of research indicating that there appear to be common design practices that transcend a single engineering design discipline.

1.1 Motivation for the Automation of Computer Design

Computer design presents many interesting challenges. Market forces demand performance increases and price decreases. At the same time, functionality must also improve in order to meet increasing customer expectations about user-friendliness, flexibility, and a host of other concerns. Thus, computer systems are becoming more sophisticated with time. A combination of the increasing complexity, the demand for reduced price, and the decreasing product lifetime provides the motivation for the automation of computer design. Each of these

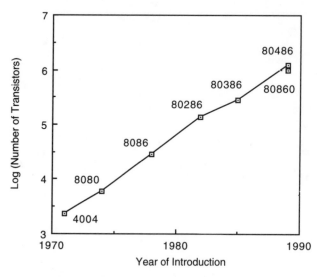

Figure 1.1. Complexity of microprocessors over the years.

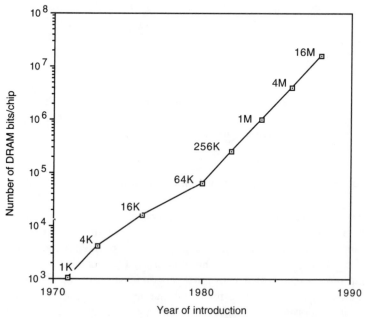

Figure 1.2. Complexity of dynamic memory chips over the years.

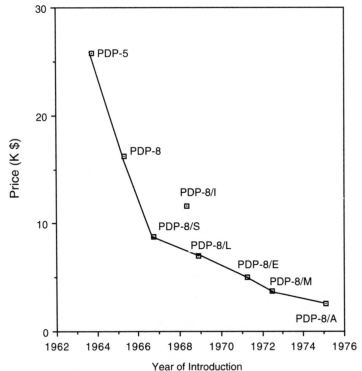

Figure 1.3. Price of DEC's 12-bit computers versus time.

issues is detailed below.

Increasing complexity: Microprocessors are a good indicator of what is to come from the computer industry. Figure 1.1 plots the complexity of Intel microprocessors (measured by number of transistors) as a function of time. Figure 1.2 plots the complexity of dynamic memory chips (measured by number of bits) as a function of time. The opinion of both industry and academia is for the trends and rates of growth indicated in the figures to continue throughout the decade and well into the next century.

Reduced price: While increasing complexity would usually result in an increased design time and hence an increased price, this contradicts[1] the continuing market demand for cheaper machines. Several computer manufacturers have been able to reduce their prices for machines of the same complexity. Figure 1.3 shows the reduction in price of DEC's 12-bit computers as a function of

---

[1] Assuming that manufacturing, distribution, and sales costs do not drop sufficiently to offset the design cost increases, which is reasonable.

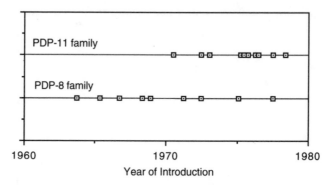

Figure 1.4. Introduction of the DEC models for PDP-8 and PDP-11 over the years.

time [6]. To meet customer expectations, a computer manufacturer must make technological innovations to support the trend of price reduction.

Decreasing product lifetime: While computer complexity and sophistication continue to increase, product lifetimes shrink. Figure 1.4 shows the date of introduction of several unique DEC models in the same family. The reduction in the time duration between the introduction of the two models substantiates the claim of reduced product lifetime[2]. In the early days of the industry, computers had a useful sales life of at least five years. In the early 1990's market, a computer's sales life is as little as 1.5 years; this time is expected to shrink to as little as six months by the middle of the decade. The ability of a computer manufacturer to reduce design time is essential to staying in business.

The combination of circumstances described here is beneficial to the computer consumer – almost continuously improving machines are available at lower prices – but can cause problems for computer manufacturers. Increased design costs and shorter design times combined with the consumer expectation of reduced product prices can quickly erode profit margins, eventually causing a manufacturer to go bankrupt.

One solution to these problems is to increase designer productivity. This reduces both design cost and time, thereby allowing the product price to drop. The computer industry has always recognized the importance of increased productivity, and has embraced the automation of various design tasks. In addition to automation, new designs are usually upgrades of older designs, not completely new; design time is reduced by reusing portions of older designs. Figure 1.5 shows the reduction in design time per unit complexity for four commercial computer systems (measured as man-months per thousand gates for processing

---

[2]Product lifetime depends on several factors, such as date of introduction, reason and date of discontinuance, market demands, etc., which are detailed in [6]. For our purpose of indicating the pressure on the engineering design team, the year of introduction of new models is sufficient.

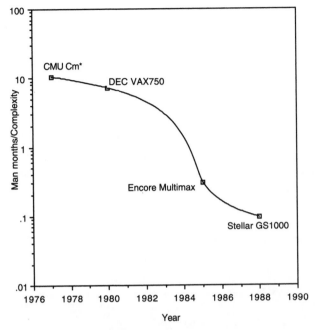

Figure 1.5. Reduction in design time per unit gate.

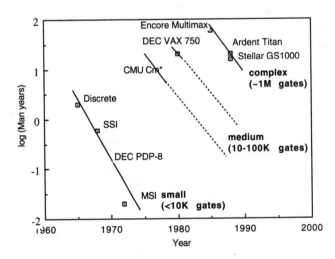

Figure 1.6. The time taken to design machines in three different complexity classes.

engine design while taking replication into account). Thus, automation together with evolving semiconductor technology and design reuse enables the computer industry to:

- increase complexity (i.e., functionality or performance) for the same cost, or
- reduce cost (i.e., design effort) for the same complexity.

Figure 1.6 shows both these trends in the typical computer design space. The time necessary to design reduces within the same complexity class, and machines in higher complexity classes can be designed for the same effort.

Before providing an introduction to the role of design tools in the industry, it is necessary to introduce a simple model of the design and manufacture of computers.

1.2   Subtasks in Computer Design

Computer design involves the development of both the hardware and software for the machine. In this book we are concerned with the design of computer hardware only. Figure 1.7 is an overview of the computer hardware development process[3] for any implementation technology, e.g., printed circuit board (PCB) or integrated circuit (IC). Each of the large blocks represents a major task; within each block are corresponding sub-tasks.

The development process typically begins with a description of the new machine [113], usually resulting from a marketing survey. This initial description may lack detail and may change as the development progresses. The hardware design task transforms this description into a detailed list of the components and their interconnections and various other pieces of information needed to build the design. The result of the hardware design process is generally a set of schematic drawings of the computer.

The physical design process then adds geometric information to the hardware design. This information constitutes the physical design: the precise location of each component, piece of conducting material, hole, or layer of semiconducting material (if an IC is being produced).

Once the physical design is complete, the manufacturing instructions are generated to create the physical artifact. For PCBs, an epoxy board is prepared using a photolithographic process which places conducting material in the proper places and drills holes to accept components. This board is then "stuffed" with components, which are soldered in place. For large computers a set of PCBs are placed in a cabinet and interconnected via a backplane. ICs also go through

---

[3]Note that the figure shows a simple sequential flow of information between these tasks; in the real world there is also feedback from downstream stages and iterations in the design process.

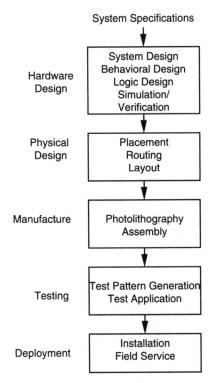

Figure 1.7. The computer hardware development process.

a photolithographic process, albeit more complex. IC assembly corresponds to bonding the silicon chip into a package.

Once a board or IC is assembled, it is tested. The purpose of testing is to determine if the artifact meets all its specifications. Testing is generally performed by applying patterns of bits, called test vectors, to the artifact and observing its behavior and performance. If both performance and behavior match the specifications, the artifact is accepted. If rejected, the artifact is either discarded (the case for ICs) or is sent back to manufacturing for re-working. Test patterns may have been generated anytime after the hardware was designed; in fact, in some cases, the hardware design task uses specific design-for-testability techniques to make the test pattern generation task easier.

All accepted designs are finally deployed, or shipped, to the customer. If an installed computer should experience trouble, field service is called for repairs. In some cases, the hardware design task uses specific design-for-dependability techniques to reduce the probability of failure at this stage.

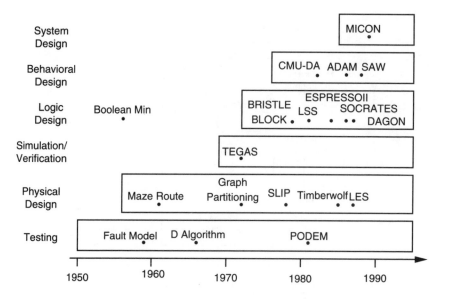

Figure 1.8. History of automation in the computer design domain.

1.3   History of the Automation of Computer Design

As mentioned earlier, automation of various steps in the design process has been central to keeping the computer industry competitive. Figure 1.8 offers an overview of when the automation of various tasks began. Note that automation typically started at the bottom of the design process and worked its way to the top. Among the earliest tasks to be automated were testing and physical design, although they are still the subject of extensive research efforts. These tasks were particularly attractive to automate because they were both routine and required considerable manpower. In addition, powerful computer-based techniques were developed that were very successful, such as the D-Algorithm [105] and later PODEM [54] for testing, the maze router [78] for routing, and graph partitioning [107] for placement. Simulation and verification tools were also early candidates for automation as successful tools, such as TEGAS [125], showed how simulation-based design methods, as opposed to prototyping, could dramatically reduce design time [113].

Research directions in physical design and testing changed as integrated circuits became popular; emphasis shifted from PCBs to ICs. New generations of tools were developed to aid with laying out ICs – the process of placing semiconducting material to form active devices such as transistors. These tools

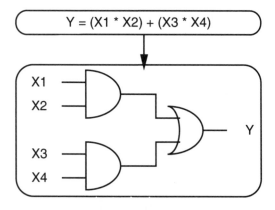

Figure 1.9. Logic design example.

include compaction tools that shrink the size of layouts (e.g., [24, 36]), a variety of placement and routing packages (e.g., [80, 103, 106, 108]), and silicon compilers that compile logic or circuit descriptions into silicon (e.g., [68, 118]).

One of the first hardware design subtasks to be automated was logic design. Logic design is the process of implementing Boolean expressions and finite state machines as circuits of gates and memory devices. Figure 1.9 illustrates a simple example of mapping a Boolean expression into logic gates. Logic design is well-suited for automation because of its strong theoretical basis, Boolean logic. Pioneering work in the field commenced over 35 years ago [38, 30, 91]. In recent years, logic synthesis has experienced a rebirth due to the popularity of ICs and the introduction of techniques, including AI-based approaches, that have significantly improved the quality of designs (e.g., [129, 18, 56, 72, 10]).

In the late 1970s, investigations into automatically synthesizing the register transfer level structure began. In this phase of the hardware design process, termed behavioral synthesis, an algorithmic description of a portion of a computer, such as the central processing unit (CPU), is transformed into a set of register-transfer (RT) elements, which, in turn, are bound either to logic gates or to transistor circuits. Register-transfer level elements include such things as arithmetic-logic units (ALUs), multiplexers (MUX), and registers. An example of mapping a simple algorithm into RT elements is given in Figure 1.10. The result of this design phase is typically a component, be it an IC or PCB, that implements the algorithm. The early work in behavioral synthesis [4, 116, 35] developed into a very active research community (e.g., [130, 90, 126, 127, 102, 101, 50]). Behavioral synthesis is also termed high-level synthesis. Research in this area has benefited from the use of AI techniques for

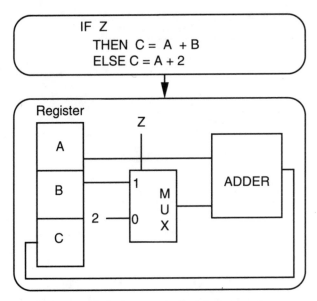

Figure 1.10. Register transfer level design example.

both problem representation and search control (e.g., [75, 20, 21]).

The design task most recently automated, and the subject of this book, is system-level synthesis. The objective of system-level synthesis is to create a complete and operational computer system capable of performing general-purpose or special-application computing. This is done by integrating sets of components into a larger system. The emphasis, therefore, of system-level synthesis is different than that of previous synthesis research efforts. Since system-level synthesis is a relatively new term, some explanation is warranted.

1.4 System-Level Synthesis

The system-level synthesis task can be illustrated through two models, the DEMETER model [113] and the Y-chart [51, 133]. Figure 1.11 shows the DEMETER model of digital system design.

- The first and highest level of design is the *task description*. This level encompasses all the preliminary study phases that try to position the future product in the market and to establish a suitable set of design goals. The general structure of the future product is established in this phase as are broad notions about the required performance, cost, design resources, etc.

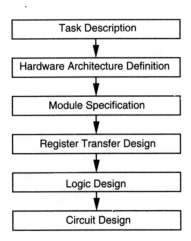

Figure 1.11. DEMETER model of subtasks in digital system design.

- The *architecture definition* phase refines the task description to produce a precise specification of the future system, including the decomposition of functionality into hardware and software.

- The *module specification* phase is split between the hardware and software development processes. This phase completely specifies the behavior (function) of and the structural interfaces between all the building blocks in the system being designed.

- In the *register transfer design* phase, the behavior of the modules is expressed as registers whose value can be affected by a specific set of instructions. This behavior is refined into a structure of data paths, control sequences, and timing diagrams.

- *Logic design* implements the functional blocks in the data paths and the controller state machine in terms of logic expressions and logic gates.

- *Circuit design* realizes logic gates as a network of transistors, resistors, and capacitors.

The system-level synthesis task includes the Hardware Architecture Definition and Module Specification tasks. If the building blocks at the Module Specification phase correspond to existing components, this is analogous to the process of designing a hardware structure and then choosing components to implement that structure.

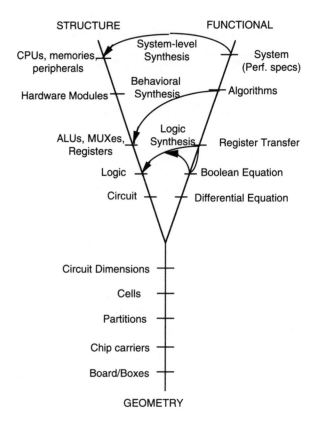

Figure 1.12. Synthesis tasks on the Y-chart.

The Y-chart combines levels of abstraction with views of a design. The Y-chart was originally intended to demonstrate the behavior of very large scale integration (VLSI) component design tools but can be extended to illustrate the system level task as shown in Figure 1.12. The markings on the axes of the chart indicate levels of abstraction in digital design. The axes represent three perspectives of the design process: (1) *function*, or behavior, is the input/output response of the system; (2) *structure*, is the interconnection of components to realize the required function; and, (3) *geometry*, is the spatial relationship between the components themselves and the environment. The highest level on the function axis is the system level, which describes the behavior of the system as a set of performance specifications, or gross operational characteristics; it is concerned with pieces of hardware that manipulate data and store results, without being concerned with the algorithms describing the details of how this occurs [133]. In Figure 1.12, system-level synthesis is shown as mapping the system level on the function axis to CPUs, memories, and other peripherals on the structure axis. The mapping for behavioral and logic synthesis is also shown to highlight the differences.

System-level synthesis differs from lower-level synthesis tasks in that it is more loosely defined. There is no equivalent of a hardware description language nor a set of Boolean equations to define clearly the function for the artifact being designed. For example, specifications for the Intel System 310, Model 35, are shown in Figure 1.13. This specification does not mention either the complete structure of the components nor the algorithm to execute. Presently, there is no complete and well-defined theory for relating behavior and structure at the system level, so the approaches used in logic and behavioral design cannot be directly extended to system-level design. Since approaches used at lower levels are inapplicable, a novel knowledge-based approach to design has been developed and is used in the MICON system. Not much research has been devoted to automated system-level design aids. However, it is one of the most significant phases during the design process, since decisions made at this level have a large impact on the lower levels of the designs and in some cases on the feasibility of the complete design. The MICON project has concentrated on providing tools for system-level synthesis, an overview of which is given in the next chapter.

Functionality Specifications:

CPU	8086, 8 MHz
Numeric Coprocessor	8087, 8 MHz
Memory	640 KB, 0 wait state dual ported on-board RAM
I/O	One RS-232 serial communications port
	One Centronics parallel port
Mass Storage	320 KB Flexible disk drive
	20 MB Winchester drive
DC Power Output	220 watts maximum (Expansion)
	+5V @ 30A (17A)
	+12V @ 4.7A (1.1A)
	-12V @ 4.7A (4.5A)
MULTIBUS Expansion Slots	5 @ 0.625 inches

Environmental Specifications:

Operating	10°C to 35°C
	26°C maximum Wet Bulb temperature
	20% to 80% Relative Humidity, non-condensing
Altitude	Sea Level to 2400 meters
Shock	30 G Non-operating
Vibration	5 Hz to 1 kHz Random
	0.001 G2/Hz (1G rms) Operating

Regulatory Agency Specifications:

Meets	UL 114-Safety
	CSA 22.2 Safety
	Docket 20780 Class A - RFI/EMI
Designed to meet	IEC 435-Safety
	VDE 0871 Class A - RFI/EMI

Dimensions:

Height	165 mm
Width	432 mm
Depth	508 mm
Weight	25 kg/51 lb

Figure 1.13. Product specifications for the Intel System 310, Model 35.

2

The MICON System

The MICON project has developed a system that automates the synthesis of computer systems using microprocessor family components. This chapter gives an overview of all the tools in the MICON systems, describes the type of designs produced using the system, discusses relationships with other knowledge-based design tools, and provides a brief history of the project.

2.1 Overview

The MICON system is shown in Figure 2.1. The goals of the MICON system are to generate error-free designs and to reduce the product design time typically from months to hours. These goals are achieved through the capture and dissemination of design expertise through a set of tools that support the design of digital electronic computer systems.

Each of the constituent MICON tools is described below.

M1 [58, 60] (MICON Synthesizer Version 1) is the synthesis module of the MICON system. Input to M1 is a set of high-level specifications that describe the functionality required of the computer. For example, a user may specify the type and clock-speed of the microprocessor, amount and type of memory, and the number and type of input/output devices required.

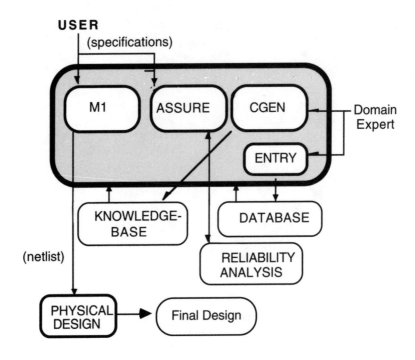

Figure 2.1. The MICON system.

An additional set of parameters describing ceilings on resources (e.g., board size, cost) are also input to the program. An example input for an Intel 8086-based design is shown in Figure 2.2. M1 uses its knowledge of components and microprocessor system structures to develop a design that satisfies the requirements given to the system. Once the design is complete, M1 produces netlists representing the design in a variety of formats. An M1-generated netlist, converted by hand into a schematic, realizing the specifications given in Figure 2.2, is shown in Figure 2.3.

M1 is implemented as an expert system written in OPS83 [67]. The knowledge base contains information about the components M1 can design with, microprocessor-based system design techniques, and design-for-reliability techniques. In order for the MICON system to produce competitive designs, the knowledge base must be updated with new components and design techniques as they are developed. M1 is described in detail in Part II of this book.

Query	Inputs	Query	Inputs
System Constraints		PIO	
Board area <sq. in.>	100	Number of PIO units	1
Amount of board cost <dollars>	250	PIO chip	?
Amount of power <mW>	1000	PIO generate interrupts	Y
System modules		Interrupt priority level	1
Is a CO_PROCESSOR needed	N	PIO port direction	IN/OUT
Is PIO needed	Y	PIO connector type	MALE
Is SIO needed	Y	PIO Connector size	9
Is TIMER needed	N	PIO port drive	NONE
Is DRAM needed	N	SIO	
Is SRAM needed	Y	Number of SIO units	1
Is ROM needed	Y	External interface	RS-232
Processor		Baud rate <Hz>	9600
Processor name	8086	SIO generate interrupts	Y
Minimum clock speed <MHz>	1	Interrupt priority level	2
ROM		External port size	3
ROM BYTES needed	2K	Type of port	DTE
Name of ROM chip	?	Communication mode	SYNC
SRAM		Connector polarity	MALE
SRAM BYTES needed	512K	Connector size	25
Name of SRAM chip	?		

Figure 2.2. Example inputs for an Intel 8086-based computer.

CGEN [8, 14] (Code GENerator) is the knowledge acquisition tool for the M1 module. Typically, a knowledge base can only be updated by those intimately familiar with the program, making the acquisition of new knowledge difficult. CGEN allows a hardware designer not familiar with M1's implementation details to add expertise to the knowledge base. Inputs to CGEN consist of schematic drawings and simple equations. An example of these is shown in Figure 2.4. CGEN has facilitated the growth of M1's knowledge base to over 3,500 rules, representing about 15 man-years of digital design experience. CGEN is described in detail in Part III of this book.

ASSURE [19, 37] (Automated SynthesiS for REliability) analyzes designs produced by M1 and suggests modifications for improved reliability. M1 carries out the modifications and passes the results back to ASSURE for further analysis. Thus, ASSURE acts like a *design advisor* for the dependability domain and interacts with M1 using a well-defined advisor-designer paradigm. ASSURE's input from the user consists of reliability

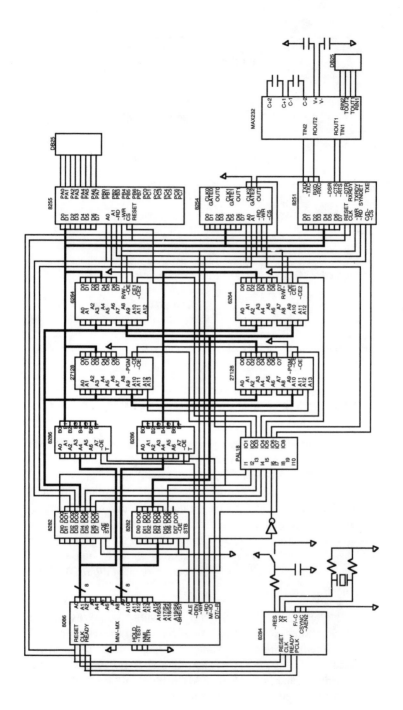

Figure 2.3. An M1 generated 8086-based design (reproduced with permission from [64]).

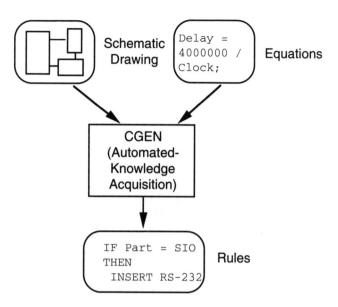

Figure 2.4. Example inputs to CGEN.

criteria, such as mean time to failure (MTTF). ASSURE uses an external reliability analysis tool to analyze the quality of the evolving design. Designs failing to meet the user specified criteria are modified by a variety of techniques, ranging from simple integrated circuit package changes to the addition of entire structures (e.g., error correcting codes on memory). ASSURE merely suggests the modifications to M1, which is responsible for implementing them – a strict separation of tasks and associated design knowledge is maintained. ASSURE is described in detail in Part V of this book.

Physical design and manufacture are performed by a suite of commercial tools. There are three steps to physical design:

1. placement and routing of the netlist for a board,

2. board fabrication using either wire wrap or printed circuit board (PCB) technologies, and

3. board population and testing.

Since the physical design process is not a research area explored by MI-CON, it is not discussed any further in this book.

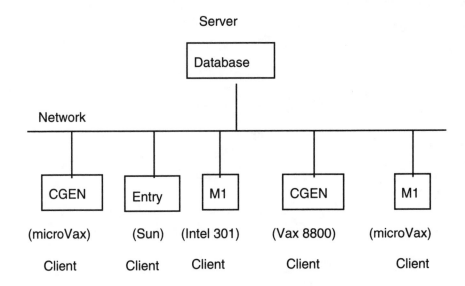

Figure 2.5. Multiple clients being supported simultaneously by the database server.

Database (DB) is the central repository for part information used by all modules
in the system and is built on a commercially available relational database
that supports the Standard Query Language (SQL). Communication between the DB and other modules is managed by a server that recognizes
high-level commands, hiding the tables and relations of the DB from the
client programs. The DB is described in more detail in Section 5.3 of this
book.

MICON is a tightly integrated environment, wherein all tools communicate via
UNIX[1] interprocess communication (IPC) links to the database. The database
uses a server to establish communication links with each tool or client. This
scheme allows the database to run as a separate process. In addition to providing
a great deal of flexibility, such as allowing a large number of clients to be served
simultaneously, this scheme allows the dedication of a single workstation on
the network as the database node. This centralizes the database management
functions and eliminates many data consistency problems. Figure 2.5 depicts
the database server communicating with a set of clients running on separate
workstations across the network.

Note that a distinction is made between a *MICON system user* and a *trainer*
or *domain,* or *hardware, expert.* The domain expert teaches M1 through CGEN

---

[1] UNIX is a trademark of AT&T Bell Labs.

how to design and uses the data entry tool, ENTRY, to add new part models to the data base. The user's goal is to create designs with M1, exploiting the work of the domain expert. If the domain expert imparts sufficient knowledge to M1, the user can be a novice hardware designer. Any M1 user can exploit the design knowledge added to M1 by multiple domain experts. Thus, the system provides a design expertise dissemination capability. Since M1 can produce a design in a short period of time, the system also provides a rapid prototyping capability.

2.2 Design Domain

MICON assists in the design of microprocessor-based computer systems. These systems range in functionality from computer workstations to application-specific computers such as embedded controllers. The computers designed by MICON consist of any of the following subsystems:

Processor: Designs utilize a microprocessor as the central processing unit (CPU).

Memory: Designs contain read-only memory (ROM) and either static or dynamic memory (SRAM or DRAM). In addition, MICON supports cache memories.

Peripheral: All input/output (IO) is performed by dedicated parts, such as serial IO (SIO) and parallel IO (PIO) devices. IO devices may utilize standard interfaces, such as RS-232-C for SIO.

Bus interface: A selection of standard bus interfaces is supported.

Support circuitry: A set of circuitry provides support functions that includes address decoders, wait state generators, oscillators, and bus drivers. Included in support circuitry are specialized structures for improving system reliability, such as Hamming encoders/decoders.

Through the design of these subsystems, a variety of computers can be built with varying degrees of sophistication. M1 has been used to generate hundreds of designs based on five microprocessor families. Two of these designs, a simple 68008-based computer and a sophisticated 80386-based workstation, have been fabricated; Chapter 13 provides more details.

MICON can synthesize individual modules in addition to complete systems. For example, if a designer needs to generate a Multibus II compatible memory card, then a design with only memory and a Multibus II adapter is created. A schematic of this design, which MICON can accept as input, is shown in Figure 2.6. By repeating this process for each board, a designer can generate a set of boards to be used in a larger system, where all the boards are interconnected

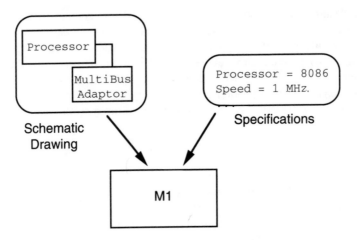

Figure 2.6. Schematic input to MICON for Memory-Multibus design.

via a backplane. As another example of MICON's use, a designer can create a module library consisting of a mother board and an array of I/O and memory boards. From this library a wide variety of products can be easily assembled.

The synthesis techniques used by MICON are not limited to designing computers. MICON can be generalized as a *synthesis engine* that is applicable to engineering design problems in a variety of different domains. Chapter 15 presents the results of applying MICON to mechanical and software engineering problems.

2.3   Related Knowledge-Based Design Tools

M1 is a knowledge-based design tool that produces a design from a library of components, a task often called *configuration*. As discussed later in Section 3.1, with even a small number of components in the library a large number of designs can be enumerated. In fact, the number is large enough that it precludes a *selection* approach, i.e., choosing a solution from an enumerated set of possible designs, suggesting that construction is a more reasonable approach to the design problem [86, 95]. The constructive approach builds a design by selecting parts from a library that meet both specifications given by the user and a set of constraints imposed by the selection of other parts in the design. For example, part *A*, selected from a library containing parts *(A B C D)*, may introduce a set of constraints that eliminate parts *(C D)* from further consideration in the design process.

Configuration problems are common to many areas. Systems have been reported in such areas as elevator design [86], computer arrangement [88], mechanical component design [22], and photocopier components [94]. M1 has much in common with these systems, but is unique in several aspects. While these differences are discussed in detail throughout the book, we summarize them here.

Dynamic subproblem ordering: Because the interaction between various subtasks are not known before runtime, M1 dynamically schedules its tasks. This scheduling is based on information dependencies.

Multiple function units per component: The parts used can provide multiple functions simultaneously. For example, some peripheral chips contain IO and memory. Most other systems have assumed only a single function per part.

Part and structure selection: M1 must both choose components and create complex structures that depend upon the components chosen, i.e., the relationships between components are not fixed. This significantly impacts M1's architecture.

Integrated knowledge acquisition: Since design requires a great deal of knowledge, MICON recognized the need for an integrated knowledge acquisition tool, CGEN (as did [85] for their system). In the rapidly evolving computer design domain, CGEN is necessary to allow M1 to continue to produce state-of-the-art designs. In addition, CGEN allows M1 to be customized for each installed site, which is important for maintaining proprietary design knowledge.

As alluded to earlier in this section, constraints play a large role in configuration design tasks. Some of these tasks, although not all, can be formulated as constraint satisfaction problems (CSP), and can be solved using CSP solution techniques [32]. The CSP captures the constraint relationships between various components and configurations of components. These relationships are then exploited to choose new components that are consistent, thereby producing valid designs. However, M1's task cannot be easily formulated as a CSP, and hence it does not use these techniques.

2.4 Project History

The MICON project began in 1983; Figure 2.7 shows the evolution of the project over the past seven years. MICON began with M0 (a name bestowed

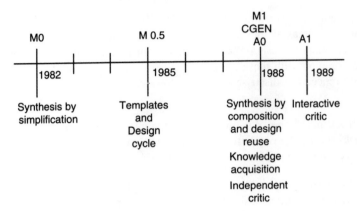

Figure 2.7. History of the MICON project.

by historical perspective) [7, 12], a knowledge-based system that assessed the feasibility of automated single board computer synthesis based on commercially available microprocessors. M0 embodied, in a less sophisticated form, many of the concepts used in the current system, M1. Several microprocessor families were programmed into the system, a number of designs were produced, and a Zilog Z80-based design, shown in Figure 2.8, was built. M0 initiated the idea of using templates, a representation for structure similar to a schematic, for synthesis. M0 had general purpose templates that represented the entire design. These templates were customized (simplified) for each design. M0, however, had a number of drawbacks which limited its general applicability. In particular, it lacked a general design model and required the design to be decomposed into a *fixed* sequence of subtasks.

These drawbacks led to the development of M0.5 [3, 13]. While M0.5 was not fully implemented, the ideas acquired from it were essential to the development of M1. In particular, M0.5 introduced component abstraction which enables M1 to have much more freedom in choosing components, thereby improving the quality of designs. In addition, M0.5 introduced the idea of templates as representing individual subsystems, not entire systems. However, M0.5 added only two additional levels of component abstraction. The design representation was too specific – there were a fixed number of abstraction levels, a fixed set of specifications for each subsystem, a fixed set of attributes for parts. A general representation for the design and the design process was lacking. This made the growth of the knowledge base difficult and automated knowledge acquisition impossible.

These drawbacks led to the development of M1 [58, 60]. M1 greatly refined the concepts of component abstraction and templates. M1 also introduced a well-

Figure 2.8. M0-synthesized Z80-based single board computer.

defined problem-solving method for computer design. M1 identified the need for knowledge acquisition, and, thus, CGEN was developed. The combination of M1 and CGEN, along with the other tools, yielded a cogent system that provides complete, integrated support for the computer system designer. At the end of the first experimental stage, this system synthesized a 68008-based single board computer shown in Figure 2.9. Subsequently, the system has been used to synthesize a high-performance 80386-based workstation with an AT bus interface (see Figure 2.10).

As reliability considerations became more important in the computer industry and to the design community at large, ASSURE was integrated into MICON. ASSURE version 0 (A0) [19] introduced the idea of an independent advisor that observed the progress of a design and made modifications to improve its reliability. ASSURE version 1 (A1) [37] formalized the concepts introduced by A0, developed a clean advisor-designer paradigm for the A1-M1 interface, and identified the kinds of knowledge used in design for dependability.

Research is continuing on MICON. A design for testability advisor, similar to ASSURE, is being developed [65]. A redesign mechanism has been developed and is being extended [28, 11]. Currently, the domain expert has to add sufficient design knowledge to ensure that M1-generated designs are correct and do not violate any timing constraints. A tool that automatically ensures timing correctness is also being developed [59].

Figure 2.9. M1-synthesized 68008-based single board computer.

Figure 2.10. M1-synthesized 80386-based AT workstation.

Part II

Automated System-Level Synthesis

3

An Introduction to Synthesis

Design synthesis is the process of producing an artifact that satisfies some high level behavioral and structural specifications. We address a particular instance of this process where an artifact is formed by integrating several primitive components. Specifically, in our domain, design synthesis produces a computer system by selecting and interconnecting parts from a library. In this chapter, we describe the problem of synthesizing computer systems, present an overview of a model for the synthesis process, and illustrate the process in our model using an example.

3.1   The Design Synthesis Problem

The synthesis problem is complex for the computer system design domain due to several reasons:

- **The design space (the set of possible designs) is very large.** For example, consider the simplified case where there are only five different processor chips, five SRAM chips, five ROM chips, and five SIO chips. If the design is to have one of each kind of chip, there is a total of $5^4 = 625$ possible combinations from which one is to be selected. Now consider the fact that each of the parts has on an average 20 pins, giving (20 x 5

31

x 4) = 400 pins in all. The design space includes all possible ways of interconnecting these pins. Since p pins can be interconnected in $O(p!)$ ways, this results in a combinatorial explosion of design possibilities. A similar analysis for the general configuration task can be found in [95]. The large number of possibilities rules out any brute-force exploration approach, such as breadth-first search, depth-first search, and generate and test [5].

- **There is interaction between steps in the design process.** For example, the processor design imposes timing constraints on memory design, and both, in turn, impose timing constraints on the design of the address-decoder. Additionally, these interactions cannot be predicted before the design begins, since they may change when new parts or design styles become available. For example, when a Direct Memory Access (DMA) controller is added to the IO subsystem in the design, it would impose additional timing constraints on the design of the memory.

- **There is no good evaluator for partially designed artifacts.** One cannot tell from a fragment of a design whether that fragment is part of a satisfactory complete solution. For example, a memory design that meets zero wait-state timing constraints may not be part of the final solution, which would use slower and cheaper memory chips in a one wait-state configuration so that peripherals can be accommodated within the budgeted cost.

- **A formalized theory of specifying and designing complete computer systems does not exist.** There is no theory or formal language for describing specifications and artifacts at the system level. Using a lower-level description (e.g., Boolean algebra, hardware description languages) would result in an explosion of detail. For example, a microprocessor would require several pages of hardware description language code. Furthermore, due to the large amount of detail, mapping from specifications to a realizable artifact using the lower level description would be unmanageably complex, if at all possible.

- **Evolving IC fabrication technology results in improved components and new design styles.** To be effective, the solution approach has to incorporate new components and design styles easily.

3.2   The Design Model

In order to build a tool that automates the synthesis process, we impose an organization and formalization on the process. The design model provides this formalism and gives the basis of the architecture of the synthesis tool M1. A brief overview of the design model is given in this section before describing the M1 architecture in detail in the next chapter. This design model has evolved from the DEMETER Design Model [113]; relationships between these models are discussed in Appendix A.

Designing computer systems requires selecting and interconnecting a suitable set of components from a library of existing components. This select-and-integrate process successively refines each portion of the design to create a design that satisfies the input specifications. In our model this process is viewed as two distinct, but closely related, searches:

- *Search for function (SFF):* selecting components that satisfy the specifications for the design.

- *Search for structure (SFS):* integrating the selected components into the design.

The decomposition into two subtasks reduces the complexity of each subtask. It is also appropriate as issues involved in both searches are significantly different, as will be shown later. The model also provides a mechanism for handling interactions between portions of the design and deciding which portion is to be designed next.

3.2.1   Search for Function: Functional Hierarchy

A brute-force search for function is not suitable as it would take an unreasonable amount of time. Two techniques are employed to reduce the size of the design space: abstraction and problem decomposition. Abstraction hides details, thereby reducing complexity. Problem decomposition, which naturally follows abstraction in our domain, provides further reduction in information by partitioning and providing a logical organization for the design problem. Since the function of the part is the criterion used for abstraction and problem decomposition, the resulting hierarchy is termed the *functional hierarchy*.

The functional hierarchy is a tree-like[1] structure of nodes, where each node represents a part. The leaf nodes correspond to available off-the-shelf components, and are termed *physical parts*. All other nodes correspond to a functionality and are formed by abstracting the nodes beneath them in the hierarchy,

---

[1] Actually, it is a directed acyclic graph, as explained in the next chapter.

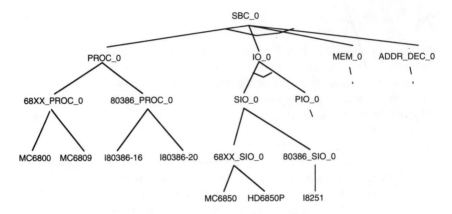

Figure 3.1. Functional hierarchy in single board computer design domain.

and so are termed *abstract parts*. The search for function subtask traverses the hierarchy. Nodes at which an abstract part is decomposed into several successor parts are termed *AND nodes*; no selection needs to be done at these nodes. Nodes at which an abstract part is refined into one of the successor parts are termed *OR nodes*; the successor part that best meets the input specifications is selected at these nodes.

An example functional hierarchy is shown in Figure 3.1. AND nodes are shown by drawing an arc through all links from its successor parts. The single board computer (SBC_0)[2] is decomposed into the processor (PROC_0) subsystem, the memory (MEM_0) subsystem, the input-output (IO_0) subsystem, the address decoder (ADDR_DEC_0), etc. The generic processor PROC_0 is refined into processor-family specific parts (e.g., 68XX_PROC_0, 80386_PROC_0) that in turn are refined into physical parts (e.g., MC6800, MC6809, MC6502). The IO subsystem is decomposed into serial input-output (SIO_0) and parallel input-output (PIO_0). The rest of Figure 3.1 can be interpreted in a similar manner. The dashed lines indicate links to portions of hierarchy that are omitted from the figure.

3.2.2 Search for Structure: Templates

The search for function subtask selects the successor part(s) in the functional hierarchy. The structural integration of the selected successor parts(s) is done using *templates*. Templates are essentially fragments of a schematic drawing that indicate the appropriate connections for the mapping. An example template detailing the integration of all the successors of the SBC_0 AND node

---

[2]A loose convention has all abstract parts ending with "_0", although this is not required.

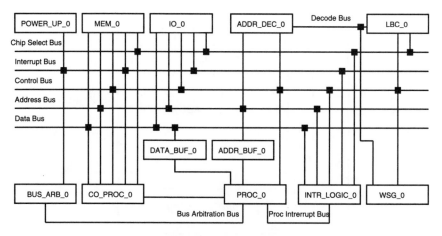

Figure 3.2. Template for SBC_0.

is shown in Figure 3.2. Another example template detailing the integration of the 80386_PROC_0 successor of the PROC_0 OR node is shown in Figure 3.3. Designs are created by integrating combinations of templates as the functional hierarchy is traversed. Templates are discussed in greater detail in the next chapter.

3.2.3   Handling Subproblem Interactions

Each abstract part in the functional hierarchy corresponds to the subproblem of designing that abstract part to meet certain specifications. Since these subproblems can be interrelated, a mechanism for handling interactions between them is needed. Our model handles these in the following manner:

- After each subproblem is solved, relevant design information is generated.

- Information generated during the design of one abstract part may be used as specifications for the design of another abstract part.

Consider the case where the design of abstract parts A_1 and A_2 are related. Some design information is generated after A_1 is designed. This information is subsequently used as a specification for the design of A_2 to make A_2's design compatible with the design of A_1. For example, the design of processor and memory subsystems are related. Once the processor subsystem is designed, the timing constraint it imposes on the memory is computed. This timing information is used as a specification of the memory subsystem's design; the search for function subtask for memory design ensures that the selected memory chip satisfies the timing constraint imposed by the processor design.

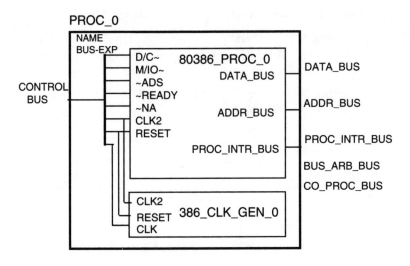

Figure 3.3. Template mapping PROC_0 to 80386_PROC_0.

3.2.4 Subproblem Ordering

The abstract parts in the functional hierarchy merely give a list of subproblems to be attempted; no ordering on solving these subproblems is imposed. A partial ordering is implicit in the subproblem interactions: if the design of A_2 requires some design information from the design of A_1, then obviously A_1 has to be designed before A_2. A novel feature of our design model is that the subproblem ordering is dynamically determined. No subproblem ordering knowledge is hardwired into the model in terms of plans or agendas, as are used in other systems [22, 62]. Instead, any design subproblem can be attempted if the information needed to complete the task, that is, the specifications for the corresponding abstract part, is available. In doing so, the partial ordering imposed by the subproblem interactions is satisfied. For example, the memory system may be designed only after a certain timing specification is known. Since it so happens that the timing specification is computed using information generated by the processor subsystem, this leads to an ordering where the processor subsystem is designed before the memory subsystem. In our domain, subproblem ordering cannot be computed *a priori* as newly added parts may introduce unforseeable interactions.

3.2.5 Putting It All Together: The Simplified Design Model

The synthesis process can be viewed as successive top-down refinement of the abstract part at the root of the functional hierarchy into a set of integrated parts at the leaves. The select-and-integrate process progresses down the functional hierarchy one level and one abstract part at a time. Each traversal step involves a search for function (i.e., selecting the successor parts) followed by a search for structure (i.e., invoking the template for integrating the successor parts). These alternate searches for function and structure continue until the entire design has been refined into physical parts. To handle design interactions, each traversal step starts with computing requirements using current design information and ends with generating new relevant design information. This traversal step is embodied in the design cycle procedure in the M1 architecture. The design process essentially keeps repeating design cycles for abstract parts until all abstract parts have been refined. The ordering of the design of abstract parts is determined dynamically in an opportunistic manner that satisfies the partial ordering implicit in the subproblem interactions.

This model forms the basis of the M1 architecture detailed in the next chapter. The actual M1 architecture is more complex due to several reasons:

- The functional hierarchy is a lattice since parts can have several functions and multiple functional units, which must be utilized effectively.

- There are several functional hierarchies linked together dynamically depending upon which templates are used.

- Design information needs to be formally and unambiguously represented and its scope clearly defined.

3.3 An Illustrative Example

To illustrate the design process in our model, we describe a trace of the design of a simple single board computer using the functional hierarchy of Figure 3.1.

In the design cycle for SBC_0, the user is queried for resource ceilings on cost, power and area of the entire board. Since this is an AND node, no selection needs to be done in SFF. In SFS a template is instantiated to integrate all the successors of SBC_0, as shown in Figure 3.2.

The design now has several abstract parts, the design of any of which may be attempted next. Let us assume that the design of MEM_0 is attempted. The user is queried on the types of memory needed. Since, however, the timing specification is computed using timing information not yet generated, the memory subsystem is not designed. Eventually the processor subsystem design is

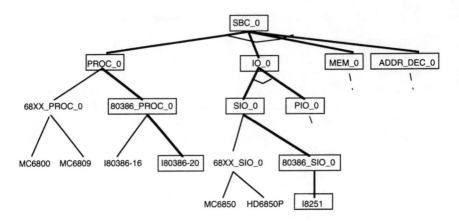

Figure 3.4. Functional hierarchy traversed for 80386-based design.

completed, and the timing information is generated. In this manner, subproblem ordering is dynamically determined.

In the design cycle for PROC_0, the user is queried for the name and minimum clock speed of the processor. In SFF, a suitable processor family specific part, say 80386_PROC_0, is selected. In SFS, a template mapping PROC_0 to 80386_PROC_0, shown in Figure 3.3, is instantiated. Design information indicating that a 80386 class processor is being used is generated.

In this manner, design cycles for abstract parts are applied until all abstract parts have been refined into physical parts. The functional hierarchy, with darkened lines indicating the links traversed in the design process, is shown in Figure 3.4.

The model presented in this chapter is a simplification of the one on which M1's problem-solving architecture is based, which is described in the next chapter.

4

An Architecture for Automated Design Synthesis

M1's problem-solving technique is based on an algorithm called the *design cycle*, which implements search for function and search for structure. Search for function (SFF) selects a part; search for structure (SFS) integrates the selected part into the design. SFF takes place along the functional hierarchy, and SFS occurs in a library of interconnecting structures called templates.

In this chapter, we first describe the formal representation of parts and related information used in the design. The design process composed of SFF and SFS is described next. Finally, the two searches are put together into a description of design cycles and their sequencing.

4.1 Design Representation

There are two kinds of information about the design:

Part-related information describes the parts that can be integrated to form the design. This information is *static*, in that it does not change during the design process. Of course, it must be updated as new parts are introduced. It also has to be edited to correct errors, update attributes (e.g., cost),

39

reflect availability, etc. All part-related information must be input from the domain-expert into the MICON database.

Design-related information describes the current system being designed. This information is *dynamic* in that it is continually updated during the design process. All design-related information is created and utilized using knowledge provided by the domain expert.

The following subsections on the functional hierarchy, part model, and functional boundary of abstract parts describe the static information. Subsequent subsections on the design hierarchy, subproblem interactions, and the design state describe the dynamic information.

4.1.1 The Functional Hierarchy

The simplified functional hierarchy described in the previous chapter had a tree-like structure. In general, the hierarchy used by M1 is a directed acyclic graph (DAG) denoted as G_{FH}. Formally, let

$$\mathcal{A} = \{p_i \mid p_i \text{ is an abstract part}\} \text{ and}$$
$$\mathcal{P} = \{p_i \mid p_i \text{ is a physical part}\}.$$

Then $G_{FH} = (N_{FH}, E_{FH})$,

where $N_{FH} = \{n_i \mid n_i \text{ is a node corresponding to part } p_i, p_i \in (\mathcal{A} \cup \mathcal{P})\}$,
$E_{FH} = \{(n_i, n_j) \mid n_i, n_j \in N_{FH}, \text{Edge-type}(n_i, n_j) \neq NIL\}$, and

$$\text{Edge-type}(n_i, n_j) = \begin{cases} \text{is-abstracted-to} & \text{if } p_i \text{ is abstracted to } p_j \\ \text{is-part-of} & \text{if } p_i \text{ is part of } p_j \\ NIL & \text{otherwise.} \end{cases}$$

Some other useful definitions are given below:

- Immediate predecessor set $P(n_i) = \{n_j \mid \exists (n_i, n_j) \in E_{FH}\}$,

- Immediate successor set $S(n_i) = \{n_j \mid \exists (n_j, n_i) \in E_{FH}\}$,

- n_i is an OR node if $\exists (n_j, n_i) \in E_{FH}$, and
  Edge-type$(n_j, n_i) = $ is-abstracted-to,

- If n_i is not an OR node, and $p_i \in \mathcal{A}$, then n_i is an AND node. For most AND nodes n_i, $\exists (n_j, n_i) \in E_{FH}$, such that Edge-type$(n_j, n_i) = $ is-part-of.

A portion of the actual functional hierarchy used by M1 corresponding to the simplified version presented previously in Chapter 2 is shown in Figure 4.1. This hierarchy is more complex in the following ways:

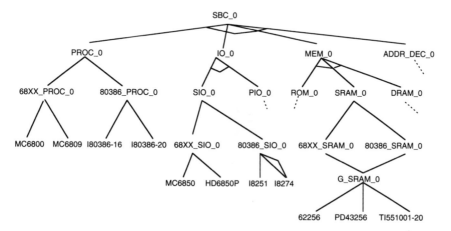

Figure 4.1. Actual functional hierarchy used by M1.

- It contains over 600 parts.

- While the functional abstraction shown was based on processor family designs, mixing components from different families is possible. In fact, a design using the Z8002 processor and Intel peripherals was added to M1.

- A single part can implement only one of several functions, i.e., a part can have more than one predecessor in the hierarchy. For example, the MC6850 can be used as an SIO for either 68XX_SIO_0 or 68008_SIO_0. This forces the functional hierarchy to be more connected than shown, leading to a lattice instead of a tree. A functional hierarchy fragment illustrating this is shown in Figure 4.2.

- Some physical parts can have multiple *functional units*, i.e., a part can perform more than one function, and hence have more than one predecessor in the hierarchy. For example, the I8155 has 256 bytes of SRAM and three PIO ports. Note that the part here has all the functions and this case is distinct from the part satisfying only one of several functions as indicated above. This also increases the connectivity of the functional hierarchy, as illustrated in Figure 4.3.

- There are actually a number of functional hierarchies in MICON where each one represents a "significant" set of functions. For example, there are hierarchies for logic gates and crystals, as shown in Figures 4.4 and 4.5. The reason for separating these functionalities is that it would not make "intuitive" sense to merge them into the main SBC hierarchy.

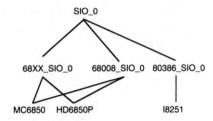

Figure 4.2. Hierarchy fragment for MC6850.

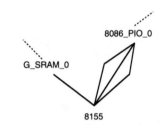

Figure 4.3. Hierarchy fragment for I8155.

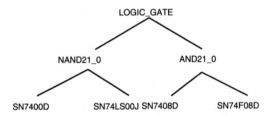

Figure 4.4. Hierarchy for logic gates.

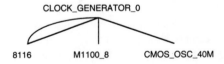

Figure 4.5. Hierarchy for crystals.

4.1.2   Part Model

A *part model* organizes information about each part and is stored in a relational database. The part models are accessed during the design process. A conceptual view of a part model is a set of attributes attached to each node of the functional hierarchy. The attribute types are given below:

Characteristics: The properties of a part. They are represented as 2-tuples (char-name, value). Both abstract and physical parts can have any number of characteristics. Let $\text{Char}(n_i)$ denote the set of characteristics for the part corresponding to node n_i.

Specifications: The requirements that an abstract part is designed to satisfy. Specifications are represented as 3-tuples (spec-name, value, group-number), but unlike characteristics the value is calculated at run time. For example, MIN_CLOCK_SPEED is a specification for the generic processor part PROC_0 that is provided by the user. Let $\text{Spec}(n_i)$ denote the set of specifications for the part corresponding to node n_i; $\text{Spec}(n_i)$ contains information used in refining n_i to $S(n_i)$. Only abstract parts can have specifications since physical parts are not refined.

The specification tuples for a part can be classified into groups where information in any group is sufficient to proceed with the design of that part. For example, a NAND21_0 part can be designed when either the PROP_DELAY or the TECHNOLOGY is specified[1]; hence both these specifications are classified into different groups and represented in the part model as (PROP_DELAY, - , 1) and (TECHNOLOGY, - , 2).

Links: The functional relationships between a part and its predecessors in the functional hierarchy, i.e., the edges in E_{FH}. They are represented as 3-tuples (predecessor-name, edge-type, functional-unit-number). Both abstract and physical parts can have any number of links. Multiple links with the same functional-unit-number means that the part can be used to satisfy the functionality of any one of the predecessor parts. For example, the MC6850 shown in Figure 4.2 has the links (68XX_SIO_0, OR, 0) and (68008_SIO_0, OR, 0). Physical parts with multiple functional units have a unique number for each unit. Multiple links with a different functional-unit-number mean that the part can satisfy the functionality of all of the predecessor parts. For example, the I8155 shown in Figure 4.3 has the links (G_SRAM_0, OR, 1), (8086_PIO_0, OR, 2), (8086_PIO_0, OR, 3), and (8086_PIO_0, OR, 4).

---

[1] Since a particular TECHNOLOGY, e.g., F series, implies a certain PROP_DELAY for a two input NAND gate.

Name: SN74LS00D		Chip name: 7400
Specifications		
spec-name		*group-number*
Characteristics		
char-name		*value*
PROP_DELAY		10
NUM_GATES		4
Links		
predecessor-name	*edge-type*	*func-unit-number*
NAND21_0	OR	1
NAND21_0	OR	2
NAND21_0	OR	3
NAND21_0	OR	4
Pins		
pin-name	*pin-index*	*pin-isa*
VCC	-	NIL
GND	-	NIL
A1	-	NIL
..	..	..

Figure 4.6. Part model for SN74LS00D.

Pins: The part's signals represented as the 3-tuple (pin-name, pin-isa, pin-index). For physical parts these correspond to actual pin names; for abstract parts these correspond to generic signals or buses (a collection of functionally similar pins). For example, the address pins, A0-A15, on an I8086 are grouped to form a pin ADDRESS_BUS on the 8086_PROC_0. Let Pins(n_i) denote the set of pins corresponding to node n_i. In addition to the pin-name, the part model also includes the pin-isa which is one of DATA_BUS, ADDRESS_BUS, NIL and indicates the functionality. For pins that are collected to form buses, the pin-index is the numeric part of the alphanumeric pin-name; e.g., D0 has pin-index = 0. The pin-isa field is used only in part expansion described in Section 5.2.3 and is not discussed further in this chapter. Motivation and mechanisms for formulating the functional boundary for abstract parts are detailed in the next section.

Each manufacturer, technology and package-specific part has a unique name and a distinct part model. For example, MC6850, MC68A50, MC68B50 and HD6850P are four distinct parts in the database. Each part also has a logical

Name: NAND21_0		Chip name: NAND21_0
Specifications		
spec-name		*group-number*
PROP_DELAY		1
TECHNOLOGY		2
Characteristics		
char-name		*value*
NUM_INPUTS		2
Links		
predecessor-name	*edge-type*	*func-unit-number*
LOGIC_GATE	OR	0
Pins		
pin-name	*pin-index*	*pin-isa*
A	-1	NIL
B	-1	NIL
Y	-1	NIL

Figure 4.7. Part model for NAND21_0.

name termed *chip_name*. Several parts may be logically equivalent, and must have the same chip_name. These parts, n_i, where i is such that chip_name(n_i) is the same, can share the following information:

- Pins(n_i).

- A subset of Char(n_i). For example, (NUM_GATES, 4) is a shared characteristic for all parts that have chip_name = 7400, such as SN74LS00D, SN74F00J and SB74S00D, while PROP_DELAY is different for each of them. A list of all legal characteristics and indication of which ones are shared between parts with the same chip_name is maintained.

- Templates.

Example part models are shown in Figure 4.6 and 4.7.

4.1.3   Functional Boundary for Abstract Parts

The functional boundary of an abstract part n_i is defined by Pins(n_i). The functional boundary of n_i is formed by abstraction of signals on successor parts (usually physical parts), such that Pins(n_i) are consistent with the functional abstraction of that part. This abstraction is manifested by grouping together

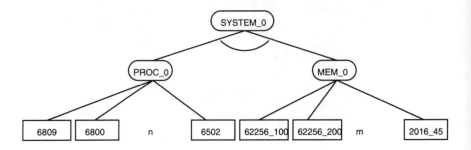

Figure 4.8. Functional hierarchy for a simple processor-memory system.

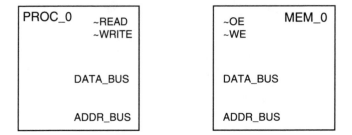

Figure 4.9. Functional boundary for generic processor and memory parts.

several signals on successor parts that share a common function. For example, a control bus is a group of signals with different names that realize the same function in a broad sense, providing control to some part of the design. Data bus and address bus are groups of signals that differ by an index. Grouping of signals is shown in templates by special "bus-expander" symbols. By using pin abstraction to form a functional boundary for an abstract part, we can integrate that abstract part into the design in a general manner; the details of each of the bus signals is determined subsequently as the design evolves.

Let us illustrate this by an example. Consider a simple processor-memory system whose functional hierarchy is shown in Figure 4.8. To obtain the functional boundary for the generic processor and memory parts (PROC_0 and MEM_0), the following pin abstractions are made:

- Data lines D0 through D7 on the physical parts are grouped into a DATA_BUS signal.

- Address lines A0 through A15 on the physical parts are grouped into an ADDRESS_BUS signal.

SYSTEM_0

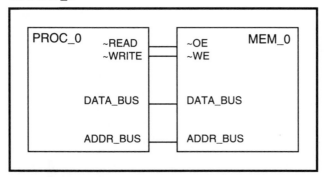

Figure 4.10. General processor memory interconnection template.

Also, generic signal names are used at the abstract part level instead of physical part specific signal names. In this manner the functional boundary for PROC_0 and MEM_0 shown in Figure 4.9 is obtained. These abstract parts can be interconnected in a template in a general manner irrespective of the size of the respective buses (as shown in Figure 4.10). After the processor is designed, it propagates the width of the buses to the memory subproblem; the memory is then designed to be compatible with the processor. Note that we could use a general template at the higher abstraction level, since we could obtain a general functional boundary for the abstract parts. The design after example templates for processor and memory subsystems have been invoked is given in Figure 4.11.

A mechanism for resolving the bus group connections into actual signal connections is needed to complete the design. In the example above, we need to connect the pins that have the same index across the data bus. These connection mechanisms are general, that is, they are applicable to a wide range of designs. The following mechanisms have been incorporated into M1:

- **Connect by index:** All pins with the same index, grouped into the bus anywhere in the design, get connected. For example, in Figure 4.12, pin D0 on part A connects to pin IO0 on part B, pin D1 to pin IO1, and so on.

- **Connect by name:** All pins with the same name, grouped into the bus anywhere in the design, get connected. For example, in Figure 4.13, pin READ on parts A, B and C are connected together.

- **Connect one-to-one arbitrarily:** Exactly one pin at an input end of the bus gets connected to a pin at the output end of the bus. While these

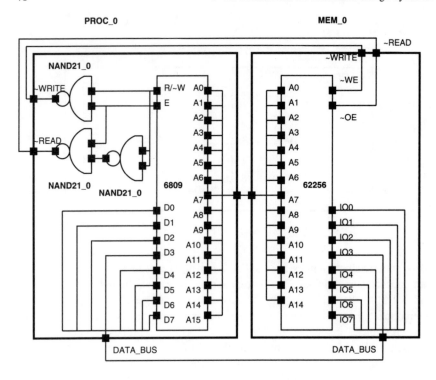

Figure 4.11. Complete design of processor memory system.

connections can be done arbitrarily, they in turn become specifications for lower-level logic synthesis tools. For example, in the design depicted in Figure 4.14, address decoding is performed with a programmable array logic (PAL) component whose outputs are programmable. A device requiring a chip-select signal needs exactly one connection to any unconnected PAL output. Here, pin O1 on the PAL gets connected to pin CS on part A, pin O2 on the PAL gets connected to pin CE on part B, and so on; later the PAL has to be designed according to these connections.

This completes the description of the part-related or static information. The next three subsections focus on design-related or dynamic information: the design hierarchy, subproblem interactions, and the design state.

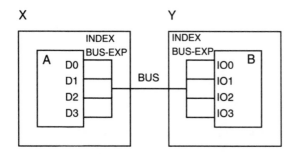

Figure 4.12. Connect by index mechanism.

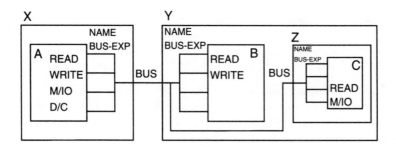

Figure 4.13. Connect by name mechanism.

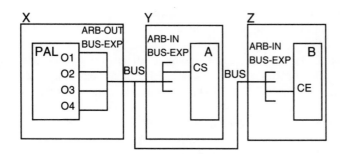

Figure 4.14. Connect one-to-one mechanism.

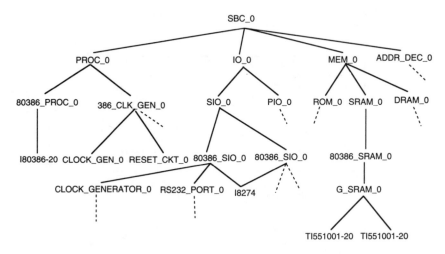

Figure 4.15. Design hierarchy for example 80386-based design.

4.1.4   The Design Hierarchy

M1 builds a design by successive refinement along the functional hierarchy. The hierarchy it builds in the design process is termed the *design hierarchy*. An example design hierarchy for a 80386-based design is shown in Figure 4.15. It is distinct from the functional hierarchy in following ways:

- It is a pruned version of the functional hierarchy; since only one node is selected at an OR node, subtrees for all the other successor nodes are pruned. For example, the 68XX_PROC_0 node and its successors do not appear in the example design hierarchy.

- In addition to the corresponding successors in the functional hierarchy, successors of a node in this hierarchy also include any other parts that are used as support circuitry in mapping that node to its successors (i.e., that are included in the corresponding template). For example, in addition to the 80386_PROC_0 successor in the functional hierarchy, the PROC_0 also has a 80386_CLK_GEN_0 successor. Thus, parts in other functional hierarchies may be linked together into the main hierarchy to form the design hierarchy. While there may be several functional hierarchies, each for a significant set of functions, there is just one design hierarchy for the current design.

- Each functional unit on all parts in this hierarchy is linked to at most one abstract part; even though a functional unit can perform several functions, it can be used for at most one function in the current design. For example, unlike the functional hierarchy, the G_SRAM_0 has only one link in the design hierarchy (to the 80386_SRAM_0 function for which it is being used).

Parts corresponding to nodes in the design hierarchy have the same part model as described previously. $P_{DH}(n_i)$ and $S_{DH}(n_i)$ denote the set of immediate predecessor and immediate successor nodes respectively of a node n_i in the design hierarchy.

4.1.5 Subproblem Interactions

The problem-decomposition strategy divides the problem into smaller, logically organized subproblems, finds a solution to these subproblems, and then integrates the results into a total problem solution [115]. For example, the functional hierarchy indicates that the single board computer consists of traditional computer subsystems, such as memory, processor, and so forth. Thus, by synthesizing a design for each subsystem and integrating each subsystem through a common bus, an entire computer system can be created.

Subproblems formulated by problem decomposition usually interact, and a mechanism for handling these interactions is needed. M1 handles subproblem interactions by constraint propagation [124, 120], which supports passing information from one subproblem to another; one subproblem creates the information that is utilized by the other subproblem. For example, the value for ACCESS_TIME, computed using the equation

```
ACCESS_TIME  =  PROCESSOR_CYCLE_TIME  *  NUMBER_OF_WAIT_STATES,
```

is propagated from the processor design subproblem to the memory and IO design subproblems. The propagated information is represented as reports. Reports are 2-tuples of the form (report_name, value), where report_name is the name of the propagated variable; and value is the value of the variable. Reports can be created in one abstract part's design and used to fill in specifications of other abstract parts. In this example, the report ACCESS_TIME could be created in the processor design and used to fill in the MAX_ACCESS_TIME specification of the memory and IO abstract parts.

In several cases, the name of the propagated variable is not unique for the entire design; this results in ambiguity when the value of this variable is to be utilized by other subproblems. For example, the NAND_PROP_DELAY report created by the NAND21_0 gate design subproblem in Figure 4.16 is utilized to compute the access time in the memory subproblem; however, this report may not be unique since there may be several NAND21_0 gates in the design. For these cases, local reports are used for propagating values between hierarchically

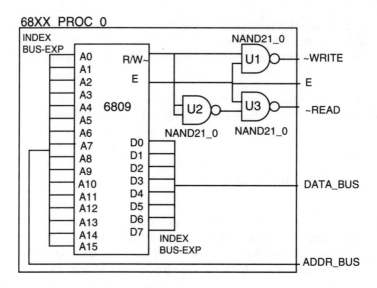

Figure 4.16. Template mapping 68XX_PROC_0 to a 6809.

related subproblems. Local reports are 3-tuples of the form (local_report_name, value, instance_tag), where local_report_name and value are the same as for reports, and instance_tag identifies the subproblem instance that created the variable. In the example, the local report (NAND_PROP_DELAY, value, U1) is created by the subproblem of designing instance U1 of the NAND21_0 gate; since the instance_tag is unique for the entire design, this variable is unique and can be used to compute the access time of memory. The set of local reports created by the design of an abstract part corresponding to node n_i is represented as $Local\text{-}report(n_i)$.

The decision about which reports should be propagated between subproblems and whether the reports should be local or not is made by the domain expert while adding knowledge to the system. If the solution of a subproblem creates information that would be useful for other subproblems, appropriate reports must be created. If several instances of the subproblem exist in the design, and if it is desirable to distinguish the information created by each, then local reports must be created. Reports are accessible anywhere - i.e., they have global scope; local reports created for part n_i are accessible only in the design of $P_{DH}(n_i)$ and $S_{DH}(n_i)$ - i.e., they have local scope. Note that local reports can provide the functionality of reports also; however, they may require repeated propagation along the hierarchy due to their limited scope.

4.1.6   The Design State

The *design state* characterizes the state of M1 at any time. The total design state consists of all arts (organized hierarchically), characteristics, specifications, reports, and local reports. For designing a node n_i, however, a more compact form, termed the design state for n_i, denoted as DesignState(n_i), is used. The design state for n_i is defined as follows:

$$\text{DesignState}(n_i) \;=\; \text{Reports}$$
$$\bigcup_{n_j \in P_{\text{DH}}(n_i) \cup \{n_i\}} \text{Spec}(n_j)$$
$$\bigcup_{n_j \in S_{\text{DH}}(n_i) \cup P_{\text{DH}}(n_i) \cup \{n_i\}} \text{Char}(n_j)$$
$$\bigcup_{n_j \in S_{\text{DH}}(n_i) \cup \{n_i\}} \text{Local-reports}(n_j).$$

Thus, from the perspective of scope of design variables, the specifications, characteristics, and local reports of n_i are like local variables with their scope limited to the portion of the design involving the predecessor and successors of n_i. Reports are analogous to global variables since they are visible across the entire design.

4.2   The Design Process

The design proceeds down one level of the hierarchy, one abstract part at a time. This design process adds successors in the hierarchy and creates information that may be used by abstract parts anywhere in the hierarchy. In this way, the design of an abstract part can trigger the design of other abstract parts anywhere in the hierarchy. At each level, it consists of the following steps:

- a search for function,

- a search for structure, and

- communicating information between subproblems.

Each of these is described in detail.

4.2.1   The Search for Function

At an AND node no action is taken in the search for function; the refinement is done using a template in the search for structure phase. At an OR node n_i,

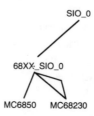

Figure 4.17. Functional hierarchy fragment for 68XX_SIO_0.

the search for function selects only one of the successor nodes $n_j \in S(n_i)$; the objective is to find the n_j that most closely matches n_i.

The functional hierarchy reduces the search space by presorting the nodes according to function. Function is the primary criterion for selecting a part and is automatically covered in the search procedure by following the links. Without the links, the set $S(n_i)$ would necessarily include all parts in the database instead of just the greatly reduced number given by the in-degree of n_i. Based on experimental data, the typical in-degree is less than 10, while the number of parts in the database at this point is over 600; the hierarchy reduces search almost two orders of magnitude. (A more detailed discussion is given in [8]).

Before searching for a new part from among elements of $S(n_i)$, a check is made for unused functional units on parts that are already in the design. Using existing functional units is preferred since it reduces the total number of parts in the design. This step is necessary in order to exploit parts with multiple functional units.

Two points need to be highlighted here. First, our approach can result in locally optimal but globally sub-optimal solutions. While our approach can exploit all units on a part once it has been brought into the design, we do not address the issue of globally selecting an optimal set of parts to be brought into the design (since the parts are selected locally at each node). For example, consider the functional hierarchy shown in Figure 4.17. The 6850 has one 68XX_SIO_0 unit while the 68230 has two such units. If a design requires two SIO ports, the 68230 is a better choice from the global perspective (assuming one 68230 is cheaper than two 6850s). However, since our approach would design each SIO port independently, it would select a 6850 for both ports (assuming one 6850 is cheaper than one 68230); this is clearly a locally optimal but globally sub-optimal choice. Of course, the user can force M1 to select the 68230 for one of the SIO ports by explicitly specifying the chip to be used; M1 is capable of subsequently utilizing the unused unit on the 68230 for the second SIO port.

Second, note that even though an unused functional unit exists, it may or may not be found to be suitable. Using the other functional units on that part in

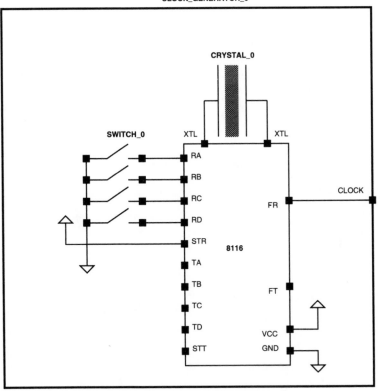

Figure 4.18. Design of a CLOCK_GENERATOR_0 using a functional unit on a 8116.

the design could possibly constrain it to be unsuitable for the specifications of another abstract part. For example, consider the 8116 physical part that contains two clock generators. A design using the first clock generator unit on the 8116 is shown in Figure 4.18. This would constrain the second clock-generator to have a frequency that is a submultiple of the frequency chosen for CRYSTAL_0 by the first clock generator design. Later in the design process, if there is a CLOCK_GENERATOR_0 abstract part to be refined, the second clock generator unit on this existing 8116 chip could be used only if the frequency specification of this second CLOCK_GENERATOR_0 is a submultiple of the frequency of CRYSTAL_0.

The sequence of steps for SFF are given below:

1. If there exists a part in the design with an unused functional unit that is suitable, then select it and exit.

2. All parts $n_j \in S(n_i)$ are candidates.

3. Reject candidates that do not satisfy constraints. Constraints are expressed as relationships between specifications of n_i and characteristics of n_j. For example, a constraint may require the ACCESS_TIME characteristic of memory chips to be less than the MAX_ACCESS_TIME specification on the memory abstract part; all chips that do not satisfy this constraint would be rejected.

4. If no candidates are left, SFF has failed and the failure-handling module FAILURE is invoked (see Chapter 6 for details).

5. If exactly one candidate is left, select it and exit.

6. If more than one candidate is left, compute the penalty points for each using the equation

$$\text{penalty points}(a) \ = \ \sum_{r_i \in R} \left(\begin{array}{c} \dfrac{\text{Amount used of } r_i}{\text{Total amount allocated of } r_i} \\[2ex] \times \dfrac{\text{Amount of } r_i \text{ used by } a}{\text{Total amount allocated of } r_i} \end{array} \right)$$

where R is the set of resources utilized by the part. Resources are items consumed by the design, and a ceiling on these is initially specified by the user. Examples of resources are power budget, board area budget, cost budget, and so forth. The function assigns a normalized penalty for each candidate based on the amount of resource it uses. Also, the penalty is weighted by the criticality of the resource; if the design is running out of a particular resource, the resource's criticality increases.

7. Select the candidate with the fewest penalty points.

The search procedure has an interesting property that should be noted. The weight on the penalty for each resource is the only global variable used in the selection process; the effect of these weights is dependent on when in the overall design process the selection for an abstract part is done. If the selection is done at the beginning of the design process, the weights for each resource are fairly uniform; toward the end of the design prcess, the plentiful resources tend to have lower criticality and hence lower weight. Hence, in the beginning, M1 might select parts that consume large portions of a critical resource; later in the design process, M1 will make more discriminating choices.

As a result of this property, M1 may make poor component selections in the context of the entire design. Consider the example design space shown in Table 4.1. Suppose M1 is selecting a memory chip with ACCESS_TIME $\leq$ 151 ns,

Chip name	Access time	Cost	Power
A	100 ns	$5	200 mW
B	150 ns	$2	250 mW

Table 4.1. Design space of memory chips.

the available cost resource is $500, and the available power resource is 1000 mW. M1 would choose chip A; this is a good local decision at this stage of the design process. Now, further suppose that for the same design, M1 is at the end of the design process and needs to select an IO chip, but the cost resource is down to $1 and the least costly IO chip is $3. The impact of the memory chip decision is now felt; if M1 had chosen chip B, which would also have violated no constraints, the extra $3 saved would have allowed the design of the IO to be completed successfully.

Simple solutions to this problem such as adding a heuristic that always prefers the least costly (where cost refers not just to monetary cost but to cost in the general sense) will not work, because of unforeseen interactions between variables in the design. For example, in the previous example it is conceivable that memory chip A may have been the best global choice. Consider the case where drivers added to the memory subsystem would add an additional 10ns to the delay of the memory; selecting chip B would then have violated the ACCESS_TIME $\leq$ 151 ns constraint when drivers would be introduced into the design. Other common schemes, such as allocating budgets to various subsystems [128, 21], are also susceptible to problems, where the decision now becomes one of proper allocation. The budgets are merely a guess of the actual resource needs, and therefore may unnecessarily overconstrain or underconstrain a subsystem's design. These limitations are analogous to those of M1's selection scheme.

As a result, M1's selection process can be viewed as an intelligent guess-making process. Since guesses are sometimes wrong, M1 may have to backtrack to some earlier decision, try another guess, and redesign. As discussed later in Chapter 6, this is a property of design problems where interactions between design parameters, or design subtasks, are not totally forseeable.

4.2.2 Search for Structure

The representation of complex structural information is critical to M1's operation as the system essentially integrates various "pieces of structure". M1 uses a simple declarative representation for structure called a *template*. A template is a chunk of knowledge about structural design for a particular part in a particular

68XX_SIO_0

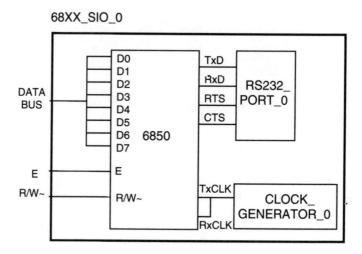

Figure 4.19. Template showing integration of 6850 to 68XX_SIO_0.

design situation. An example template detailing the integration of a 6850 SIO physical part to a 68XX_SIO_0 abstract part is shown in Figure 4.19. Salient features of a template are

- **Boundary pins:** The functional boundary of the abstract part being refined constitutes the boundary of the template. Integrating the parts in the template with this boundary effectively integrates them into the rest of the design. In Figure 4.19, the pins on the 68XX_SIO_0 constitute the template boundary.

- **Major functional component:** The selected successor part is the major functional component (only for OR nodes). The 6850 is the major functional component in Figure 4.19.

- **Support circuitry:** Circuitry may be required to support the operation of parts in the template. In Figure 4.19 the RS232_DRIVER_0 and the CLOCK_GENERATOR_0 support the 6850's operation.

- **Invocation preconditions:** Many parts may be used in a variety of ways, each requiring different interconnections or support parts. M1 requires that each part usage have a different template. To aid SFS, each template is marked with a unique, unambiguous set of invocation preconditions. Invocation preconditions for the template in Figure 4.19 are shown in

```
REPORT name = BOARD_AREA value > 0
REPORT name = BOARD_COST value > 0
REPORT name = REMAINING_BOARD_AREA value > 0
REPORT name = REMAINING_BOARD_COST value > 0
SPECIFICATION name = SIO_TAG value <> ||
SPECIFICATION name = CHIP_NAME value <> ||
SPECIFICATION name = EXT_INTERFACE value = |RS-232|
SPECIFICATION name = BAUD_RATE value <= 6850_MAX_BAUD_RATE
SPECIFICATION name = BAUD_SWITCH value <> ||
SPECIFICATION name = INTERRUPTS value <> ||
SPECIFICATION name = INTR_MASKABLE value <> ||
SPECIFICATION name = INTR_PRIORITY_LEVEL value >= 0
SPECIFICATION name = PORT_SIZE value >= 3
SPECIFICATION name = PORT_TYPE value = |DTE|
SPECIFICATION name = CONNECTOR_SIZE value >= 3
SPECIFICATION name = CONNECTOR_TYPE value <> ||
SPECIFICATION name = MAX_ACCESS_TIME value >= -1
```

Figure 4.20. Invocation preconditions for template mapping 68XX_SIO_0 to 6850.

Figure 4.20[2]. Note that an RS232 port is required for this template; another template would be used if an RS422 port was required instead.

SFS chooses the proper template from among those stored in M1's knowledge base. The search process is simple: The design state is compared to the template's preconditions, and the template that matches the design state is selected and incorporated into the design. This reduces SFS to match [88]. For example, given that an MC6850 has been selected for 68XX_SIO_0 and an RS232 port interface is required, the single template that integrates the MC6850 and the RS232 port to the 68XX_SIO_0 is chosen.

If more than one structure matches the design state, more information must be added to disambiguate them. For example, the 6850 can be connected to the RS232 port in two ways depending upon whether the SIO port is being used as a Data Terminal Equipment (DTE) or a Data Communication Equipment (DCE); to distinguish these structures, an additional specification PORT_TYPE, which can be either one of these two values, is added to the 68XX_SIO_0 part. Alternatively, both structures could be abstracted to separate parts and the selection process could select one of them based on some new criterion. If neither alternative is possible, both structures are equivalent in all known respects and the system needs just one. Thus, requiring a unique

---

[2]The ``value <> ||'' indicates that the variable could have any non-null value, i.e., it is a don't care.

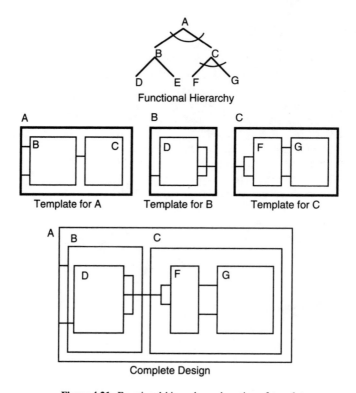

Figure 4.21. Functional hierarchy and nesting of templates.

solution for SFS is not a limitation of the framework; on the contrary, it disam-
biguates conflicts and forms the basis for the knowledge-acquisition framework
(discussed in detail in Chapter 8).

Templates represent knowledge of how M1 maps from one level in the functional hierarchy to a lower level in a structural sense. A simple functional
hierarchy and a set of templates are shown in Figure 4.21; if D is selected in
the SFF for B, the complete design formed by nesting of templates is also shown
in Figure 4.21. Designs are created by combining templates in such a way as
to satisfy the designer's requirements. Thus, given a functional hierarchy and a
set of templates, the designs that a system can produce are enumerable *a priori*
(except as noted in Section 5.2.3). In order to cover a wide range of designs, a
large number of templates are needed.

4.2.3 Report Propagation

As pointed out previously, subproblem interactions are handled by propagating reports (or local reports) from one subproblem to another. Let the design of $n_1 \in N_{DH}$ and $n_2 \in N_{DH}$ interact, and let there be a report that is computed after n_1 is designed and is used in the design of n_2. The interaction process consists of the following two steps:

Report calculation: After SFF and SFS, a suitable report R based on the solution of the n_1 design subproblem is created, and its value is calculated using any of the variables in the design state.

Specification filling: Before starting SFF for the n_2 design subproblem, the report R, together with other variables in the design state, is used to fill in the value of a specification in $\text{Spec}(n_2)$.

The equations used to compute the value of the report and the specification could be arbitrarily complex functions of the variables in the respective design state.

4.3 Putting It All Together

The design process described above is put together into a sequence of steps termed the *design cycle*, which is executed for each abstract part. The other issue is ordering these design cycles, i.e., deciding which abstract part should go through its design cycle next. These two procedures together form M1's problem-solving method.

4.3.1 The Design Cycle

The design cycle refines a node n_i into one or more of the successor nodes in $S(n_i)$, possibly introducing additional support circuitry parts into the design. The sequence of steps in the design cycle is illustrated in Figure 4.22. Each step, denoted by $d_{\text{step\_name}}$ for brevity, is explained below:

Specification (d_{spec}): Each $s_k \in \text{Spec}(n_i)$ is assigned a value using either of the following two mechanisms:

- *Query:* The user is prompted with an appropriate question and the response is used to fill in the specification.

- *Formulation:* The reports, specifications, and characteristics of $P_{DH}(n_i)$ are used to fill in the specification.

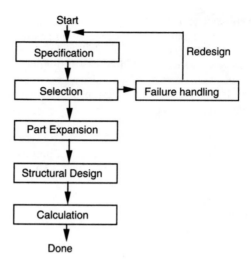

Figure 4.22. The design cycle.

For each specification, the mechanism to be used is given by the domain expert while adding knowledge to the system. For query, the domain expert must provide the appropriate question to be posed to the user. For formulation, the domain expert must provide the appropriate equation to compute the value. A design cycle is executed for a node only when all its specifications are filled.

Selection (d_{select})**:** At an OR node, one of $S(n_i)$ is chosen; no action is taken at an AND node. This step has been described in detail in Section 4.2.1.

Structural synthesis[3]$(d_{\text{casc}} + d_{\text{temp}})$**:** A template is asserted for the n_i to one or more of the $S(n_i)$ mapping, as described in Section 4.2.2.

Report generation (d_{calc})**:** Reports are generated in one of the following ways:

- *Immediate* calculation $(d_{\text{calc\_imm}})$: Reports are generated immediately. Any of the variables in DesignState(n_i) may be used to compute the value of the report.

- *Delayed* calculation $(d_{\text{calc\_delayed}})$: Structural synthesis may bring several abstract parts into the design, and the reports to be generated at this point may depend on reports generated by the design of those abstract parts. Hence, generation of some reports is delayed until all abstract parts introduced by a template are completely designed

---

[3]The step is actually composed to two substeps as described in the next chapter.

(i.e., have been driven to physical parts). Also, the purpose of some reports is to signal the completion of an abstract part's design. The generation of these reports is delayed until all abstract parts within the abstract part have been completely designed.

Failure analysis: When selection fails, the cause of the failure is analyzed to create *failure reports*. For example, while designing the memory array, we may find that none of the memory chips satisfy the ACCESS_TIME specification; a failurereport is created that indicates that the ACCESS_TIME specification was not satisfied and the amount by which it was violated.

Failure handling: Corrective action for failure handling is taken, which involves redesigning n_i and possibly other abstract parts in the design. For the memory design example above, a wait-state may be inserted and the memory array redesigned. This process is performed by the module FAILURE (see Chapter 6).

4.3.2 Subproblem Ordering

The functional hierarchy, while dividing the problem into smaller, simpler subproblems, does not give an ordering for solving the subproblems. For example, the hierarchy does not imply that the processor should be designed before memory or vice-versa. Ordering depends upon the interaction, or dependencies, between subproblems; a report generated during the design of one abstract part may be needed to fill the specifications of another.

In the simplest type of problem (e.g., [88]) the dependencies between subproblems are determined by analysis of the problem domain, and an ordering is derived such that each subproblem is attempted only after other subproblems that provide information for it have been solved. For this problem type the subproblem ordering is fixed. In a less restrictive problem class (e.g., [22]) the ordering is fixed but there is interaction between subproblems, possibly leading to backtracking and redesign. For example, the solution to subproblem A assumes a value that is computed later in subproblem B; if the assumed value is incorrect, A can be redesigned.

In our case, ordering is more complex than that for any of these problem types. It is not possible to find a reasonable, invariant subproblem ordering since the dependencies can change. Recall the formula used to calculate the access time for memory and IO:

```
ACCESS_TIME  =  PROCESSOR_CYCLE_TIME  *  NUMBER_OF_WAIT_STATES.
```

Note that the PROCESSOR_CYCLE_TIME value depends on the selection of a processor part. So, it is clearly advantageous to wait for the processor to be

chosen before deciding on memory and IO. Under normal conditions memory
and IO subsystems can be designed independently. If a particular design, however, requires a direct memory access controller, then the access time of IO will
affect the access time of memory and vice-versa, and the subproblem ordering
will change. It is not practical to enumerate all possible subproblem interactions
a priori, especially considering that, as new parts or subsystems are added and
technology evolves, new, unforeseeable interactions may arise.

The inability to order subproblems *a priori* has an important implication for
M1. M1 cannot use a fixed control scheme, such as plans [45, 44] for designing
a system [22, 62]; the order in which subproblems are attacked must be dynamically computed. This dynamically determined subproblem ordering is a novel,
powerful feature of our design model. The subproblem of designing the part
associated with a node is solved by the application of the design cycle to that
node. Before a design cycle can be started for a node its specifications must
be filled. Thus, conceptually, the algorithm for subproblem ordering is given
below:

$$\text{if } \forall s_i \in \text{Spec}(n_i), \exists s_i \in \text{DesignState}(n_i)$$
$$\text{then activate design cycle for } n_i.$$

This procedure results in a data-driven search process which is only dependent on a node's specifications being filled. As soon as a node is eligible to
be designed, it will be. This provides the flexibility needed to add new parts
(subproblems) that might change the dependencies. Also, the partial ordering
imposed by the subproblem interactions is satisfied. Note that conceptually several design cycles could be active simultaneously. To keep the design process
manageable in M1, however, each design cycle is scheduled as shown in Figure
4.23. Scheduling continues until the queue is empty. If no progress is being
made, then a deadlock is reported to the user, who may take corrective action,
such as changing specifications or modifying the knowledge base.

In the algorithm in Figure 4.23, the queue contains both nodes that can be
designed and nodes waiting for additional design information to be generated
by other nodes. subproblems are attempted in an ad hoc depth-first search of
the design hierarchy (since new nodes in d_{template} are added to the front of the
queue). Performance of the algorithm can be improved by using heuristics for
queueing. In the improved algorithm shown in Figure 4.24, a queue of only
those nodes that can be designed is maintained; other nodes are kept in sets of
nodes waiting for additional design information, or for successors to be designed.
After each design cycle, all nodes in the waiting sets are re-evaluated to check
if they are eligible to be designed. If so, the nodes are added to the queue.
The heuristics used to order this queue are the *abstractness* and *complexity*, as
described below:

Let each n have a slot status,
 status $\in \{$ new, waiting_spec, waiting_calc, designed$\}$
Subproblem_Ordering ();
{
 $Q = 0$;
 AddEnd (Q, Booting-part);
 loop
  n = First (Q);
  DesignCycle (n);
  if (n.status $\neq$ designed) AddEnd (Q, n);
 until ($Q = 0$);
}
DesignCycle (n);
{
 if (n.status = new $\vee$ n.status = waiting_spec) {
  d spec;
  if ($\neg$ SpecComplete(n)) { n.status = waiting_spec; return; }
  d select;
  d casc;
  d template; /* $\forall$ $m \in$ $S_{DH}(n)$, AddFront (Q, m) */
  d calc_now;
  if ($\neg$ SuccDone(n)) { n.status = waiting_calc; return; }
  d calc_delayed;
  n.status = designed; return;
 }
 else if (n.status = waiting_calc) {
  if ($\neg$ SuccDone(n)) { n.status = waiting_calc; return; }
  d calc_delayed;
  n.status = designed; return;
 }
}
function SpecComplete (n); /* Returns T iff all specifications are filled */
{
 $\forall$ $s_i \in$ Spec(n), if ($\neg$ $\exists$ $s_i \in$ DesignState(n)) return(F);
 return(T);
}
function SuccDone (n); /* Returns T iff all successors are designed */
{
 $\forall$ $m \in$ $S_{DH}(n)$, if (m.status $\neq$ designed) return(F);
 return(T);
}

Figure 4.23. Algorithm for subproblem ordering.

Abstractness is the depth of a node (i.e., distance from the root node) in the design hierarchy. Nodes that are higher up in the design hierarchy are more abstract. The queue is ordered such that more abstract nodes are towards the head of the queue. This results in a breadth-first traversal of the hierarchy, which has the following advantages:

- it gives a more global view, unlike depth-first traversal that can introduce unnecessary detail early in the design process, and

- violated constraints and failures, if any, are usually detected earlier in the design process.

Complexity is a qualitative measure indicating the relative size and resource consumption of the abstract part's design and thus its impact on the design. This is the secondary parameter on which the queue is ordered; for the nodes with the same abstractness, nodes with higher complexity are toward the head of the queue. Example values in order of reducing complexity are VLSI, LSI, MSI, SSI, discrete connectors, and discrete components. This results in the following advantages:

- parts that have greater ramifications on the design are designed first, and

- violated constraints and failures, if any, are detected earlier.

These heuristics are captured in the `AddQ` procedure in Figure 4.24. Also, since procedures `DesignCycle1` and `DesignCycle3` are repeated often, they use data structures that enable them to reason incrementally, making them more efficient than their conceptual description in Figure 4.24.

In this chapter, we have described the design representation and the problem-solving method, the design cycle, at a conceptual level. In the next chapter, we discuss their implementation in an expert system.

```
Subproblem_Ordering ();
{
    Q = 0;
    AddQ (Q, Booting-part);
    loop
        n = First (Q);
        DesignCycle2 (n);
        DesignCycle3 (CalcWaitSet);
        DesignCycle1 (SpecWaitSet);
    until (Q = 0);
    if (SpecWaitSet ≠ φ) Error("Some Spec cannot be filled");
}
DesignCycle1 (SpecWaitSet);
{
    ∀ n ∈ SpecWaitSet {
        d spec;
        if (SpecComplete(n)) { Delete (SpecWaitSet, n); AddQ (Q, n); }
    }
}
DesignCycle2 (n);
{
    d select;
    d casc;
    d template;
    d calc_now;
}
DesignCycle3 (CalcWaitSet);
{
    ∀ n ∈ CalcWaitSet
        if (SuccDone(n)) { Delete (CalcWaitSet, n); d calc_delayed; }
}
AddQ (Q, n)
{
    m = Q;
    while ((m ≠ 0) ∧ (Abstractness(m) ≥ Abstractness(n)) ∧
            (Complexity(m) ≥ Complexity(n))) move m down the Q;
    Insert n after m in Q;
}
```

Figure 4.24. Improved algorithm for subproblem ordering.

5

The M1 System

This chapter describes an implementation of the concepts and algorithms described in the previous chapter in a program called M1. M1 is implemented as a knowledge-based expert system. We describe M1's knowledge base and the MICON part database with detailed examples.

5.1 Knowledge-Based Implementation

Expert systems (ES) are composed of two major elements: the problem solver and the knowledge base. The problem solver describes a general method for solving the problem; M1's problem-solving method is the design cycle and the subproblem ordering algorithm. The knowledge base contains knowledge specific to the task that is used by the problem solver to find the solution. In a properly designed ES all control knowledge – decisions about which step to take next to solve a problem – resides exclusively in the problem solver. A knowledge-based approach to implementing M1 was chosen for several reasons:

- The programming paradigm easily supports data-driven computation. The subproblem ordering task can be conveniently cast in a data-driven approach.

- Generally, human designers are unable to provide a complete well-defined algorithm for solving the design synthesis problem; however, they can describe the approach in terms of specific situations and corresponding solutions. Rules naturally represent this design knowledge. A rule-based system can automate the task at least for similar situations, although not for a general case.

- A knowledge base is easily extensible as compared to modifying procedural code. This allows M1 to track technology changes, which is necessary in the computer design domain.

M1 is implemented as a rule-based expert system in the OPS83 [67] production language. The remainder of the book assumes a working knowledge of rule-based programming concepts. A review of rule-based programming can be found in Appendix B.

Part models, i.e., characteristics, specifications, links, and pins for all parts are stored in the central MICON database described in Section 5.3. The knowledge that M1 uses while creating a design is stored in the knowledge base. A detailed description of M1's knowledge base is given in Section 5.2. Since the performance of a knowledge-based system depends strongly on both the quality and breadth of its knowledge, especially in knowledge-intensive application areas such as design [87], building the knowledge base is a critical part of the development process. The knowledge acquisition process is described in detail in Part III of this book. Issues on how the knowledge base has been engineered to support automated knowledge acquisition is also described in Part III. Here we describe the structure, representation, and utilization of the knowledge base.

5.2 Knowledge Base

M1's knowledge base is divided into disjoint partitions, each corresponding to a particular step in the design cycle. The knowledge base consists of a set of rules with each rule residing in one and only one partition. Strict separation of rules eliminates interactions in the rule base (which hinders the growth of an ES) and facilitates knowledge acquisition. (See Chapter 8 for more information.)

Each of the following knowledge base partitions in M1 correspond to steps in the design cycle as defined in Section 4.3.1:

- Specification knowledge (k_{spec}) supports d_{spec};

- Selection knowledge (k_{select}) supports d_{select};

- Structural synthesis (composed of two partitions, see Section 5.2.3 for details)

– Part expansion knowledge (k_{casc}) supports d_{casc},

– Structural design knowledge (k_{template}) supports d_{template};

• Calculation knowledge (k_{calc}) supports d_{calc}.

Knowledge in all the above partitions is associated with the design cycle and is termed *design knowledge*. Note that part models are stored in the database and are not considered design knowledge.

Knowledge in each of the above partitions has a specific role in the overall design process. An ordering is imposed on the sequence in which these partitions are activated. These activated knowledge partitions are termed *contexts*. An activated partition executes several rules to accomplish a specific task; in this way contexts behave similarly to subroutines or functions in procedural languages in that all side effects have limited scope. Each rule in a context has a special working memory element (WME), termed *context element*, as a condition on the left-hand side (LHS). In M1, for all rules, the context element is the `goal` WME that has the design cycle step as an attribute. Selective activation of contexts is effected by creating and deleting these `goal` WMEs.

An additional partition, architectural and support knowledge (k_{arch}), is responsible for sequencing through the contexts to effect the design cycle. It also includes the subproblem ordering algorithm, input and output routines, database interaction functions, other support functions for maintaining data structures (e.g., netlists), and the conflict resolution strategy.

The total knowledge in M1 is the union of all the partitions:

$$K_{\text{T}} = k_{\text{spec}} \cup k_{\text{select}} \cup k_{\text{casc}} \cup k_{\text{template}} \cup k_{\text{calc}} \cup k_{\text{arch}}.$$

Similarly, we can define design knowledge as the following:

$$K_{\text{D}} = k_{\text{spec}} \cup k_{\text{select}} \cup k_{\text{template}} \cup k_{\text{calc}}.$$

Knowledge in each of the partitions is described in detail in the following subsections. Example rule formats are provided for each case. Some detail of the actual implementation has been abstracted for clarity. For example, symbolic pointers between WMEs in the examples are actually unique integers in the implementation.

5.2.1 Specification

The d_{spec} design cycle step has to assign a value to the specification for abstract parts in a template using either query or formulation. The method or equation for assigning the value is represented as a rule. Example rules for each of the formulation and query cases are given in Figure 5.1(a) and 5.1(b),

```
Rule memory_access_time
  If (goal design_cycle_step = specification for_part = MEM_0) and
     (part name = MEM_0 predecessor = SBC_0) and
     (template_tag name = SBC_0_GENERAL for_part = SBC_0) and
     (report name = ACCESS_TIME value = X) and
     (specification for_part = MEM_0 name = MAX_ACCESS_TIME)
  Then
       create (specification, for_part = MEM_0,
       name = MAX_ACCESS_TIME value = X - SKEW_DELAY);
```

(a)

```
Rule memory_sram_needed
  If (goal design_cycle_step = specification for_part = MEM_0) and
     (part name = MEM_0 predecessor = SBC_0) and
     (template_tag name = SBC_0_GENERAL for_part = SBC_0) and
     (specification for_part = MEM_0 name = SRAM_NEEDED)
  Then
       get_response(''Do you need SRAM memory <Y,N>'', X);
       create (specification, for_part = MEM_0,
                           name = SRAM_NEEDED, value = X);
```

(b)

Figure 5.1. Specification rules for MEM_0.

respectively. In the first rule illustrating the formulation mechanism, the LHS of the rule checks that the current context is the specification design step, that the part MEM_0 is being used in the template for SBC_0, and that a report named ACCESS_TIME is available. The rule's right-hand side (RHS) creates a specification for the part MEM_0 using the equation shown. In the second rule illustrating the query mechanism, no reports are needed on the LHS, and the RHS has a question to ask the user.

Note that the method for computing a specification of an abstract part is specific to a particular template in which that part is being used. For example, if the part MEM_0 was being used in the design of a memory board instead of within a template for SBC_0, the value of the MAX_ACCESS_TIME specification could be obtained from the user (using the query mechanism). If MEM_0 was being used to provide memory within another abstract part, such as parity, then it would be appropriate to compute MAX_ACCESS_TIME using some other information in the design state (the formulation mechanism). To make each specification rule specific to a template, the rule includes a special template_tag condition element (CE) that has a unique name for each template. This WME is created when the template for the predecessor part was invoked in the d_{template} design step (see Section 5.2.3).

The specification step exploits the data-driven nature of rule-based systems. The antecedents of the rule represent the reports or specifications needed by

```
Rule compare_PROC_0_clock_speed.
  If (goal design_cycle_step = selection_check_constraint
          for_part = PROC_0) and
      (candidate name = P is_successor_of = PROC_0) and
      (characteristic name = CLOCK_SPEED of_part = P value = X) and
      (specification name = MIN_CLOCK_SPEED for_part = PROC_0 value > X)
  Then
      mark candidate as rejected
```

Figure 5.2. Example selection rule.

the equation generating the value of the specification. The rule executes only if WMEs corresponding to the antecedents are available in the design. If an abstract part n_i's design depends on another abstract part n_j's design, the rule for generating some specification in $\text{Spec}(n_i)$ will have as an antecedent a report that is generated in the calculation step for n_j. This rule will not execute until the design of n_j has been completed, which would generate the required report. Since the design of an abstract part proceeds only when all its specifications are complete, n_i would have to wait until n_j had completed its design cycle. In this way, the data-driven nature of rule-based systems is used to determine when the design of an abstract part can be started.

5.2.2 Part Selection

The d_{select} design cycle step executes the algorithm given in Section 4.2.1 to select parts. This algorithm requires two kinds of knowledge. The first kind, in subpartition $k_{\text{select\_rule}}$, provides constraints for comparing a candidate part's characteristics with the specifications of the abstract part. This subpartition is specific to the abstract part. Figure 5.2 shows a rule for selecting between all the possible candidates of PROC_0 (e.g. 8086_PROC_0 and 68XX_PROC_0) with regard to clock speed. The LHS of the rule checks if the current context is the check constraints substep in the selection design cycle step, and if the MIN_CLOCK_SPEED specified for the PROC_0 part is greater than the CLOCK_SPEED of the candidate. The RHS rejects the candidate if the LHS is matched. Note that a manifestation of the implementation is that the rules in $k_{\text{select\_rule}}$ check for constraints being violated, not satisfied, and actually reject candidates. M1's knowledge base contains rules of this type for specifications of virtually all parts; parts that are used exclusively in AND nodes do not require these rules. The second subpartition, $k_{\text{select\_func}}$, realizes the penalty function described in Section 4.2.1; this knowledge is fixed since the types of resources are fixed.

5.2.3 Structural Synthesis

Structural synthesis instantiates a part chosen in the selection step and integrates
that part into the design. The number of parts to be instantiated depends on
specifications that are filled at run time. For example, the number of 8086_SIO_0
to be brought into the design depends upon the number of SIO ports desired by
the user; the number of SRAM physical parts to be instantiated depends upon
the amount of memory required by the user. As the specifications cover a large
range of values, the amount of integration knowledge can explode. Fortunately,
parts can be viewed as constituting a structure, and the knowledge of forming
the structure is independent from the knowledge of integrating this structure
into the design. For example, the SRAM chips can be viewed as constituting an
array structure; the knowledge of designing an array of SRAMs is independent
of the knowledge needed to integrate the array into the memory subsystem. This
dichotomy leads to the division of the structural synthesis step into the following
two separate substeps:

Part expansion (d_{casc})**:** A variable number of successor parts are instantiated
and integrated into the structure as described below.

Structural design (d_{template})**:** The successor parts in the structure are integrated
with the abstract part.

There are two common structures used in part expansion:

- **Independent:** Each instance of the successor part is independent of the
  other. For example, each 8086_SIO_0 instantiated is independently integrated to SIO_0. This structure is used when the keyword AMOUNT is a
  specification for an abstract part.

- **Array:** The successor parts are organized as an array with variable dimensions. d_{template} is used for the boundary parts in the array only. Integration
  of the other parts of the array is decoupled from d_{template} and also from the
  dimensions of the array. For example, memory chips are organized as an
  array with dimensions depending upon the data bus width and the amount
  of memory required; the address bus pins and chip select signals connect
  across rows while the data bus pins connect across columns. This structure is used when the keyword ROWS and COLUMNS are specifications for
  an abstract part.

Knowledge for forming these structures, k_{casc}, is best represented in procedural
form (given in the rule's RHS). Examples of this knowledge are shown in Figures
5.3 through 5.5. To avoid confusion, some context sequencing information is
not shown in these rules. The rule in Figure 5.3(a) is the default – if a successor

```
Rule instantiate_part_default
  If (goal design_cycle_step = part_expansion for_part = X) and
     (selected part = Y for = X);
  Then
     instantiate_part (Y);
                              (a)
```

```
Rule instantiate_independent_structure
  If (goal design_cycle_step = part_expansion for_part = X) and
     (specification name = AMOUNT for_part = X value = A) and
     (selected part = Y for = X);
  Then
        for (i = 1; i <= A; i++) instantiate_part (Y);
                              (b)
```

```
Rule instantiate_array_structure
  If (goal design_cycle_step = part_expansion for_part = X) and
     (specification name = ROWS for_part = X value = R) and
     (specification name = COLUMNS for_part = X value = C) and
     (selected part = Y for = X);
  Then
        for (i = 1; i <= R; i++)
            for (j = 1; j <= C; j++) instantiate_part (Y[i][j]);
                              (c)
```

Figure 5.3. Example part expansion rules for instantiating parts.

```
Rule update_indices_array_structure
   If (goal design_cycle_step = part_expansion for_part = X) and
      (part name = Y predecessor = X row = r col = c) and
      (characteristic of_part = Y[r][c] name = DATA_BUS_WIDTH value = W) and
   P (pin of = Y[r][c] index <> -1 index = I is_a = DATA_BUS);
   Then
        modify (P index = I + (c - 1) * W);
```

Figure 5.4. Example part expansion rules for updating indices in array elements.

```
Rule connect_rows_array_structure
   If (goal design_cycle_step = part_expansion for_part = X) and
      (part name = Y predecessor = X row = r col = 1) and
      (part name = Y predecessor = X row = r col = c) and
   P1(pin of = Y[r][1] index = I is_a = ADDRESS_BUS);
   P2(pin of = Y[r][c] index = I is_a = ADDRESS_BUS);
   Then
        connect (P1, P2);
```

```
Rule connect_columns_array_structure
   If (goal design_cycle_step = part_expansion for_part = X) and
      (part name = Y predecessor = X row = r col = c) and
      (part name = Y predecessor = X row = r col = c) and
   P1(pin of = Y[1][c] index = I is_a = DATA_BUS);
   P2(pin of = Y[r][c] index = I is_a = DATA_BUS);
   Then
        connect (P1, P2);
```

Figure 5.5. Example part expansion rules for making connections within array.

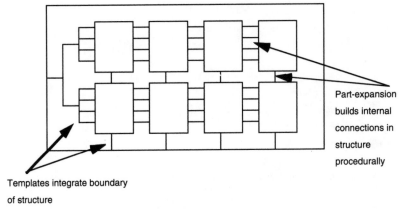

Part-expansion
builds internal
connections in
structure
procedurally

Templates integrate boundary
of structure

Figure 5.6. Interconnections for an array structure.

part has been selected for an abstract part, it is instantiated once. The rule in
Figure 5.3(b) instantiates a suitable number of parts in the independent structure;
nothing else needs to be done in the d_{casc} step for this structure. The rule in
Figure 5.3(c) instantiates a suitable number of parts into an array structure. The
rule in Figure 5.4 modifies the indices of pins on the parts so that they reflect the
position of the part in the array. The rules in Figure 5.5 make the connections
across rows and columns internal to the array. Note that if structural synthesis
was done using only templates, a separate template would be required for each
array organization, resulting in a total of

maximum number of rows × maximum number of columns

templates for each part configured as an array. Also, if the part expansion
connections were to be made using additional templates for each pair of adjacent
parts in the array, a total of

(maximum number of columns − 1) × maximum number of rows

column interconnect templates and

(maximum number of rows − 1) × maximum number of columns

row interconnect templates would be required. Here we exploit the repetitive
nature of the connections and the fact that a connection of pins on several parts
configured as arrays can be generalized by considering the functionality (is_a)
and the index of the pin instead of its name. This completes the d_{casc} step
for arrays. Connections to the boundary elements of the array are done in the
$d_{template}$ step, as illustrated in Figure 5.6.

At an OR node n_i, structural design integrates the selected successor part in the structure with n_i. At an AND node n_i, structural design instantiates all successor parts and integrates them with n_i. Structural design is done using templates, which are represented as a single rule. Different types of structures require different template forms, thus the format of the LHS is unique to the type of structure. The template types and corresponding structures are listed below:

- **Type AND:** Used for an AND node (see Figure 5.7).

- **Type OR-simple:** Used for an OR node, when the successor part is not organized into an array structure and has just one functional unit (see Figure 5.8).

- **Type OR-functional-unit-specific:** Used for an OR node, when the successor part is not organized into an array structure but has multiple functional units; some connections on these parts (e.g., power and ground lines) are common between all functional units; this template shows the connections specific to the functional unit being used (see Figure 5.9).

- **Type OR-common-connections:** Used for an OR node, when the successor part is not organized into an array structure but has multiple functional units; it shows the connections common to all functional units on the successor part (see Figure 5.10).

- **Type OR-row-of-array:** Used for an OR node, when the successor part is the boundary element on Row 1 of an array structure (see Figure 5.11).

- **Type OR-column-of-array:** used for an OR node, when the successor part is the boundary element on Column 1 of an array structure (see Figure 5.12).

Templates are easily represented as rules. The LHS describes the context and the design state when the template is applicable. The RHS asserts the template's parts and connections. The `instantiate_part` routine instantiates a new part into the design, the `connect_net` routine makes a connection between two pins, and the `connect_net_bus` routine indicates that the second pin is a bus of a particular type (INDEX, NAME, or ONE-TO-ONE) and that the first pin is one of the pins on this bus. The RHS also creates the `template_tag` WME with a unique name for that template. This WME is used as a CE in the specification and calculation rules to make them specific to the invocation of a particular template (as discussed in Sections 5.2.1 and 5.2.4). Thus, the `template_tag` threads together the knowledge in k_{template}, k_{calc}, and k_{spec}. The rule form of the template shown in Figure 4.19 is given in Figure 5.8.

```
Rule Template_SBC_0
    If (goal design_cycle_step = template for_part = SBC_0) and
       (specification name = TOTAL_BOARD_COST for_part = SBC_0 value > 100) and
      (specification name = TOTAL_BOARD_AREA for_part = SBC_0 value > 5000000) and
       (template_tag for_part = SBC_0 type = 1);
    Then
        create (template_tag name = SBC_0_GENERAL
                             for_part = SBC_0 type = 1);
        instantiate_part (PROC_0);
        instantiate_part (MEM_0);
        ....
        connect_net (MEM_0, DATA_BUS, PROC_0, DATA_BUS);
        ....
```

Figure 5.7. Example template rule (AND).

```
Rule Template_68XX_SIO_0_to_6850_for_RS232
    If (goal design_cycle_step = template for_part = 68XX_SIO_0) and
       (part name = 6850 predecessor = 68XX_SIO_0) and
       (characteristic MAX_BAUD_RATE of_part = 6850 value = X) and
       (specification name = BAUD_RATE for_part = 68XX_SIO_0 value <= X) and
      (specification name = DRIVER_TYPE for_part = 68XX_SIO_0 value = RS232) and
       (specification name = INT_TYPE for_part = 68XX_SIO_0 value = ASYNC) and
       (report REMAINING_BOARD_COST value > 120)
       (report REMAINING_BOARD_AREA value > 100)
       (template_tag for_part = 68XX_SIO_0 type = 2);
    Then
        create (template_tag name = 68XX_SIO_0_6850_RS232
                             for_part = 68XX_SIO_0 type = 2);
        instantiate_part (CLOCK_GEN_0);
        instantiate_part (RS232_PORT_0);
        connect_net (6850, TxD, RS232_PORT_0, TxD);
        connect_net_bus (6850, D0, 68XX_SIO_0, DATA_BUS, INDEX);
        ....
```

Figure 5.8. Example template rule (Simple-OR).

```
Rule Template_NAND21_0_to_7400_unit1
    If (goal design_cycle_step = template for_part = NAND21_0) and
       (part name = 7400 predecessor = NAND21_0) and
       (specification name = PROP_DELAY for_part = NAND21_0 value >= -1)
       (template_tag for_part = NAND21_0 type = 2a);
    Then
        create (template_tag name = NAND21_0_7400_UNIT1
                             for_part = NAND21_0 type = 2a);
        connect_net (7400, A1, NAND21_0, IN1);
        connect_net (7400, B1, NAND21_0, IN2);
        connect_net (7400, Y1, NAND21_0, OUT);
        ....
```

Figure 5.9. Example template rule (OR-functional-unit-specific).

```
Rule Template_NAND21_0_to_7400_common
    If (goal design_cycle_step = template for_part = NAND21_0) and
       (instantiated part = 7400 for = NAND21_0) and
       (specification name = PROP_DELAY for_part = NAND21_0 value >= -1)
       (template_tag for_part = NAND21_0 type = 3);
       (connection pin_of = 7400);
    Then
       create (template_tag name = NAND21_0_7400_COMMON
                            for_part = NAND21_0 type = 3);
       connect_net (7400, VCC, POWER_SUPPLY, VCC);
       connect_net (7400, GND, POWER_SUPPLY, GND);
       ....
```

Figure 5.10. Example template rule (OR-common-connections).

```
Rule Template_G_SRAM_0_62256_row
    If (goal design_cycle_step = template for_part = G_SRAM_0) and
       (part name = 62256 predecessor = G_SRAM_0 row = 1 col = C) and
       (specification name = ROWS for_part = G_SRAM_0 value >= -1)
       (specification name = COLUMNS for_part = G_SRAM_0 value >= -1)
       (specification name = ACCESS_TIME for_part = G_SRAM_0 value >= -1)
       (report REMAINING_BOARD_COST value > 0)
       (report REMAINING_BOARD_AREA value > 0)
       (template_tag for_part = G_SRAM_0 type = 4 col = C);
    Then
       create (template_tag name = G_SRAM_0_62256_ROW
                            for_part = G_SRAM_0 type = 4 col = C);
       connect_net_bus (62256, D0, G_SRAM_0, DATA_BUS, INDEX);
       connect_net_bus (62256, D1, G_SRAM_0, DATA_BUS, INDEX);
       ....
```

Figure 5.11. Example template rule (OR-column-of-array).

```
Rule Template_G_SRAM_0_62256_col
    If (goal design_cycle_step = template for_part = G_SRAM_0) and
       (part name = 62256 predecessor = G_SRAM_0 row = R col = 1) and
       (specification name = ROWS for_part = G_SRAM_0 value >= -1)
       (specification name = COLUMNS for_part = G_SRAM_0 value >= -1)
       (specification name = ACCESS_TIME for_part = G_SRAM_0 value >= -1)
       (report REMAINING_BOARD_COST value > 0)
       (report REMAINING_BOARD_AREA value > 0)
       (template_tag for_part = G_SRAM_0 type = 5 row = R);
    Then
       create (template_tag name = G_SRAM_0_62256_COL
                            for_part = G_SRAM_0 type = 5 row = R);
       connect_net (62256,   OE, G_SRAM_0,   READ);
       connect_net (62256,   WE, G_SRAM_0,   WRITE);
       connect_net_bus (62256,   CE, G_SRAM_0, CHIP_SELECT_BUS, ONE-TO-ONE);
       connect_net_bus (62256, A0, G_SRAM_0, ADDRESS_BUS, INDEX);
       connect_net_bus (62256, A1, G_SRAM_0, ADDRESS_BUS, INDEX);
       ....
```

Figure 5.12. Example template rule (OR-row-of-array).

```
Rule 8086_PROC_0_max_access_time
    If (goal design_cycle_step = imm_calculation
            for_part = 8086_PROC_0) and
        (template_tag name = 8086_PROC_0_8086 for_part = 8086_PROC_0) and
        (characteristic name = CLOCK_SPEED of_part = 8086 value = X) and
        (characteristic name = PROC_SETUP_TIME of_part = 8086 value = Y)
    Then
        create (report name = MAX_ACCESS_TIME value = 10**9/X - Y);
```

Figure 5.13. Calculation rule for 8086_PROC_0.

Since the following situations do not occur, we do not have separate template types for these:

- successor part with multiple functional units organized into an array,

- AND node with a successor part having multiple functional units and only a subset of the functional units being used.

The SFS is performed by the conflict resolution process of the rule-based system. The LHS of each template is efficiently matched against the design state (represented in working memory) as a natural consequent of the rule-based programming paradigm. If more than one template matches the design state, an error condition is detected (since a template's preconditions are guaranteed to be unique according to the design model) and reported to the user. If no template matches the design state, then knowledge acquisition is automatically triggered, as explained in Part III of the book.

5.2.4   Calculation

The d_{calc} design cycle step computes reports and local reports using equations involving other variables in the design state. The equation for creating each report or local report is represented as a rule. This partition is divided into two subpartitions, $k_{calc.imm}$ and $k_{calc.delayed}$, corresponding to design cycle substeps $d_{calc.imm}$ and $d_{calc.delayed}$, respectively. An example rule for the $k_{calc.imm}$ is given in Figure 5.13. The LHS of the rule checks if the current context is the calculation design cycle step for the part 8086_PROC_0 after the template integrating the 8086 with the 8086_PROC_0 has been used. If the characteristics of the 8086 are present, the rule's RHS creates a report MAX_ACCESS_TIME using the equation shown. Delayed calculation rules are similar except for that the name of the design cycle step in the goal CE becomes delay_calculation.

Note that the method for computing a report is specific to a particular template that has been used for an abstract part. For example, if some additional interfacing logic is used in the template for interfacing the 8086 with the 8086_PROC_0, the equation for computing the MAX_ACCESS_TIME would be different. To make each calculation rule specific to a template, the rule includes a special `template_tag` CE which has a unique name for each template. This WME is created when the template for the abstract part was invoked in the $d_{template}$ design step as described in Section 5.2.3.

5.2.5   Architectural Knowledge

The architectural knowledge is responsible for sequencing through the contexts in M1 to effect the design process in accordance with the design model. k_{arch} provides the control for the M1 problem solver and maps directly into three distinct levels of control:

Subproblem ordering layer: Decisions about which abstract part's design is to be attempted next is made at this level. The subproblem ordering algorithm described in Section 4.3.2 provides the control. Decisions to execute external analysis tools are also made. For example, control is passed to ASSURE, which analyzes the design for reliability metrics and makes suggestions for enhancing system reliability.

Design cycle sequencing layer: Sequencing of the design cycle for each abstract part is done at this level. For each design cycle step, a corresponding knowledge-base partition is activated by setting the `goal` context element suitably.

Conflict resolution layer: Decisions about which rule in a particular knowledge-base partition is to be fired is made at this level. The control is provided by a simple conflict resolution strategy, which is based on the recency of the first CE and the specificity of the rule (and is similar to MEA [47]).

This layering of control knowledge is similar to that in [120]. In addition to simplifying the implementation of the control structure, the multi-layered approach also allows for easy modification of control at any level. For example, adding another step to the design cycle would just influence the middle layer; passing control to an external advisor tool like ASSURE would influence just the top layer.

In addition to control, k_{arch} also includes support functions such as input and output routines (e.g., `get_response`), database interaction functions (e.g., `instantiate_part`), and routines for maintaining data structures (e.g., `connect_net`). These functions have been used in the example rules presented in the previous sections.

5.3   The MICON Database

Part models are stored in the central MICON database, which is built on a commercial relational database. The part model is actually implemented in the database as a set of tables that are linked together by common fields. These tables are detailed below:

Part table includes the part-name, chip-name, package type and pin-mapping-descriptor.

Characteristic table includes the characteristic-name, value, and a pointer to a specific chip-name or part-name (depending upon whether the characteristic is applicable to all logically equivalent parts or not).

Specification table includes the specification-name, type, group-number, and a pointer to a specific part-name.

Link table includes the predecessor-name, edge-type, functional-unit-number, and a pointer to a specific chip-name.

Logical pins table includes the pin-name, index, is_a, and a pointer to a specific chip-name.

Physical pins table includes a pin-number for each pin-name in the logical pins table for a specific pin-mapping-descriptor in the parts table.

Package table includes the package-type and the number of pins on it.

Package pins table includes the location in the Cartesian space for each pin-number on a package-type.

Recall the relationship between part-name and chip-name described in Section 4.1.2. By keeping separate logical and physical pin tables, pin-related information between logically equivalent parts can be shared. Similarly, separating package information allows all parts to share package information. The tables for the part models described previously in Figures 4.6 and 4.7 are shown in Figure 5.14. Note that in the actual implementation, all pointers between tables are unique integers and not symbolic.

Data can be accessed from these tables using the Structured Query Language (SQL) supported by the relational database. A database server has been built on top of the database and can simultaneously service multiple clients over a computer network, as was shown in Figure 2.5. In addition to supporting direct SQL, the server provides a high level interface to access the part model. For example, a client program can use a set of procedures to access the part name and chip name of all parts that have characteristics COST $\leq$ 100 and AREA $\leq$ 500.

Part			
Part-name	*Chip-name*	*Package-type*	*Pin-mapping*
NAND21_0	NAND21_0	NONE	NONE
SN74LS00D	7400	DIP14	1

Characteristic		
Char-name	*Value*	*Pointer to part*
NUM_INPUTS	2	NAND21_0
NUM_GATES	4	7400
PROP_DELAY	10	SN74LS00D

Specification			
Spec-name	*Type*	*Group-number*	*Pointer to part*
PROP_DELAY	Integer	1	NAND21_0
TECHNOLOGY	Symbol	2	NAND21_0

Link			
Predecessor-name	*Edge-type*	*F-unit-number*	*Pointer to part*
LOGIC_PART	OR	0	NAND21_0
NAND21_0	OR	1	7400
NAND21_0	OR	2	7400
NAND21_0	OR	3	7400
NAND21_0	OR	4	7400

Figure 5.14. Part models for NAND21_0 and SN74LS00D represented as tables in the database.

These procedures, however, support only frequently used queries; in other cases, direct SQL has to be used.

Human designers can access part models in the database using ENTRY, an interactive data-entry tool. ENTRY allows the user to check out a complete model of a part from the database, make additions or changes to it, and store it back into the database. Like other MICON tools, it also operates as a client program that connects to the central database server.

All information about parts is stored as attribute-value_pairs (characteristics). At any stage of the overall design process, only a subset of these characteristics is relevant. For example, M1 reasons with the function-related characteristics. ASSURE, however, requires package-related, not function-related, information. To avoid overwhelming each tool with unnecessary information, a separate filter table that lists relevant characteristics is maintained for each tool. After connecting to the database server, the tool specifies the filter table, and only the characteristics permitted by the filter are returned.

Name: 80386_SIO_0		Chip name: 80386_SIO_0
Specifications		
spec-name		*group-number*
EXT_INTERFACE		1
BAUD_RATE		1
BAUD_RATE_SWITCH		1
MAX_ACCESS_TIME		1
SIO_TAG		1
CHIP_NAME		1
INTERRUPTS		1
INTR_MASKABLE		1
INTR_PRIORITY_LEVEL		1
PORT_SIZE		1
PORT_TYPE		1
CONNECTOR_SIZE		1
CONNECTOR_TYPE		1
Characteristics		
char-name		*value*
PROC_FAMILY		80386
Links		
predecessor-name	*edge-type*	*func-unit-number*
SIO_0	OR	0
Pins		
pin-name	*pin-index*	*pin-isa*
DATA_BUS	-1	NIL
..	..	..

Figure 5.15. Part model for the 80386_SIO_0.

```
(part name = 80386_SIO_0 predecessor = SIO_0)
(characteristic of_part = 80386_SIO_0 name = PROC_FAMILY value = 80386)
(template_tag name = SIO_0_80386_SIO_0 for_part = SIO_0)
(part name = SIO_0 predecessor = IO_0)
. . . . .
```

Figure 5.16. Working memory at beginning of design cycle.

```
Rule spec_80386_SIO_0_number_1
  If (goal design_cycle_step = specification for_part = 80386_SIO_0) and
     (part name = 80386_SIO_0 predecessor = SIO_0) and
     (template_tag name = SIO_0_80386_SIO_0 for_part = SIO_0) and
     (specification for_part = 80386_SIO_0 name = EXT_INTERFACE)
  Then
     get_response(''Input external interface type <RS232, RS422> '', X);
     create (specification for_part = 80386_SIO_0,
                           name = EXT_INTERFACE, value = X);

Rule spec_80386_SIO_0_number_2
  If (goal design_cycle_step = specification for_part = 80386_SIO_0) and
     (part name = 80386_SIO_0 predecessor = SIO_0) and
     (template_tag name = SIO_0_80386_SIO_0 for_part = SIO_0) and
     (specification for_part = 80386_SIO_0 name = BAUD_RATE)
  Then
     get_response(''Input baud rate for this port <1200,2400,4800,9600>'', X);
     create (specification for_part = 80386_SIO_0, name = BAUD_RATE, value = X);

Rule spec_80386_SIO_0_number_3
  If (goal design_cycle_step = specification
            for_part = 80386_SIO_0) and
     (part name = 80386_SIO_0 predecessor = SIO_0) and
     (template_tag name = SIO_0_80386_SIO_0 for_part = SIO_0) and
     (report name = ACCESS_TIME value = X) and
     (specification for_part = 80386_SIO_0 name = MAX_ACCESS_TIME)
  Then
     create (specification for_part = 80386_SIO_0,
                           name = MAX_ACCESS_TIME, value = X);
```

Figure 5.17. Specification rules for 80386_SIO_0.

5.4   Knowledge Utilization Example

In the last two sections, we have described how the knowledge in M1 and the part models are represented. In this section, we illustrate how this information is utilized by the M1 problem solver in the design cycle.

Consider an 80386_SIO_0 abstract part which has not yet been designed. The part model for this part is shown in Figure 5.15. The relevant elements in working memory at this stage are shown in Figure 5.16. Initially the 80386_SIO_0 part is in the set of nodes waiting for their specifications to be filled. Hence the goal WME corresponding to the specification step is created for 80386_SIO_0. The context for the rules shown in Figure 5.17 is active. Rules for computing other specifications are similar to these. Given the elements in WM currently, only Rules 1 and 2 are applicable since all LHS CEs for these rules are in WM. The conflict resolution layer of k_{arch} selects the rule to be fired; here Rules 1 and 2 are fired in arbitrary order since both rank equally. Since specifications are not complete for this part, its design cycle is not activated. At a later stage, the report (report name = ACCESS_TIME value = 200) is added to WM,

Name: I8251		Chip name: 8251
Specifications		
spec-name		*group-number*
Characteristics		
char-name		*value*
ADDRESS_BITS		1
ACCESS_TIME		300
Links		
predecessor-name	*edge-type*	*func-unit-number*
80386_SIO_0	OR	0
8086_SIO_0	OR	0
Pins		
pin-name	*pin-index*	*pin-isa*
D0	0	DATA_BUS
D1	1	DATA_BUS
..	..	..

Figure 5.18. Part model for the I8251.

allowing Rule 3 of Figure 5.17 to fire. Subsequently, since the specifications are complete, the design cycle for 80386_SIO_0 is activated. The design cycle sequencing layer controls the order of execution of the design cycle steps as described below.

Selection: The following sequence of substeps are executed:

1. No unused 80386_SIO_0 units are found in the design, so the selection process continues.

2. The database is searched for successors of 80386_SIO_0, and the parts I8251 and I8274 are brought into WM as candidates. The part models for these parts are shown in Figure 5.18 and 5.19. Note that both parts must have links pointing to 80386_SIO_0.

3. The `goal` WME corresponding to the checking of selection constraints is created. The WM at this stage is given in Figure 5.20. The context for the k_{select_rule} partition rule shown in Figure 5.21 is active. The rule is applicable for the I8251 candidate; it fires and the I8251 gets rejected.

4. Since only the I8274 remains, it is selected. If, however, the I8251 had not been rejected, penalty points would be computed based on

Name: I8274		Chip name: 8274
Specifications		
spec-name		*group-number*
Characteristics		
char-name		*value*
ADDRESS_BITS		2
ACCESS_TIME		200
Links		
predecessor-name	*edge-type*	*func-unit-number*
80386_SIO_0	OR	1
80386_SIO_0	OR	2
8086_SIO_0	OR	1
8086_SIO_0	OR	2
Pins		
pin-name	*pin-index*	*pin-isa*
D0	0	DATA_BUS
D1	1	DATA_BUS
..	..	..

Figure 5.19. Part model for the I8274.

```
(goal design_cycle_step = selection_check_constraint for_part = 80386_SIO_0)
(candidate name = I8251 successor_of = 80386_SIO_0)
(characteristic name = ACCESS_TIME value = 300 of_part = I8251)
(candidate name = I8274 successor_of = 80386_SIO_0)
(characteristic name = ACCESS_TIME value = 200 of_part = I8274)
(specification for_part = 80386_SIO_0 name = MAX_ACCESS_TIME value = 200)
(report name = ACCESS_TIME value = 200)
(specification for_part = 80386_SIO_0 name = EXT_INTERFACE value = RS232)
(specification for_part = 80386_SIO_0 name = BAUD_RATE value = 9600)
(part name = 80386_SIO_0 predecessor = SIO_0)
(characteristic of_part = 80386_SIO_0 name = PROC_FAMILY value = 80386)
(template_tag name = SIO_0_80386_SIO_0 for_part = SIO_0)
(part name = SIO_0 predecessor = IO_0)
.....
```

Figure 5.20. Working memory at selection step in design cycle.

```
Rule compare_80386_SIO_0_access_time
   If (goal design_cycle_step = selection_check_constraint
           for_part = 80386_SIO_0) and
      (candidate name = P is_successor_of = 80386_SIO_0) and
      (characteristic name = ACCESS_TIME of_part = P value = X) and
      (specification name = MAX_ACCESS_TIME for_part = 80386_SIO_0 value < X)
   Then
      mark candidate as rejected
```

Figure 5.21. Example selection rule.

resource usage of both parts, and the part with fewer penalty points would be selected.

Part expansion: Rule `instantiate_part_default` of Figure 5.3(a) fires, and the I8274 is instantiated into **WM**. One of the two functional units (see the part model in Figure 5.19), say the second one, on the I8274 is marked as being used in the design of this particular 80386_SIO_0.

Structural design: The `goal` corresponding to the structural design step is created. The context for the k_{template} partition rules shown in Figure 5.22 is active. The rule in Figure 5.22(c) is not applicable as it is for a different design state (when an RS422 port is needed). First, the rule in Figure 5.22(a), the common connections template rule (Type 3), is applicable, and it fires. Next, the rule in Figure 5.22(b), the functional-unit-2-specific template rule (Type 2a), is applicable, and it fires. In this way, the I8274 is interconnected into the 80386_SIO_0 abstract part. Note that a CLOCK_GENERATOR_0 and RS232_PORT_0 abstract part were introduced in the second template.

Immediate calculation: The `goal` corresponding to the immediate calculation step is created. The context for the $k_{\text{calc\_now}}$ partition rule shown in Figure 5.23 is active. The rule fires, and a `report` indicating the address occupied by this particular SIO port is created.

Since successors of the 80386_SIO_0 need to be designed, the design cycle has to wait for the delayed calculation step. The subproblem ordering layer takes control, assigns a `waiting` status to 80386_SIO_0, and designs other abstract parts in the design. At a later stage, the CLOCK_GENERATOR_0 and the RS232_PORT_0 have been designed, and the design cycle for the 80386_SIO_0 is activated again. The design cycle sequencing layer executes the following step:

Delayed calculation: The `goal` corresponding to the delayed calculation step is created. In this particular case, there are no rules in this context in the $k_{\text{calc\_delayed}}$ partition.

This completes the design cycle for the 80386_SIO_0.

While the design process was successful in this example, such is not always the case. In the next chapter, we discuss how a failure during the design process is handled.

```
Rule Template_80386_SIO_0_to_8274_COMMON_AND_ANY_EXT_INTERFACE
  If (goal design_cycle_step = template for_part = 80386_SIO_0) and
     (part name = 8274 predecessor = 80386_SIO_0) and
     (characteristic name = MAX_BAUD_RATE of_part = 8274 value = X) and
     (specification name = MAX_ACCESS_TIME for_part = 80386_SIO_0 value >= -1) and
     (specification name = BAUD_RATE for_prat = 80386_SIO_0 value <= X) and
     (specification name = EXT_INTERFACE for_part = 80386_SIO_0 value <> NIL) and
     (connection pin_of = 8274);
  Then
     create (template_tag name = 80386_SIO_0_8274_COMMON
                          for_part = 80386_SIO_0 type = 3);
     connect_net (8274, VCC, POWER_SUPPLY, VCC);
     connect_net (8274, GND, POWER_SUPPLY, GND);
     connect_net_bus (8274, D0, 80386_SIO_0, DATA_BUS, INDEX);
     connect_net_bus (8274, D1, 80386_SIO_0, DATA_BUS, INDEX);
     ....
```

                                    (a)

```
Rule Template_80386_SIO_0_to_8274_unit2_RS232
  If (goal design_cycle_step = template for_part = 80386_SIO_0) and
     (part name = 8274 predecessor = 80386_SIO_0) and
     (characteristic name = MAX_BAUD_RATE of_part = 8274 value = X) and
     (specification name = MAX_ACCESS_TIME for_part = 80386_SIO_0 value >= -1) and
     (specification name = BAUD_RATE for_part = 80386_SIO_0 value <= X) and
     (specification name = EXT_INTERFACE for_part = 80386_SIO_0 value = RS232) and
     (connection pin_of = 8274) and
     (template_tag for_part = 80386_SIO_0 type = 2a)
  Then
     create (template_tag name = 80386_SIO_0_8274_UNIT2_RS232
                          for_part = 80386_SIO_0 type = 2a);
     instantiate_part(RS232_PORT_0);
     instantiate_part(CLOCK_GENERATOR_0);
     ....
     connect_net (8274, TxDA, RS232_PORT_0, TxD);
     ....
```

                                    (b)

```
Rule Template_80386_SIO_0_to_8274_unit2_RS422
  If (goal design_cycle_step = template for_part = 80386_SIO_0) and
     (part name = 8274 predecessor = 80386_SIO_0) and
     (characteristic name = MAX_BAUD_RATE of_part = 8274 value = X) and
     (specification name = MAX_ACCESS_TIME for_part = 80386_SIO_0 value >= -1) and
     (specification name = BAUD_RATE for_part = 80386_SIO_0 value <= X) and
     (specification name = EXT_INTERFACE for_part = 80386_SIO_0 value = RS422) and
     (connection pin_of = 8274) and
     (template_tag for_part = 80386_SIO_0 type = 2a)
  Then
     create (template_tag name = 80386_SIO_0_8274_UNIT2_RS422
                          for_part = 80386_SIO_0 type = 2a);
     instantiate_part(RS422_PORT_0);
     ....
     connect_net (8274, TxDA, RS422_PORT_0, TxD);
     ....
```

                                    (c)

Figure 5.22. Example template rules for mapping 80386_SIO_0 to 8274.

```
Rule 80386_SIO_0_ADDRESS_SPACE
     If (goal design_cycle_step = imm_calculation for_part = 80386_SIO_0) and
       (template_tag name = 80386_SIO_0_8274_COMMON for_part = 80386_SIO_0) and
         (characteristic name = ADDRESS_BITS of_part = 8274 value = X)
     Then
         create (report name = SIO_ADDRESS_SPACE value = 2 ** X);
```

Figure 5.23. Calculation rule for 80386_SIO_0.

6

Failure Handling

Failure occurs during the design process when M1 is unable to create a design that meets the specifications and ceilings on physical resources given by the user. While the cause of failure is sometimes attributable to unreasonable user input, both the design cycle and the nature of the problem also make M1 susceptible to failures. This is because M1 makes design decisions using only local information, thereby attempting to optimize each individual choice without regard to its impact on later decisions. Since interactions between various subproblems, and therefore design decisions, are not predictable, the ramifications of a decision are impossible to foretell. Thus, while a decision may appear sound when made, it may cause the design process to fail later. As a result, M1 has a set of techniques for recovering from failures.

This chapter gives an overview of the failure handling module, FAILURE, within M1[1]. We first provide an overview of failure handling mechanisms, then characterize the two kinds of failure that occur in M1 and describe the techniques employed to handle them.

---

[1]This chapter is based, in part, on work done by Ajay Daga and reported in [28, 29]. The interested reader is encouraged to explore these publications for more information.

6.1 Failure Handling Mechanisms

The failure handling process is fundamentally different from the design process. While the objective of the design process is to construct a solution, the objective of the failure handling process is to reason about the actions taken by the design system, trying to determine if alternative actions can be taken that will eventually lead to a successful design. The failure handling process, therefore, considers the design decisions and the context in which they were made. Thus, the problem-solving approach used by failure handling systems is different from that used by their associated design problem solvers. The failure problem-solving process can be summarized as the following:

1. Change a variable to correct the failure.

2. Propagate the new variable through the design.

3. Reconfigure the design to account for any changes introduced by the changed variable.

Determining the cause of a failure can be difficult and often requires either domain-specific knowledge or user guidance. Similarly, changing some variable in a design (in our case this refers to a characteristic, report, or specification) also requires domain specific information. Several design systems, such as Air-Cyl [22], VT [85], and Pride [94], have specific provisions for the domain knowledge, also called fixes or suggestions, needed to perform these two tasks. Some domains with a strong algebraic foundation allow a more generalized approach, such as that used by Constraints [123] where device behavior, as represented by mathematical models, drives the failure handling process.

Propagation of changes through the design can be accomplished with a dependency network [119]. The nodes of the network correspond to design variables. There are two types of links in the dependency network: antecedent and consequent. The antecedent links indicate all the variables (reports, characteristics, or specifications) that were used to generate a given variable. The consequent dependencies are the variables that depend on the given variable, and will be affected by a change in its value. FAILURE allows no cycles in the dependency network. Further, a node that has no antecedent links is termed a *root*. Root variables correspond to either specifications that were filled by queries or some changeable characteristics.

The dependency network can be illustrated with a simple example. Assume that the functional hierarchy is traversed such that PROC_0 is designed first. Now assume that during the design of PROC_0 a report, PROC_CLOCK_SPEED, was generated. This report was subsequently used in the design of nodes MEM_0 and SIO_0. A dependency network with PROC_CLOCK_0 report as an antecedent variable and specifications on MEM_0 and SIO_0 as consequent variables is created. Subsequently, if a failure were to occur in the design of PIO_0, and it was determined that PROC_CLOCK_SPEED should be changed, the changed value must be propagated to only those nodes affected. The dependency network for PROC_CLOCK_SPEED is used to identify the parts of the design that need to be modified by the changed variable without any search. As described in the next section, the dependency network is essential to the failure handling capability.

Design state reconfiguration occurs once a new variable has been propagated through the dependency network. All parts in the design that were based on the changed variable are removed, and the design process is restarted. Any abstract part whose physical parts were removed will be visited once again by M1. The effect of this is to cause either new parts to be chosen during d_{select}, or new templates to be chosen during $d_{template}$, based on the new values propagated through dependency network. The supposition of failure handing is that these changes will remove the impasse that caused the design to fail.

6.2 Failure Characterization

Failure occurs at two points in the design cycle. The first place is $d_{template}$ due to the absence of a template. This is referred to as a *template failure* and is handled through the normal knowledge acquisition procedure (see Part III).

The second place where failure occurs is during the selection step, d_{select}. Failure occurs here because no part was able to satisfy all the selection constraints, k_{select_rule} (see Section 4.2.1). Failures due to selection constraint violations can be further divided into two categories: specification failures and resource failures. Each of these is discussed below.

6.3 Specification Failure Correction

A specification failure occurs when at least one specification of a part can not be met by its set of successors (candidate parts). In this case, the cause of the failure is simple: It is the unsatisfied specification. If more than one specification is violated, then each is taken in turn until either all eventually are satisfied or the user decides to end the failure handling process. Once the specification is identified, FAILURE takes over and performs the following steps:

1. Change variable value.

2. Variable propagation.

3. Design state reconfiguration.

Each step is discussed below.

6.3.1   Change Variable Value

A specification failure may occur due to a mismatch of values, termed a mismatch failure, or due to a value being overly constrained, called a constraint failure. An example mismatch failure is when a specification does not match any of the values of the corresponding characteristic in the database. Mismatch failures can occur for symbolic values or numeric values. When a symbolic value is the problem, a list of legal values is displayed and the user selects one. If there is problem with a numeric value, FAILURE chooses the closest arithmetic alternative.

A constraint failure is handled by changing one of the variables that generated the specification. This is done by showing the user the antecedent dependencies of the violated specification. At this point, a new value can be specified by the user or calculated by FAILURE. The user is shown the type of each variable (specification, report, or characteristic), and can, therefore, specify a change in terms of a root variable. If a non-root variable is chosen, the system recursively moves toward the root variable by considering the antecedent dependencies of each changed variable. The list of changed variables is passed to the next stage in the failure handling process.

6.3.2   Variable Propagation

A changed variable is passed throughout the design so that the design state can be reconfigured. This propagation is done via the dependency links and occurs in both the antecedent and consequent directions. The change propagates, however, in only one direction at a time. There are three types of change propagation mechanisms depending on direction and whether a new value is being passed. Each mechanism is described below.

Change without Value
This type of change takes place when a changed variable, v_1, which does not have a new value assigned to it, has links to a variable, v_2, that has not yet been changed. The variable v_2 is marked changed but does not have a new value assigned to it and waits for a value assignment. Note that this change is propagated in both the consequent and the antecedent directions.

Consequent Change with Value
This type of change takes place when a changed variable, v_1, has a new value assigned to it and is linked in the consequent direction to a variable, v_2, which

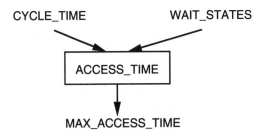

Figure 6.1. Consequent change with value example.

is either waiting for a new value or has not yet been changed. Here, the rule used to generate v_2 from v_1 and any other variables is fired, and a new value for v_2 is computed.

An example of consequent change is given in Figure 6.1. In this example, CYCLE_TIME is linked in the consequent direction to ACCESS_TIME. Thus when CYCLE_TIME is changed from 100 to 150, ACCESS_TIME is updated from 300 to 450 (assuming WAIT_STATES equals 3).

Antecedent Change with Value

Antecedent change occurs when a changed variable, v_2, has a new value assigned to it and is linked in the antecedent direction to a changed variable, v_1, which does not have a new value.

This type of propagation is more complex than a consequent change because the roles are reversed between the variables on the right hand side of the equation, termed the *generator* variables, and variable on the left hand side, referred to as the *generated* variable. Consider the simple equation $v_2 = 1/v_1$; when v_2 was first generated it was the dependent variable and was generated from v_1. Now if v_2 changes, a new value for v_1 must be computed, which is simple in this case but is not so in general. For complete generality, it would be necessary to compute the inverse function for each of the generator variables. In the above example this would be $v_1 = 1/v_2$. To limit the complexity of FAILURE, a data structure captures information about each of the generator variables, such as whether the variable is directly or inversely proportional to v_2, the constant associated with the variable, and the other variables used in the expression. An antecedent change is made by using this information to calculate the new value of v_1. The technique is general and dependent only on the type of the equation linking the variables. For example, it can represent equations of the form:

$$A = 2 * (B/(C * D)) + E/G.$$

There is no limitation on the number of expressions in an equation or terms in an expression. Each variable may appear in only one expression, and only arithmetic operations are permitted. FAILURE allows, however, only a single variable to be changed, and this variable must be specified by the user. The use of this technique is based on [123].

Change propagation takes place opportunistically; a variable is passed through the network only when it is changed. The dependency network stabilizes when no more changes need to be propagated. If the changed variable is at the root of a dependency path, changes are propagated only in the consequent direction.

6.3.3   Design State Reconfiguration

Once variables are propagated and the network has stabilized, affected parts of the design are reconfigured. This may cause portions of the design to be removed, if the variable they depended upon changed. If a specification for an OR node has been changed, then that node is redesigned because the change could affect the results of d_{select}. AND nodes are redesigned since their templates may be affected. All nodes that are rooted at the node to be redesigned are also purged from the design state, as are the consequence variables (e.g., reports that were generated). The node to be redesigned is placed in the queue of pending design tasks. Once the design state is reconfigured, the changed specifications, reports, and characteristics are shown to the user. Also shown are the nodes removed and redesigned.

The following section provides an example of the failure handling process.

6.4   A Failure Correction Example

Specification failure correction in FAILURE is illustrated in the following example. A computer is to be designed based on a Motorola 6809, 2K bytes ROM, 40K bytes SRAM, one SIO, and one PIO. The computer is to operate at a frequency of 1 MHz. A specification failure for an access time violation will occur due to a slow peripheral device. Recovery from this failure will affect a variety of other devices.

A 6809 operating at 1 MHz and zero wait states allows 395 ns for an I/O device to communicate to it. For this example, assume that all the SIOs in the database have an access time of 600 nS. Failure correction is illustrated through the actual user-system interaction during failure handling. Tool output is in `typeface`, comments are *italicized*, and user input is in $\boxed{\textbf{bold boxed text}}$.

`Activating 68XX_SIO_0 design`

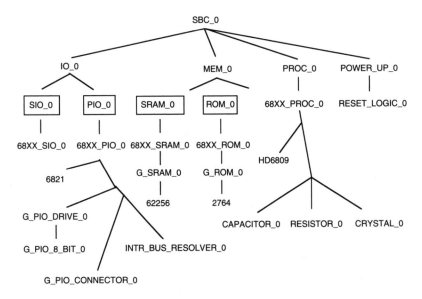

Figure 6.2. Design hierarchy at point of failure.

```
Resource check returns NONE SUITABLE
Selection
   Rejecting HD68A50 due to a larger ACCESS_TIME
   Rejecting MC68B50 due to larger ACCESS_TIME
   Selection Fails
Failure analysis
Failure handling
   Failed for 68XX_SIO_0:
   Specification: MAX_ACCESS_TIME
   Current Value: 395
   Reason:  VALUE OVER CONSTRAINED - too small by 205
```

A failure in M1's synthesis process occurred during the selection step of the design cycle. The design hierarchy at the point of failure is indicated in Figure 6.2. The failed specification, its current value, and the amount by which it failed are sent to FAILURE. Note: This failure is due to a value being overconstrained. The system now progresses to the first step in its failure handling process, changing variable value.

```
ANTECEDENT DEPENDENCIES of MAX_ACCESS_TIME
MAX_ACCESS_TIME of 68XX_SIO_0
   specification MAX_ACCESS_TIME of SIO_0
MAX_ACCESS_TIME of SIO_0
   report IO_MAX_ACCESS_TIME of 68XX_PROC_0
```

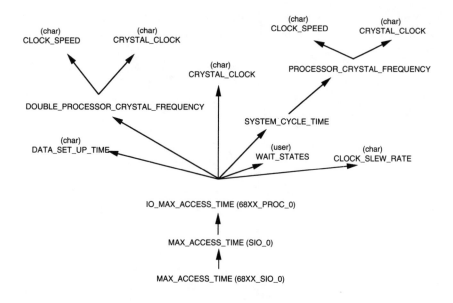

Figure 6.3. Dependency network for MAX_ACCESS_TIME.

```
IO_MAX_ACCESS_TIME of 68XX_PROC_0
    report DOUBLE_PROCESSOR_CRYSTAL_FREQUENCY of 68XX_PROC_0
    characteristic CRYSTAL_CLOCK of 6809
    characteristic CLOCK_SLEW_RATE of 6809
    characteristic DATA_SET_UP_TIME of 6809
DOUBLE_PROCESSOR_CRYSTAL_FREQUENCY
    characteristic CLOCK_SPEED of 6809
    characteristic CRYSTAL_CLOCK of 6809
```

The direct antecedent dependencies of a variable are those immediately below it and indented. A rendering of part of the dependency network is given in Figure 6.3. All reports or specifications appearing as the antecedent dependencies of a variable have their dependencies traced to root variables. Consequently, DOUBLE_PROCESSOR_CRYSTAL_FREQUENCY, *an antecedent dependency of* IO_MAX_ACCESS_TIME, *is dependent on* CLOCK_SPEED *and* CRYSTAL_CLOCK.

```
Change design state to handle this failure (Y or N):  y
Name of parameter to be changed:  CLOCK_SPEED
Type of the parameter
   (specification or report or characteristic):  characteristic
Automatic computation of new parameter value (Y or N):  y
Any further changes (Y or N):  n
```

Note that the user changed a characteristic. FAILURE allows this because it recognizes two types of characteristics: fixed and changeable. Changeable characteristics have a range of allowable values. For example, clock speed for a processor is usually specified as a range, so any value in the range is acceptable. Fixed characteristics can not be changed. Power dissipation is a fixed characteristic since its value is constant.

The root variables of IO_MAX_ACCESS_TIME *are* CLOCK_SPEED, CRYSTAL_CLOCK, DATA_SET_UP_TIME, *and* CLOCK_SLEW_RATE. *It is desirable that the user change one of these variables to handle the failure. Alternatively, the design may specify a change of a non-root variable (e.g.,* DOUBLE_PROCESSOR_CRYSTAL_FREQUENCY), *in which case the system will guide the user in ultimately specifying a root variable. Here,* CLOCK_SPEED *was specified. The system recomputed the value of* CLOCK_SPEED, *changing it to 709 KHz, and now* MAX_ACCESS_TIME *of IO_0 is 600 ns. The formulas used to calculate several of the values and the corresponding data structures are shown in Figure 6.4. In this data structure, a formula is obtained by summing all terms linked together; each term is obtained by multiplying all enclosed variables while considering the* CONSTANT *and* INVERSE *fields. FAILURE performs the second step of the fail handling process, updating the dependency network using the propagation techniques defined earlier. When the network stabilizes, FAILURE displays the changes made.*

```
6821, 62256, 2732   removed
PIO_0, SRAM_0, ROM_0, SIO_0   redesigned
POWER_DISSIPATION of SBC_0 changed: 47440 - 49000 mW
BOARD_COST of SBC_0 changed:  1785 - 2785 cents
BOARD_AREA of SBC_0 changed: 5986000 - 880000  mils
MAX_ACCESS_TIME of MEM_0 changed:  695 - 1103 ns
SYSTEM_CYCLE_TIME of 68XX_PROC_0 changed: 250 - 352 ns
LEFT_CS_ACCESS_TIME of 68XX_PROC_0 changed:  300 - 504 ns
PROCESSOR_CRYSTAL_FREQUENCY of 68XX_PROC_0   changed:
40000000 - 2836876 Hz
DOUBLE_PROCESSOR_CRYSTAL_FREQUENCY of   68XX_PROC_0
changed: 80000000 - 5673758 Hz
CLOCK_SPEED of 6809 changed: 1000000 - 709219 Hz
IO_MAX_ACCESS_TIME of 68XX_PROC_0 changed:  395 - 600 ns
MAX_ACCESS_TIME of IO_0 changed: 395 - 600 nS
```

The resultant design hierarchy list is shown in Figure 6.5. The failure has been alleviated, so FAILURE returns control to M1. FAILURE now performs the final step of its task, updating the design state. FAILURE will remove all portions of the design that depended the changed variables.

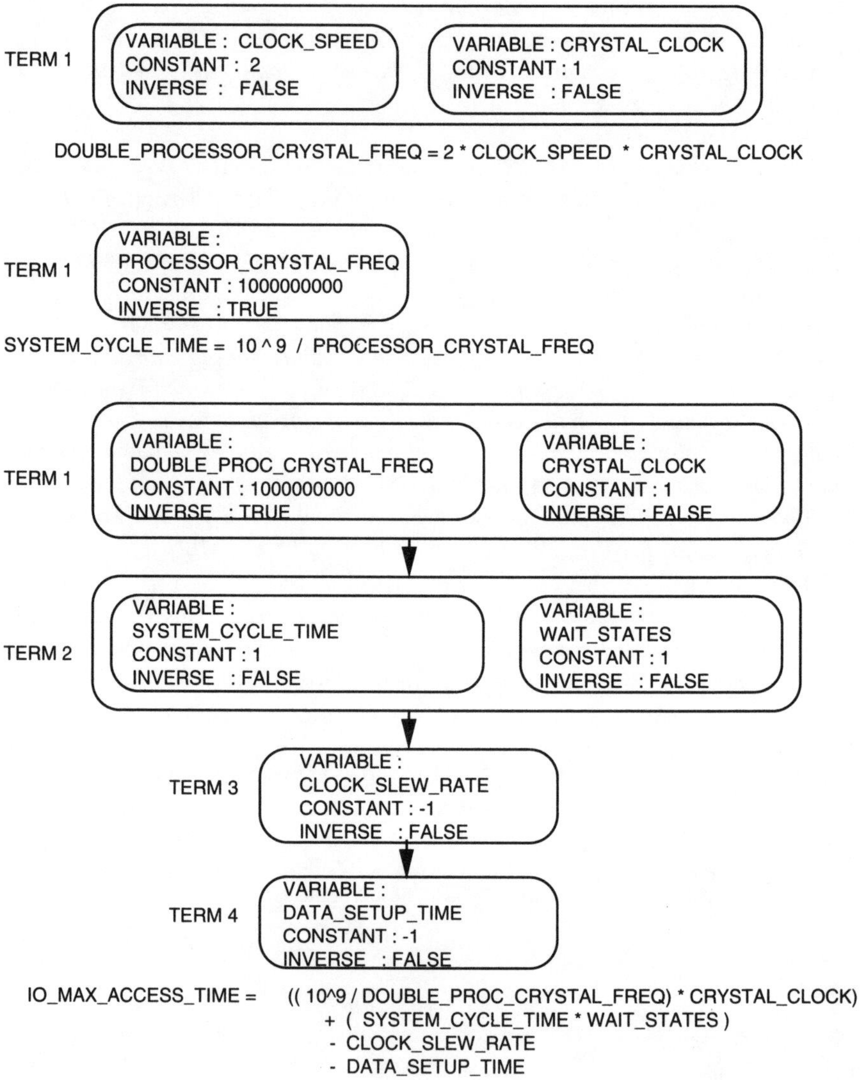

TERM 1
VARIABLE : CLOCK_SPEED	VARIABLE : CRYSTAL_CLOCK
CONSTANT : 2	CONSTANT : 1
INVERSE : FALSE	INVERSE : FALSE

DOUBLE_PROCESSOR_CRYSTAL_FREQ = 2 * CLOCK_SPEED * CRYSTAL_CLOCK

TERM 1
VARIABLE :
PROCESSOR_CRYSTAL_FREQ
CONSTANT : 1000000000
INVERSE : TRUE

SYSTEM_CYCLE_TIME = 10 ^ 9 / PROCESSOR_CRYSTAL_FREQ

TERM 1
VARIABLE :
DOUBLE_PROC_CRYSTAL_FREQ
CONSTANT : 1000000000
INVERSE : TRUE

VARIABLE :
CRYSTAL_CLOCK
CONSTANT : 1
INVERSE : FALSE

TERM 2
VARIABLE :
SYSTEM_CYCLE_TIME
CONSTANT : 1
INVERSE : FALSE

VARIABLE :
WAIT_STATES
CONSTANT : 1
INVERSE : FALSE

TERM 3
VARIABLE :
CLOCK_SLEW_RATE
CONSTANT : -1
INVERSE : FALSE

TERM 4
VARIABLE :
DATA_SETUP_TIME
CONSTANT : -1
INVERSE : FALSE

IO_MAX_ACCESS_TIME =   ((10^9 / DOUBLE_PROC_CRYSTAL_FREQ) * CRYSTAL_CLOCK)
+ (SYSTEM_CYCLE_TIME * WAIT_STATES)
- CLOCK_SLEW_RATE
- DATA_SETUP_TIME

Figure 6.4. Data structures and formulas used to compute variables in the example.

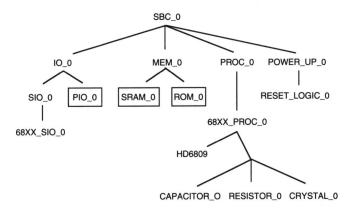

Figure 6.5. Example design hierarchy after the point of failure (before redesign).

6.5   Resource Failures

Resource failures happen when the user specified budget for a resource (e.g., power, area, cost) would be exceeded by selecting a part. This is manifested at OR-nodes when all the successors will consume more of a resource than is currently available. Resource failures are particularly difficult to handle since all components in a design are potential contributors. For example, all components consume area, so if the area resource is exhausted, then it is difficult to determine the cause for the problem. Viewed from a different perspective, if a dependency network were to be constructed for a resource, it would be very dense, making it difficult to search efficiently [33].

The assistance provided by FAILURE is limited to helping the user backtrack through the selection of parts or increasing the amount of the critical resource. If the user chooses to backtrack, then each node in the decision list is traversed in chronological order. At each node, the user is shown the alternative for a given selected part and may select the alternative. If a new component is placed in the design, then the design is reconfigured in the same way as for specification failures. An example of a resource failure correction is given in Figure 6.6. At the node 80386, M1 fails while trying to select an 80386-16 (16 MHZ version) because of a cost overrun of $100. At this point the user considers the alternative, 80386-12 (12 MHZ version) which, while substantially cheaper ($50), does not remedy the failure. The user may quit, if neither the processor nor the cost budget can be relaxed, or can move up to the PROC_0 node. In this case, the user decides to relax the processor specification and looks

102

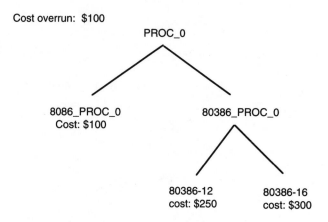

Figure 6.6. Resource failure correction example.

at the projected costs[2] of the 8086 path, which is \$150 cheaper, and decides to pursue it. The 8086_PROC_0 is then inserted into the design, reconfiguration occurs, and the design process is restarted at the 8086_PROC_0 node.

---

[2]M1 passes the minimum amount of each resource consumed by each node up the functional hierarchy.

Part III

Knowledge Acquisition

7

An Introduction to Automated
Knowledge Acquisition

The basic architecture of an expert system is shown in Figure 7.1. The problem
solver defines the method, such as M1's design cycle, for solving a problem.
The knowledge base contains the specific expertise used by the problem solver
to generate a solution. The working memory contains information about the
current problem being solved. The interface handles communication between
the expert system and the user. The expert system development process is
defined in the next section. The development process illustrates the need for
knowledge acquisition tools. The second section overviews an important class
of knowledge-acquisition tools. This chapter concludes with a discussion of
development issues for these tools.

7.1 Expert System Development

The process of building an expert system, called knowledge engineering, is performed by knowledge engineers. Knowledge engineers are highly trained in the
techniques used to construct expert systems and are familiar with the domain
in which the system will be deployed. The knowledge engineer is responsible for all aspects of expert system development: defining and implementing

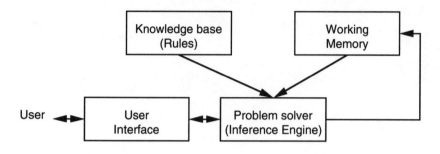

Figure 7.1. Basic architecture of an expert system.

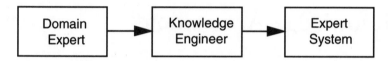

Figure 7.2. Function of the knowledge engineer.

the problem solver and constructing the knowledge base. Generally, the task of developing the problem solver is performed entirely by the knowledge engineer, while construction of the knowledge base requires cooperation with a domain expert. Since domain experts are not usually familiar with knowledge engineering techniques, they cannot transfer their expertise without assistance from a knowledge engineer. The knowledge engineer, therefore, is an interface between the domain expert and expert system, as shown in Figure 7.2.

Developing an expert system can require considerable effort for a number of reasons, including the following [11]:

- Tasks performed by expert systems are typically knowledge intensive, meaning that a large amount of expert knowledge is required to generate a solution. This is particularly true of design tasks [87].

- In addition to being knowledge intensive, design tends to be heavily dependent on technology. Since technology is rapidly evolving, especially in the computer area, knowledge bases must be constantly updated. Failure to track technological change would result in poor designs. Imagine a knowledge base for MICON built in the early 1970s and never updated – all designs would be based on the Intel 4004, a twenty-year-old microprocessor.

- The process of acquiring knowledge is often the most difficult phase of developing an expert system and has been dubbed "the knowledge-

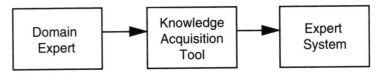

Figure 7.3. Function of the knowledge-acquisition tool.

acquisition bottleneck" [43]. The knowledge engineer must become well versed in the concepts and jargon of the application area in order to communicate effectively with the domain expert. Even so, domain experts may find it difficult to express their reasoning process.

- Expert systems are often large, complex programs written in specialized languages. All the software engineering problems associated with any large software system also apply to expert systems. Additionally, the programming languages used are difficult to master and may not support modern software engineering concepts.

Knowledge-acquisition tools reduce expert system development effort by automating various parts of the knowledge engineering process. In the same way that tools like MICON increase productivity for engineering design tasks, knowledge-acquisition tools facilitate, or in some cases eliminate, the knowledge engineer, as shown in Figure 7.3.

The benefits of knowledge-acquisition tools are shorter expert system development time and higher quality knowledge bases. These benefits are realized through the following:

- more efficient transfer of expertise through a well-defined, efficient knowledge-acquisition methodology,

- detection and elimination of various errors from expert knowledge before adding it to the knowledge base,

- ability to replicate the knowledge-acquisition tool arbitrarily, thereby creating as many knowledge engineers as necessary,

- subsumption of tedious and time consuming knowledge engineering tasks by a tool.

The development of an expert system covers a wide range of activities that range from structuring a domain to constructing a fully functional system. Because the activities vary greatly and many are not well-understood, no single knowledge-acquisition tool can provide all the functionality needed to build a

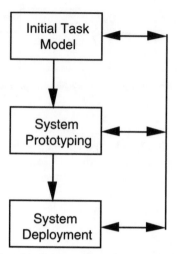

Figure 7.4. Simplified model of the stages of development of an expert system.

system. Rather, knowledge-acquisition tools and techniques have been developed for specific tasks. In fact, models of the development of expert systems provide a convenient way to understand the full range of knowledge-acquisition tools, as demonstrated by [11, 98].

In Figure 7.4 we present a simple model of expert system development[1]. Note that the development process is not typically as well delineated as implied by the model; there is often a great deal of iteration between development steps.

The first development step is creating an *initial task model* where the task that the expert system is to perform is loosely defined. In this step, relevent concepts and terminology and possible techniques for performing the task are identified. While developing the initial task model is mostly an ad hoc process, there is some computer-based assistance available. For example, knowledge acquisition tools exist that can help to organize domain vocabulary and concepts [15, 112].

Once an initial task model has been developed, a *prototype* can be built. The prototype contains an operational version of the problem solver and knowledge base which can be tested. Tests are generally limited to a small set of representative problems. When the prototype has proven its capability, it is expanded to cover a broader range of problems. During this period, the system's knowledge base grows considerably, and the problem solver may undergo minor modifications. Finally, the prototype becomes a fully operational system with a stable problem-solving method and sufficiently sized knowledge base. At this point,

---

[1]This model is based on the model presented in [11]; alternative development models are presented in [66, 98].

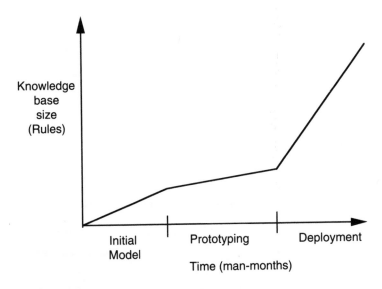

Figure 7.5. Growth in M1's knowledge base.

the system can be deployed into the field. There are a variety of knowledge acquisition tools that assist with developing the prototype into a fully operative system. These tools are discussed in the next section.

Figure 7.5 illustrates the growth of M1 during its development. Notice that there is relatively little growth in the knowledge base (as measured by rules) during the prototyping stage. At this point, a small set of example designs were used to exercise the design cycle (the problem solver) and to refine its behavior. When the problem solver became stable, an intensive knowledge-acquisition effort took place using CGEN. As reported in Chapter 12, a variety of processor families was entered by four designers roughly doubling the size of the knowledge base. Once this was complete, M1 was released for use by those outside the development group.

An expert system in the field must be maintained, which may include adding more knowledge. Maintainence, however, may include other activities such as adding new features and improving user interfaces. While some of the tools that are used for developing the prototype can be used for further knowledge base development, there are no existing knowledge-acquisition tools that specifically support maintenance activities.

Many knowledge-acquisition tools have been developed to assist with various knowledge engineering tasks. Among these, specialized knowledge tools have proven to be useful in building knowledge-based design tools. These tools are discussed in the next section.

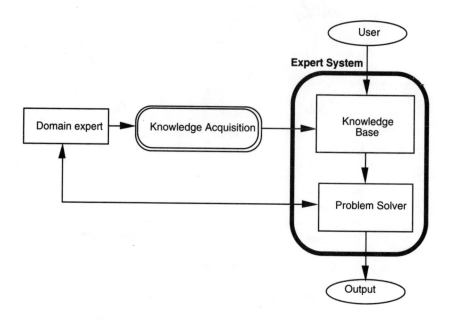

Figure 7.6. Model of specialized knowledge-acquisition tools.

7.2 Specialized Knowledge-Acquisition Tools

Specialized knowledge-acquisition tools assist with building the prototype's knowledge base. These tools are particularly powerful, able to replace the knowledge engineer completely in some circumstances by allowing the domain expert to enter expertise directly into the knowledge base. They are limited, however, to working in conjunction with a specific expert system.

A model of specialized knowledge-acquisition tools is presented in Figure 7.6 [11, 34]. The user employs the expert system to find a solution to an application task. The domain expert builds or enhances the knowledge base by using the knowledge-acquisition tool. In general, the domain expert is responsible for monitoring the performance of the expert system and for adding knowledge to it if the performance is poor. In the MICON system, however, M1 will halt when it requires knowledge and will direct the domain expert as to what to add. Notice that all knowledge is entered via the acquisition tool, thus shielding the domain expert from the expert system's implementation details.

Specialized knowledge-acquisition tools can be characterized by the following:

- The knowledge-acquisition task is composed of the following steps:

(1) acquisition of knowledge from the domain expert, (2) reformulation of the knowledge, which includes error checking and other specialized functions such as generalization, and (3) code generation.

- The expert system (i.e., the problem-solving method and knowledge base) are presupposed by the knowledge-acquisition tool.

- The scope of the tool is limited to the expert system it presupposes; specialized knowledge-acquisition tools will only work with one problem-solving method and knowledge-base organization.

The power of specialized knowledge-acquisition tools comes from the presupposition of the expert system [89, 57] , which allows the clear definition of the roles that knowledge plays in creating a problem solution and how that knowledge is operationalized[2]. This provides the following benefits [84]:

- Interaction with the expert is focused on gathering only that knowledge required by the expert system to solve a problem.

- The ability to detect errors in acquired knowledge is enhanced.

- Characterization of the knowledge base is facilitated, allowing better generation of test cases.

- Proper utilization of the acquired knowledge by the expert system is assured.

The problem-solving method contains the control knowledge that sequences the actions required to perform some task. This control knowledge defines which domain-specific knowledge is applicable for each subtask by identifying the different roles knowledge plays in the problem-solving process. Thus, the use of domain knowledge during problem solving is determined solely by its role.

In an expert system that supports automated knowledge acquisition, the knowledge base is structured by these knowledge roles. By exploiting the role, which is independent of implementation, the tool can capture knowledge in a format familiar to the expert and can anticipate what the expert might provide. This facilitates the knowledge-acquisition process and sharpens the dialogue with the domain expert. Correspondingly, the knowledge base is organized as a set of partitions, and each partition corresponds to a role. Each partition is activated only when directed by the problem solver, thereby allowing the problem solver to access all knowledge in the partition, but only in that partition. Each piece of knowledge must reside in a single partition. As the knowledge base is extended

---

[2]Converted into a format usable by the expert system.

the number of rules in each partition will increase, but the number of partitions will remain constant. This is because the problem solver is not modified.

Partitioning the knowledge base also aids operationalization in the following way: All the rules in each partition have a similar style; portions of each rule are the same, and other portions are made specific to the particular piece of knowledge captured by the rule. By enforcing such standardization, both modeling the knowledge base and code generation are made easier.

A number of specialized knowledge-acquisition tools have been developed for a variety of tasks, such as synthesis [85], diagnosis [31, 42, 70], planning [99], and report generation [74]. A recent compilation of tools is given in [134]. These tools, while operating in different domains, all share the basic characteristics outlined here.

There are alternative approaches to building knowledge-acquisition tools that are not coupled to a specific expert system. These approaches result in generalized knowledge-acquisition tools. One type of a generalized knowledge-acquisition tool is a workbench, where the knowledge engineer has access to a variety of different, highly specialized tools, each of which performs a small part of the knowledge-acquisition function [16] or provides sophisticated programming assistance [132]. Another approach is to adapt a programming methodology that supports knowledge acquisition [117]. Finally, some approaches advocate completely general purpose tools that do not presuppose any problem-solving approach [79, 97], rather they collect knowledge using a predetermined organizational scheme. The intention of these efforts is to allow any problem solver to be connected to a knowledge base.

7.3   Knowledge-Acquisition Tool Development Issues

The design of a specialized knowledge-acquisition tool is influenced by the following:

- **The expert system:** The operation of the problem solver and knowledge base defines the types of knowledge to be acquired. The organization of the knowledge base and its encoding scheme affect the knowledge-acquisition tool in much the same way as a compiler backend is affected by an instruction set.

- **The domain expert:** The knowledge-acquisition tool must use terminology that is understood by the domain expert. Furthermore, knowledge must be acquired in an order and at a level that "makes sense" to the expert; the tool should simulate as closely as possible the reasoning process used by the expert in solving problems. In a scenario with multiple experts, the tool must use terminology accepted by the majority and support customization for different experts.

The expert system must be designed before development of the knowledge-acquisition tool can begin, since the knowledge-acquisition tool presupposes it. As a practical concern, it is useful to overlap development of the knowledge-acquisition tool with that of the expert system. This can be achieved via abstracting the expert system at various stages of development into a model. This model captures key features of the evolving expert system such as the organization of the knowledge base. The model represents various syntactic features of the expert system including data structure referencing and the control scheme (e.g., goal and subgoal names), as described in Chapter 10. Development of the knowledge-acquisition tool can then proceed based on this model. ·

In this part of the book we describe the architecture and the development process of CGEN. Chapter 8 describes the impact that M1 has on CGEN, and relates this to the knowledge gathering process. The generalization of design knowledge is described in Chapter 9. Various models of M1 are given in Chapter 10; one model was used during the development of CGEN, several others are used by CGEN to generate code. The principles described in these chapters can be applied to the development of knowledge-acquisition tools in any domain or for any task.

8

Knowledge Gathering in CGEN

CGEN is an automated knowledge-acquisition tool that allows hardware engineers to add expertise directly to M1's knowledge base. This chapter presents CGEN's knowledge gathering methods. These methods are based upon the following factors: the interface between CGEN and the hardware expert and M1's problem-solving method.

8.1 The Problem

The following observations help to define CGEN's knowledge-acquisition task:

Single training case: Only a single example of the knowledge that is to be entered into the system is available. This example is called a *training case*.

Overly specific example: The example is usually applicable to a wider range of situations than is evident from the training case. This implies that a generalization technique is required to utilize each training case fully.

Knowledge from user: All knowledge comes from the domain expert. As described later, in Section 8.3.6, knowledge cannot be derived from sources existing either in M1 or in CGEN. Thus, many of the generalization schemes found in machine learning or knowledge-acquisition tools used for design problems, such as explanation-based generalization [92] or induction [2], will not work.

The experimental data in Chapter 12 shows that computer system design is knowledge intensive. It is also interesting to note the rapid rate of growth of the knowledge base, as measured by the number of rules, when new parts are added (see Table 12.1). Clearly, an efficient means of acquiring design expertise is necessary. CGEN provides the following to support the acquisition of knowledge:

Methodology: A consistent and complete methodology for the entire knowledge-acquisition process.

Expressibility: Ability to express adequately the design knowledge required by M1.

Completeness: The capability to ensure that k_{spec} knowledge is complete for the given template.

Generalization: The capability to generalize $k_{template}$ knowledge.

Operationalized representation: The capability to formulate the acquired knowledge so that it is executable by M1.

One way of viewing knowledge acquisition is as a transformation of the domain expert's knowledge into M1's representation. This transformation is accomplished by CGEN and requires establishing interfaces between

- CGEN and the domain expert, and

- CGEN and the expert system (M1).

The semantic gap between these interfaces is a major contributor to the complexity of the transformation function provided by CGEN. For example, if domain concepts (e.g., templates, selection constraints) are directly representable in the expert system, the transformation function requires only a syntactic translation. This is analogous to a computer that directly executes a high-level language. If the concepts are not directly representable, the transformation function becomes more complex. For example, most high-level languages must be translated, or compiled, into machine code. An exact means of determining the difference in interface levels seen by a knowledge-acquisition tool is not currently available; however, a quantitative method is given in Chapter 12. When the method was applied to CGEN it showed that the abstraction level of the domain-expert interface was significantly higher than that of the expert system, so CGEN does more than just syntactic translation.

In order to get a sense of the difference between the domain expert and the expert system, a broad set of characteristics for each is given in the following sections. These characteristics form the basis of the interfaces for CGEN.

8.1.1 Domain Expert Characteristics

The domain expert is considered an expert designer, knowledgeable about all aspects of the domain that will affect M1. Further assumptions about the domain expert are the following:

Non-programmer: The domain expert, a hardware designer, is not an experienced programmer and is thus not readily adaptable to new programming languages and styles. Furthermore, the domain expert is not familiar with design automation or artificial intelligence programming concepts. Therefore, it is not practical to teach a hardware designer to be a knowledge engineer. CGEN must perform any necessary knowledge-engineering activities.

Valid training cases: All training cases are assumed to be valid, and no actions are taken purposely to corrupt the knowledge base being built. CGEN does not need to detect and reject bad training cases.

Schematics and constraints: Schematic drawings are an efficient means of conveying structural information. The domain expert is fluent with the symbol system used in schematics. The expert also understands the constraints of the domain and the implications they have on design decisions. Thus, a good means of communicating with designers is via schematics and simple constraint descriptions.

Time is valuable: A domain expert's time is valuable, since the time spent with a knowledge-acquisition tool could also be spent in revenue-producing activities. Thus, CGEN must use the expert's time as effectively as possible by utilizing each training case fully.

8.1.2 Expert System Characteristics

M1's characterization is dominated by the architecture and the implementation language; i.e., everything necessary to write code to ensure proper compilation and execution in M1. Concepts used by the domain expert, such as templates and selection constraints, are not directly expressible in OPS/83, M1's implementation language. A complete characterization of M1 is given in Chapter 10, but general considerations from CGEN's perspective are outlined below:

Semantics: M1's knowledge base organization must be properly modeled by CGEN so that acquired knowledge can be properly represented.

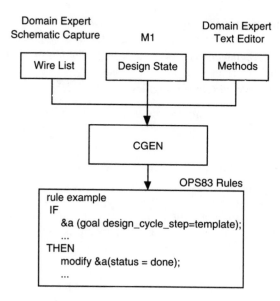

Figure 8.1. Inputs and outputs for CGEN.

Syntax: a model of the implementation language syntax is necessary so that executable code can be generated by the system.

These characteristics reveal that the challenge for CGEN is to hide M1's implementation details from the domain expert, presenting only architectural concepts, a fundamental principle of knowledge-acquisition tools [57]. These concepts include: templates, the design state, and part models. These high level concepts are more easily understood by the expert, thereby reducing the knowledge-acquisition burden.

In Figure 8.1 the inputs to and outputs from CGEN are shown. Input from the domain expert consists of a schematic drawing representing a template and a description of other design information necessary for M1's proper operation. The schematic is created with a drawing editor (schematic capture tool), automatically converted into a wire list, and finally input to CGEN. Design information is described via a file containing a collection of *methods*, explained more fully later in this chapter, created with a text editor. Design state information is supplied by M1 via the PREVIEW file. Part models are acquired separately via ENTRY (see Chapter 2).

The output of CGEN is a module of OPS/83 code representing the acquired knowledge. This code is automatically compiled into M1's knowledge base. Thus, the expert sees only the schematic diagram and the methods file; all of M1's implementation details are hidden.

8.2 Presupposing M1

M1's problem-solving method imparts an organization on its knowledge base. This organization, in turn, affects CGEN and, ultimately, what the expert sees during a training case. In this section we describe the structure of M1's knowledge base as imposed by the problem-solving method and the implications this has for CGEN.

Recall that the M1 knowledge base is composed of a set of partitions and that each partition supports a step in the design cyle. Further, recall that design cycles are initiated for an abstract part once a group of its specifications have been assigned values. The information used to fill these specifications may come from reports (if the formulation method was used) that were generated in some other design cycle. This leads to two important points:

- There is an information dependency on the design cycles; the information generated in design step d_{calc} in one cycle may "spawn" other design cycles. Thus, when adding a template to the knowledge base, k_{calc} must also be entered, otherwise the reports needed to spawn new cycles will not be available.

- Knowledge for filling the specifications for abstract parts must also be given, or else new design cycles will never start. Thus, when a template is acquired, k_{spec} knowledge must be given for each abstract part introduced.

Given these points, we define a set of relationships among the partitions called super-partitions. Design knowledge can be classified in the following way:

$$K_D = K_T^P \cup K_T^S \cup k_{select\_func} \cup k_{casc},$$

where selection knowledge, which is independent of the other partitions, is given by the part-related superpartition

$$K_T^P = k_{select\_rule}$$

and the knowledge that must be acquired concurrently when a structure is entered is given by the structure-related superpartition

$$K_T^S = k_{spec} \cup k_{template} \cup k_{calc}.$$

These super-partitions define the relationships between partitions that are important for CGEN, i.e., all the knowledge needed for a super-partition must be acquired during a training session, otherwise M1 will not behave properly. Further, it is apparent that CGEN can acquire the two super-partitions independently, although in practice both can be entered simultaneously by the domain expert.

Partition	Procedural	Declarative	Growth Rate
k_{spec}		$\checkmark$	rapid
$k_{\text{select\_rule}}$		$\checkmark$	rapid
$k_{\text{select\_func}}$	$\checkmark$		none
k_{casc}	$\checkmark$		very slow
k_{template}		$\checkmark$	rapid
k_{calc}		$\checkmark$	rapid
k_{arch}	$\checkmark$		none

Table 8.1. Summary of growth and representation knowledge.

Additional insight into the knowledge-acquisition task can be gained by considering the representation of various types of knowledge and the relative growth rates. This information is summarized in Table 8.1. Knowing the types of representation (i.e., procedural vs. declarative) and relative growth rates is important for the knowledge-acquisition effort. Since partitions $k_{\text{select\_func}}$, k_{casc}, and k_{arch} have a slow growth rate and are procedurally encoded, they are not considered in the knowledge-acquisition task. Capturing procedurally encoded knowledge presents a problem for automatic knowledge acquisition since its acquisition may require some form of programming that we are trying to avoid, although in some domains a nonprogramming technique is possible (see [98] for an example). This is not a limitation for CGEN – these partitions are programmed by M1's developers to be applicable to a large number of parts and, hence, the domain expert does not need to add to them. The remaining partitions, k_{spec}, $k_{\text{select\_rule}}$, k_{template}, and k_{calc}, are expected to grow rapidly. The knowledge-acquisition effort, therefore, is directed at these partitions.

It is interesting to note the process by which knowledge bases are initially constructed. A minimal M1 knowledge base, called the initial knowledge base K_{T}^{I}, is defined to contain only the following partitions:

$$K_{\text{T}}^{\text{I}} = k_{\text{select\_func}} \cup k_{\text{casc}} \cup k_{\text{arch}}.$$

From K_{T}^{I}, M1 is able to "boot" itself up, assuming that the functional hierarchy exists in the database. This booting process works by M1 starting at the root r of the functional hierarchy and then trying to instantiate the root's successor $S(r)$. Since no template will exist in the knowledge base for this situation, M1 will fail, and CGEN will be invoked. Once the new knowledge is compiled into M1, it will continue until the next time design cycle step d_{template} is executed causing CGEN to be invoked once again. This process continues until all needed templates are acquired. Selection knowledge can be added to M1 when new parts are added to the functional hierarchy.

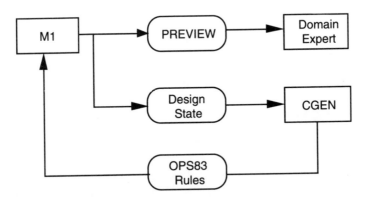

Figure 8.2. Information flow between MICON tools during knowledge acquisition.

8.3   Gathering Knowledge

In this section we discuss how CGEN gathers knowledge using inputs from both the user and M1.

8.3.1   Interfacing with M1

Before describing CGEN's knowledge-gathering process, we describe CGEN's interaction with M1. Knowledge acquisition actually begins with M1; when M1 fails to find an appropriate template during design cycle step d_{template} it halts. At this point, M1 generates the following:

1. A description of the design state for the expert so that a proper template for this particular design state can be created. (An example design state is shown in Figure 8.6.) This description is called a PREVIEW file.

2. A description of the design state that CGEN can read.

Once this information is created, CGEN begins the knowledge-acquisition process as discussed later in this chapter. When knowledge acquisition is complete, M1 continues with the design at the point where it stopped. The information flow between M1 and CGEN is shown in Figure 8.2.

The close interaction between M1 and CGEN, where M1 exactly specifies the knowledge it requires, is unusual for specialized knowledge-acquisition tools. Except for Tieresias [31], most knowledge-acquisition tools operate independently of their problem-solving system. In these cases, the domain expert is responsible for monitoring the problem solver's performance and initiating knowledge acquisition when the performance is unacceptable. Alternatively, the knowledge-acquisition tool is used only to create the expert system and not to maintain it. An advantage to the approach used by M1 and CGEN is that the knowledge-acquisition task is less ambiguous – the expert knows exactly what to add to the knowledge base. The disadvantage of this approach is that knowledge cannot be added until M1 requests it.

A description of the other inputs to CGEN and the acquisition process for K_T^S and K_T^P is given in the remainder of this chapter.

8.3.2   Methods

As mentioned earlier, methods are used by the expert to describe various information required by M1. In particular, methods capture equations and text strings; equations are used for k_{spec}, k_{select_rule}, and k_{calc} in M1, and generalization knowledge in CGEN (discussed in Chapter 9); text strings are used in k_{spec} to acquire information from the M1 user via questions. Methods are organized by the type of knowledge being described and by the data type of the arguments. The various types of methods are

- formulation, corresponding to k_{spec},

- question, corresponding to k_{spec},

- selection, corresponding to k_{select_rule},

- generalization, corresponding to $k_{generalize}$, and

- calculation, corresponding to k_{calc}.

The data types for any method are string and integer. Examples of valid method types are *integer_selection* and *string_calculation*, in which, respectively, a selection technique based on comparison by integers is described and a report is generated that contains a string. (Example methods are given in Figures 8.3, 8.4, 8.9, and 8.11 through 8.13.)

8.3.3   Drawings

Drawings[1] are used during the acquisition of $k_{template}$ to convey structural knowledge. In particular, drawings describe

- parts needed to implement a template,

- part interconnections, and

---

[1]Note that the drawings used throughout the book were drawn by hand to represent wire list information.

- information about the types of interconnections (e.g., direct connection, INDEX bus, etc.).

In actuality, drawings are not used by CGEN, rather a wire list derived from the drawing is used.

The following two sections illustrate how methods and drawings are used by the domain expert to provide knowledge to CGEN.

8.3.4   Acquisition of K_T^S

The acquisition of K_T^S is based on M1's problem-solving method, specifically the design cycle and spawning of design cycles. Recall that as new abstract parts are incorporated into the evolving design, design cycles will be spawned. In order for a design cycle to begin, complete specifications for at least one group for a part must be filled. Thus, when a template introduces new abstract parts, knowledge for filling the specifications of those parts, k_{spec}, must be included. Furthermore, calculations must be executed to create reports that will be used in the future to fill the specifications of other parts. It is necessary, therefore, that CGEN acquires knowledge for the partitions k_{calc} and k_{spec} when a template is entered.

The remainder of this section describes the knowledge-acquisition process for each type of knowledge.

Acquisition of k_{spec}

Partition k_{spec} consists of declarative knowledge used to supply values for the specifications of abstract parts in the template. As described in Section 4.3.1, two mechanisms are used for filling specifications: formulation and query. The decision to use one mechanism or the other is left to the domain expert. All specifications can be posed as questions to the user, although this will appear both verbose and redundant, since the same question may be asked repeatedly as M1 progresses down the hierarchy. Formulation assumes that variables used in the equation exist in the design state before the associated equation can be evaluated.

CGEN checks the completeness of k_{spec} knowledge supplied by the domain expert for each training session. When a template is entered, CGEN gets each abstract part's specifications from the database. Each part's specifications are then compared to the specification methods given by the expert. If a set of methods does not complete at least one group of specifications, then CGEN reports this error to the expert. At this point, the expert must add the missing specifications to the methods file.

While it can be ensured that all specifications can be "filled" by a method, the

```
method_type: integer_question
method: Amount of SRAM needed ;
```

Figure 8.3. Example query method.

```
method_type: integer_formulation
method: SPEC_ROWS = NO_OF_BYTES / 1024;
```

Figure 8.4. Example formulation method.

correctness of the methods can not be determined. Ideally, CGEN should ensure that specification methods provide values that will choose the correct part. The information necessary to evaluate the specifications, however, is only available during the actual synthesis process; therefore, validation is not possible. In addition, CGEN has no notion of what constitutes a correct part for a given template.

The method in Figure 8.3 will cause M1 to request the amount of SRAM required for a design from the user. In Figure 8.4 the method will cause M1 to translate the amount of SRAM requested, NO_OF_BYTES, into the number of rows of 1K byte memory chips needed.

Note that if a template contains multiple instances of the same abstract part, the methods for computing the specifications for each part instance must be given, even if the specifications are identical.

Acquisition of k_{template}

Of all the partitions, the acquisition for knowledge of k_{template} is the most complex. The process consists of two phases: specific rule acquisition and rule generalization. The first phase compiles k_{template} into CGEN's intermediate form. The second phase uses generalization knowledge (described in Chapter 9) to relax the preconditions of the rule.

Phase 1: Several mappings may exist between a part n_i and it successors $S(n_i)$, so a number of templates may exist. To differentiate between templates a unique set of preconditions are given to each. The preconditions are defined in terms of the design state, which is directly extracted from the M1-generated input file and form a rule's LHS. The wire list provides the structural knowledge, forming the rule's RHS. The combination of these two inputs produce a k_{template} rule, as illustrated in Figure 8.5. An example design state, the template, and the resulting rule are shown in Figures 8.6, 8.7, and 8.8 respectively.

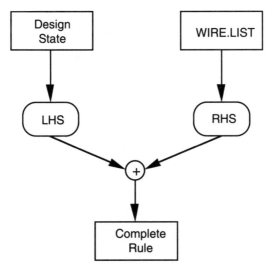

Figure 8.5. Representation of the $k_{template}$ creation process.

Phase 2: The rule created during Phase 1 is specific to the design situation. As is typical, in the case illustrated in Figure 8.6, a number of preconditions derived from the design state are overly specific. In particular, consider preconditions PC1 through PC6, PC11, and PC12. PC11 is overly specific because the template is applicable for all SRAM parts, not only to those situations where the designer has no preference of which chip to use[2]. PC12 is overly specific since the template is applicable to a wide range of memory sizes. Preconditions PC1 through PC6, generated from initial user input, provide resource bounds on the

```
PC1:  (report name = BOARD_AREA value = 121000000000)
PC2:  (report name = BOARD_COST value = 99999900)
PC3:  (report name = POWER_DISSIPATION value = 99999)
PC4:  (report name = REMAINING_BOARD_AREA value = 1212528256)
PC5:  (report name = REMAINING_BOARD_COST value = 99999300)
PC6:  (report name = REMAINING_POWER_DISSIPATION value = 98424)
PC7:  (report name = ADDRESS_BUS_WIDTH value = 16)
PC8:  (report name = SYS_PROC_FAMILY value = 68XX)
PC9:  (report name = SYSTEM_PROCESSOR value = 6809)
PC10: (report name = DATA_BUS_WIDTH value = 8)
PC11: (specification name = SRAM_CHIP_NAME  value = ?)
PC12: (specification name = NO_OF_BYTES value = 40000)
```

Figure 8.6. Design state information created by M1 at point of failure in the search for structure.

---

[2]The ? for this specification indicates the designer has no preference in SRAM chips.

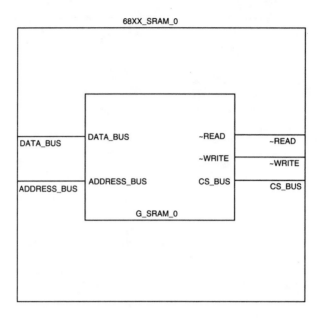

Figure 8.7. Template for mapping 68XX_SRAM_0 to G_SRAM_0.

```
rule example_1
  If (goal design_cycle_step = template for_part = 68XX_SIO_0) and
     (report name = BOARD_AREA val = 121000000000) and
     (report name = BOARD_COST value = 99999900) and
     (report name = POWER_DISSIPATION value = 99999) and
     (report name = REMAINING_BOARD_AREA value = 1212528256) and
     (report name = REMAINING_BOARD_COST value = 99999300) and
     (report name = REMAINING_POWER_DISSIPATION value = 98424) and
     (report name = ADDRESS_BUS_WIDTH value = 16) and
     (report name = SYS_PROC_FAMILY value = 68XX) and
     (report name = SYSTEM_PROCESSOR value = 6809) and
     (report name = DATA_BUS_WIDTH value = 8) and
     (specification name = SRAM_CHIP_NAME  value = ?) and
     (specification name = NO_OF_BYTES value = 40000) and
  Then
     create (template_tag name = 68XX_SRAM_0
                          for_part = 68XX_SRAM_0 type = 1);
     connect_net (G_SRAM_0,DATA_BUS,68XX_SRAM_0,DATA_BUS);
     connect_net (G_SRAM_0,ADDRESS_BUS,68XX_SRAM_0,ADDRESS_BUS);
     connect_net (G_SRAM_0, READ,68XX_SRAM_0, READ);
     connect_net (G_SRAM_0, WRITE,68XX_SRAM_0, WRITE);
     connect_net (G_SRAM_0,CS_BUS,68XX_SRAM_0,CS_BUS);
```

Figure 8.8. Resulting rule from the combination of the drawing in Figure 8.7 and the design state in Figure 8.6.

```
method_type: integer_generalization
method: BOARD_AREA   > 0;

method_type: integer_generalization
method: BOARD_COST > 0;

method_type: integer_generalization
method: POWER_DISSIPATION > 0;

method_type: integer_generalization
method: REMAINING_BOARD_AREA > 0;

method_type: integer_generalization
method: REMAINING_BOARD_COST > 0;

method_type: integer_generalization
method: REMAINING_POWER_DISSIPATION > 0;

method_type: integer_generalization
method: NO_OF_BYTES > 0;

method_type: string_generalization
method: SRAM_CHIP_NAME <> NIL;
```

Figure 8.9. Example generalization methods for the relaxation of preconditions in Figure 8.6.

evolving design. The template in Figure 8.7 contains only abstract parts which have no physical characteristics; therefore, the template is not affected by the resource preconditions. This implies the template preconditions are not strictly defined by the resource bounds issued by the user. If, for example, the user had increased the board area bound PC1 to 400000000 from 121000000 the template would not be applicable as defined by the preconditions even though it is still valid.

To overcome this problem, the preconditions are relaxed. The domain expert and CGEN supply knowledge to direct a generalization process. During generalization this knowledge indicates which preconditions are to be relaxed and to what extent. The generalization knowledge is applied to the intermediate form of the rule LHS, allowing the rule's application range to be fully exploited.

An example set of methods for relaxing the preconditions in Figure 8.6 are given in Figure 8.9. The methods represent the absolute bounds on each precondition. The result of the application of this knowledge is shown in Figure 8.10.

```
PC1: (report name = BOARD_AREA value > 0)
PC2: (report name = BOARD_COST value > 0)
PC3: (report name = POWER_DISSIPATION value > 0)
PC4: (report name = REMAINING_BOARD_AREA value > 0)
PC5: (report name = REMAINING_BOARD_COST value > 0)
PC6: (report name = REMAINING_POWER_DISSIPATION > 0)
PC7: (report name = ADDRESS_BUS_WIDTH value = 16)
PC8: (report name = SYS_PROC_FAMILY value = 68XX)
PC9: (report name = SYSTEM_PROCESSOR value = 6809)
PC10: (report name = DATA_BUS_WIDTH value = 8)
PC11: (specification name = SRAM_CHIP_NAME  value <> ||)
PC12: (specification name = NO_OF_BYTES value > 0)
```

Figure 8.10. Relaxed preconditions based on the application of generalization methods in Figure 8.9 to the design state in Figure 8.6.

```
method_type: integer_calculation
method: NUM_MEM_CHIPS = MEM_REQ/1024
```

Figure 8.11. Example method for a $k_{\text{calc\_now}}$ rule.

Acquisition of k_{calc}

In partition k_{calc} the domain expert describes equations to be evaluated either when the template is asserted, $k_{\text{calc\_now}}$, or when each abstract part in the template has been realized as a physical part, $k_{\text{calc\_delay}}$. In Figure 8.11 the $k_{\text{calc\_now}}$ method calculates the number of 1K bit chips necessary to realize the amount of memory given by MEMORY_REQ.

Delayed calculations, $k_{\text{calc\_delay}}$, are also useful for determining when the design for an abstract part or subsystem is complete. In Figure 8.12 a report is generated when the SRAM subsystem is completed.

8.3.5 Acquisition of K_T^P

K_T^P includes only k_{select}, and its acquisition is independent of any particular template. This is because, in M1, part selection is not dependent on a design situation, so, unlike K_T^S, K_T^P is entered only once for a given abstract part.

```
method_type: string_completion
method: 68XX_SRAM_0_COMPLETED = DONE;
```

Figure 8.12. Example method for a $k_{\text{calc\_delay}}$ rule.

```
method_type: integer_selection
method: G_PIO_CONNECTOR_CONNECTOR_SIZE >= DB9_SIZE;

method_type: string_selection
method: G_PIO_CONNECTOR_CONNECTOR_TYPE <> DB9_CONNECTOR_TYPE;
```

Figure 8.13. Example method for a k_{select} rule.

The knowledge given by the domain expert determines which characteristics on a candidate successor part $n_j \in S(n_i)$ are compared to which specifications of an abstract part n_i and the constraint to use. The general form of a k_{select_rule} equation is

specification OP characteristic,

where OP is a relational operator from the set $\{=, \neq, \geq, \leq, <, >\}$.

Example methods are given in Figure 8.13 for the selection of a connector, the DB9, given size and connector type, *male* or *female*[3]. These methods reject all connectors that are less than the specified size of the G_PIO_CONNECTOR_0 (which will be refined into a DB9) and that are not of the specified connector type.

8.3.6 Correctness and Completeness

CGEN is not capable of independently verifying the correctness and completeness of most of the incoming knowledge. Some syntactic checks are provided to validate the following:

- that a complete set of specifications are given for all abstract parts in a template,

- that the syntax on equations given in the methods for k_{spec}, k_{select_rule}, k_{calc} is correct,

- that incoming knowledge is grouped into the correct super-partition, and

- that the proper template component is used in a template.

Table 8.2 summarizes important information about the partitions.

Verifying the correctness and completeness of all incoming knowledge is not presently possible for two reasons, lack of a reference and the piecemeal

---

[3]G_PIO_CONNECTOR_SIZE and G_PIO_CONNECTOR_TYPE are specifications of G_PIO_CONNECTOR_0. DB9_SIZE and DB9_CONNECTOR_TYPE are characteristics of the DB9, one of the successors of the G_PIO_CONNECTOR_0.

Partition	Generalized	Correctness	Completeness
k_{spec}			√
k_{select}			limited
$k_{template}$	√	√	limited
k_{calc}		limited	

Table 8.2. Summary of major features of the knowledge partitions.

style of knowledge acquisition. CGEN cannot independently determine the functionality of knowledge entered. This would require either a formal proof mechanism, similar to explanation-based generalization, or a simulation. Formal proofs are impossible since the domain is not yet rigorously defined. Simulation is difficult because the following are required: (1) simulation models of all the components, (2) a comprehensive set of test vectors (stimuli for the models), and (3) a means of interpreting the results of the simulation. Unfortunately, simulation models are not readily available for all the parts in M1's knowledge base. Furthermore, test vectors cannot practically cover all possible situations, so complete verification cannot be assured. Test vector generation has been shown to be NP-complete for the type of circuits designed by M1. In addition, automatically interpreting the results of a simulator is a significant research issue.

The piecemeal knowledge-acquisition process also makes verification difficult. Knowledge is acquired as separate chunks, and, while each chunk is well-specified, it is possible that an assumed piece of information, such as a report, needed to enable a rule to execute, is not present. Thus, to ensure that all assumed information will be available at run time, the design must actually be produced.

9

Generalization Technique

The initial formulation of a newly acquired chunk of $k_{template}$ knowledge is usually too specific with respect to its preconditions. Since it is desirable for each template to be applicable to all valid design situations, overly restrictive preconditions must be identified and generalized by either removal or relaxation. Some of the generally applicable knowledge for performing this generalization task resides in CGEN's knowledge base; other specific generalization knowledge must be provided by the domain expert for each template.

This chapter discusses the second task in the knowledge- acquisition process, CGEN's generalization process.

9.1   Problem Definition

During the formulation of $k_{template}$, structural knowledge is concatenated with a set of preconditions. The preconditions are based on the definition of the design state given by M1 at the point of failure in the search for structure. The initial formulation of preconditions coincides exactly with the design state, yielding the tightest possible set of invocation conditions describing when the new piece of knowledge can be applied. This definition is necessary to comply with the M1 problem solver's requirement that each $k_{template}$ rule have a unique set of preconditions. Figure 8.6, recreated in Figure 9.1, provides an example

```
PC1:  (report  name = BOARD_AREA value = 121000000)
PC2:  (report  name = BOARD_COST value = 99999900)
PC3:  (report  name = POWER_DISSIPATION value = 99999)
PC4:  (report  name = REMAINING_BOARD_AREA value = 1212528256)
PC5:  (report  name = REMAINING_BOARD_COST value = 99999300)
PC6:  (report  name = REMAINING_POWER_DISSIPATION value = 98424)
PC7:  (report  name = ADDRESS_BUS_WIDTH value = 16)
PC8:  (report  name = SYS_PROC_FAMILY value = 68XX)
PC9:  (report  name = SYSTEM_PROCESSOR value = 6809)
PC10: (report  name = DATA_BUS_WIDTH value = 8)
PC11: (specification name = SRAM_CHIP_NAME  value = ?)
PC12: (specification name = NO_OF_BYTES value = 40000)
```

Figure 9.1. Design state information created by M1 at point of failure in the search for structure.

of preconditions formed from a design state.

Often the preconditions derived from the design state are overly specific, indicating the template will not be applied in all design states in which it is perfectly valid. Specifically, preconditions are overly specific because of the following:

- **Equality:** Equality is used as the test on a design state variable.

- **Constants:** Constants derived from the design state are used for comparison.

- **Irrelevant preconditions:** Superfluous preconditions are sometimes included.

The key to the generalization process is to identify each precondition that exhibits one of these characteristics and apply an appropriate fix to it. As described later, the generalization process is knowledge intensive; specific domain knowledge is needed to implement each fix.

Fixes consist of the following:

- **One- or two-sided constraint substitution:** Equality test is removed and a single- or double-sided interval is used to test a variable.

- **Variable substitution:** Variables are used whenever possible.

- **Delete precondition:** Superfluous preconditions are removed.

A simplified example of the relaxation problem is given in Figure 9.2. Consider part (a) of the figure that has a design space with two variables, A and B. The point represents the acceptable values each variable can take for the template to be selected. Application of the generalization process results in a larger

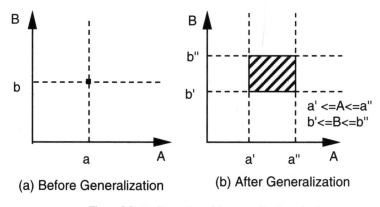

Figure 9.2. An illustration of the generalization of values.

acceptable interval. The shaded box in part (b) of the figure illustrates the new interval of the variables' values under which the preconditions are satisfied.

Generalization can be viewed as a search problem, where the search objective is to find the correct generalization for each variable given a specific design situation. Traditional machine learning techniques guide this search process by either a large number of training examples for which a system can induce underlying patterns [2] or by a kernel of domain knowledge, domain theory, which controls a deductive search [92]. These techniques are not suitable for CGEN because no domain theory exists and only a single training case is available. CGEN, therefore, employs a knowledge-intensive generalization technique.

9.2 The Generalization Approach

The knowledge used for CGEN's generalization procedure identifies both the interaction between design state variables and the proper range those variables can take. The knowledge used to guide the generalization process comes from two sources: the domain expert who supplies generalization methods for each training case and CGEN's knowledge base. Thus, generalization knowledge is actually two separate bodies:

- the set of methods for each training case, denoted as $k_{\text{general\_method}}$, and

- the generalization rules in CGEN's knowledge-base, denoted as $k_{\text{general\_rule}}$. These rules capture variable relationships that are generally applicable to all training cases; however, the rules cover only a small subset of all potential generalizations.

The $k_{general\_rule}$ knowledge partition is created by the CGEN knowledge engineer in the following way. The $k_{general\_method}$ knowledge for a large number of training cases is examined. Any set of commonly occurring methods are encoded into CGEN rules, thereby making these methods available for all future training cases. Ideally, after enough training cases are seen, a large set of $k_{general\_rule}$ rules will exist in CGEN, drastically reducing the number of methods needed for a training case.

It is necessary to look over many training cases because some generalization methods are applicable to only a specific template. Including all methods as part of $k_{general\_rule}$ would cause two problems. First, a large number of methods would exist that would never be used, wasting memory. Second, and more importantly, some methods may be applied inappropriately, resulting in improper generalizations that would cause templates to be used in the wrong design situation.

Recall that methods and preconditions are encoded in an intermediate representation. Knowledge partition $k_{general\_rule}$, however, is encoded as a set of rules. The LHS of each $k_{general\_rule}$ rule represents the precondition to which its associated fix applies; the RHS asserts a generalization method in intermediate form. When the rule fires, a method appears in CGEN's working memory exactly as if supplied by the domain expert (after being parsed). Generalization is performed by the following procedure after the generalization methods have been parsed:

```
Generalize_Template_LHS
{
  Fire all applicable k general_rule rules;
  /* this asserts new generalization methods */
  Apply all generalization methods to template LHS;
};
```

The execution of this procedure is illustrated next by providing examples of generalization methods and rules for an example template.

9.3   An Example

A brief example set of preconditions and generalization methods for an SIO template are shown in Figures 9.3 and 9.4, respectively. Figure 9.5 illustrates a $k_{general\_rule}$ rule. In the first method of Figure 9.4, which removes the precondition SYSTEM_PROCESSOR_FAMILY, the domain expert indicates that the template applies to all processor families known to M1, so the precondition is superfluous and is removed. In the second method, the domain expert indicates the specified baud rate for the SIO part, BAUD_RATE, must be less than or equal to SIO's

```
PC1: (report name = BOARD_COST value = 400000);
PC2: (report name = SYSTEM_PROCESSOR_FAMILY value = 68XX);
PC3: (specification name = BAUD_RATE value = 300);
```

Figure 9.3. Example preconditions.

```
method_type: string_generalization;
method: SYSTEM_PROCESSOR_FAMILY = DELETE ;

method_type: integer_generalization
method: (BAUD_RATE <= MAX_6850_BAUD_RATE) AND
        (BAUD_RATE >= MIN_6850_BAUD_RATE)
```

Figure 9.4. Example generalization methods.

maximum baud rate, MAX_6850_BAUD_RATE, and greater than or equal to its minimum baud rate, MIN_6850_BAUD_RATE.

The method asserted in the $k_{general\_rule}$ rule of Figure 9.5 indicates that the remaining board cost, REMAINING_BOARD_COST, must be greater than or equal to the sum of the cost of all parts asserted by the template.

The flexibility allowed in the types of calculations performed in $k_{general\_rule}$ is greater than in other partitions (e.g., k_{spec}, k_{calc}) because $k_{general\_rule}$ rules are handcrafted and the restrictions of the method language do not apply. For example, a general procedure for summing the cost of parts in a template can be used in the calculation.

The generalization procedure is applied to all the preconditions. This results in the preconditions given in Figure 9.6. Note that the final version of a precondition can either be compared to a constant or to a variable at M1's run time. In this example, the variables MAX_6850_BAUD_RATE and MIN_6850_BAUD_RATE

```
Rule general_board_cost
  If (precondition name = REMAINING_BOARD_COST)
  Then
   Assert_method
   method_type: integer_constraint
   method: REMAINING_BOARD_COST >= total of template part cost;
```

Figure 9.5. Example generalization rule.

```
PC1: (report name = BOARD_COST value >= 325);

PC2: (specification name = BAUD_RATE
                 value = ((BAUD_RATE <= MAX_6850_BAUD_RATE) /\
                          (BAUD_RATE >= MIN_6850_BAUD_RATE)))
```

Figure 9.6. Final preconditions resulting from the application of methods.

are characteristics of the 6850 SIO chip. The actual value of these variables will be assigned during the synthesis process depending on the particular part used in the design. For the other precondition, the constant 325 is computed using the general procedure in Figure 9.5; it is fixed and will not be re-evaluated even if the cost of template parts changes later, resulting in an incorrect generalization; this is a manifestation of CGEN's limitation of not allowing procedure calls in preconditions.

9.4   Issues in Generalization

When preconditions are generalized, there is the possibility of over-generalization and shifting. Over-generalization occurs when a set of preconditions is relaxed too far, causing an illegal application of the template. CGEN assumes the correctness of the generalization methods and, hence, cannot directly detect an over-generalized template. In some cases, however, over-generalization is manifested in M1 by having more than one template applicable to a given design state. A two-dimensional view of over-generalization with respect to template preconditions is illustrated in Figure 9.7. The cross-hatched area in the figure illustrates the range of variable values for a correctly formed set of preconditions, and the dotted box shows the range of application for an over-generalized set of preconditions. Since the dotted box covers the cross-hatched box, M1 will not be able to determine correctly which template to choose and will need to rely on conflict resolution for the final decision. This will violate a tenet of M1's problem solver.

Over-generalization can be detected and reported by M1 at run time. Once detected, the domain expert can then modify the generalization methods, re-run CGEN on the training case, and produce a more specific set of preconditions. It is possible that the generalization is correct, but the design state does not have enough resolution, i.e., enough design state variables to differentiate correctly two apparently similar design states. For these cases, the domain expert needs to augment the design state through the introduction of new reports or

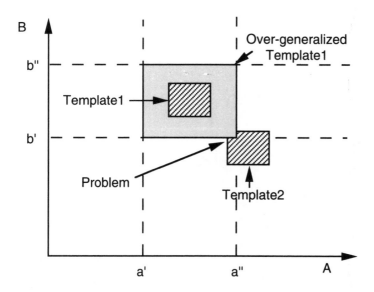

Figure 9.7. Over-generalization of a set of preconditions.

specifications, thereby increasing the number of preconditions. For example, assume a domain expert enters a template illustrating the connection between a 6850 and an RS-232 port. If the expert believes only an RS-232 port will be used with the 6850, no indication of port type is necessary on the LHS of the template rule. Now, suppose another domain expert would like to connect the 6850 to an RS-422 port. An additional specification, or report, for PORT_TYPE would need to-be introduced by the expert to allow the two 6850 templates to be differentiated. A report is introduced by declaring it in the methods file when adding a template for the predecessor part, such as for the template mapping the SIO_0 to the 68XX_SIO_0. The declared report becomes part of the design state when its method (actually the rule compiled from the method) executes and will become the design state for the 68XX_SIO_0 template. A new specification is introduced by updating the part model for the 68XX_SIO_0 with the name of the new specification. When the part 68XX_SIO_0 is used in a template, a method for the SIO_0 will be written for the new specification.

Note that introducing a new specification for a part may require all templates using that part to be updated. If the specification is added to an already existing group of specifications, then a specification method must be added to the methods file for all templates using the part. Otherwise, a complete set of specifications for the part will never be generated, and a design cycle for that part will never occur.

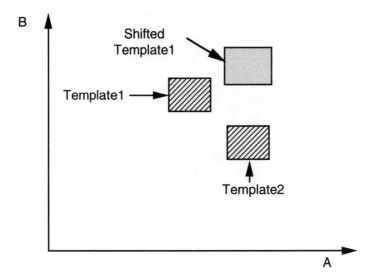

Figure 9.8. Shifting a set of preconditions.

```
PC1: (report name = BOARD_COST value < 325)
PC2: (specification name = BAUD_RATE
             value = ((BAUD_RATE > MAX_6850_BAUD_RATE) OR
                      (BAUD_RATE < MIN_6850_BAUD_RATE)))
```

Figure 9.9. Shifted preconditions.

An extreme case of over-generalization called shifting occurs when the preconditions are satisfied only for design states where they are incorrect. Thus, the template will always be used in the wrong design situations. Figure 9.8 illustrates how the application range for a set of preconditions has been moved from the correct area, shown by cross-hatching, to an incorrect area, shown by a dotted box. The problem is also illustrated in Figure 9.9, where the preconditions in Figure 9.6 have been improperly generalized.

Since CGEN has design state information, it is possible to detect when shifting has occurred. This is done by applying the design state to the generalized preconditions and ensuring that they are satisfied. If the preconditions are not met, then the offending preconditions can be reported. Note that CGEN does not presently detect shifting due to limitations in its implementation, although the extension is simple. Experimental evidence shows, however, that over-generalization and shifting have not occurred.

9.5   The Nature of Generalization Knowledge

The role of generalization knowledge is different from other types of knowledge collected and used by CGEN. This partition is not design knowledge in the same sense as the other partitions; it does not indicate how to connect parts, how to fill in part specifications, and so forth. Instead, generalization knowledge describes relationships between parameters in the design, i.e., how variables in the design state interact and what the limits on these variables should be for a given design situation.

Generalization knowledge should represent a set of invariant relationships for a domain. Upon collecting such a set of relationships it may be possible to begin to characterize a domain, perhaps leading to the development of a domain theory. This theory could then be used to guide the search for generalization for all training cases, eliminating altogether the need for generalization methods.

At present, generalization knowledge is distributed. Each template requires its own set of methods, and methods are not automatically shared between different templates (except for $k_{general\_rule}$). While sharing common knowledge is desired, identifying such knowledge is difficult. A broad understanding of the specific way each method relates to a design state and relationships between them is missing.

Even more importantly, a systematic method for analyzing and consolidating generalization methods to form a broad-based set of $k_{general\_rule}$ is missing. The present scheme for acquiring $k_{general\_rule}$ knowledge is to consider a set of training cases and to detect generalization methods that frequently occur. In fact, even the definition of "frequently" is not precise. The CGEN knowledge engineer associates a set of preconditions with the generalization methods to indicate applicable design states and converts them into $k_{general\_rule}$ rules. The behavior of the $k_{general\_rule}$ is examined over more training cases. If the rules are improperly applied, their preconditions are tightened. Through this process the performance of CGEN with respect to generalization improves over time.

While a complete characterization of $k_{general\_rule}$ rules does not exist, some general classes are emerging. The classes are described below.

Physical resource bounds: Ensuring that sufficient power, area, and cost resources are available for the parts asserted by the template.

Calculation-only reports: A subset of reports used only for calculating other design information. For example, the size of the address space is used in generating address decoding equations but is never used as a template precondition. Reports belonging to this class should always be removed from the set of preconditions.

Processor-family compatibility: Relaxation of some design variables to include all processors in a family can often be applied.

As more classes are identified, a framework for automatically acquiring generalization knowledge will be closer to definition; this is a topic of ongoing research.

10

Modeling M1

The development of the knowledge-acquisition tool typically lags behind that of the expert system. This is because the implementation of the expert system must be fixed before the code generator of the knowledge-acquisition tool can be written. Ideally, the development of both systems should proceed in parallel, thereby reducing the overall development time of the expert system and its knowledge-acquisition tool. Furthermore, parallel development can ensure that both the expert system and the knowledge-acquisition tool are being designed to support each other's operation. Consider that the expert system must be implemented to support knowledge acquisition; attempting to add knowledge-acquisition capabilities to an expert system after the system has been developed is, at best, very difficult, sometimes requiring the re-implementation of the expert system, and at worst it is impossible.

To facilitate parallel implementation of CGEN and M1, the following was done. First, M1 was expressly developed to support CGEN. This was done because of the knowledge-intensive nature of the design task; thus, without domain knowledge all other features of M1 would be meaningless. This decision had ramifications on the resulting implementation of M1. Second, a model of M1's knowledge-base partitions was developed by frequent design reviews. This model was critical, since the partitions represent M1's control structure for CGEN. The initial interface between the tools was based on this model. The following sections describe both these efforts.

rule *rule_name*
  If
    < *partition condition elements* > – group 1
    < *design state condition elements* > – group 2
  Then
    < *partition control actions* > – group 3
    < *design state manipulation actions* > – group 4

Figure 10.1. Canonical rule model.

10.1 Engineering M1's Knowledge Base

To ease knowledge acquisition, an organization was imposed on the representation of rules in M1's knowledge base, as described below.

10.1.1 The Canonical Rule

The bane of knowledge-acquisition system developers is a proliferation of rule types. At one extreme, each rule in a system's knowledge base can be hand-crafted and unique in form. In this case, the task of code generation for a knowledge-acquisition tool becomes impossible. At the other extreme, one rule format is used exclusively throughout the system. While possibly ideal for the developer of the knowledge-acquisition tool, a single format can severely limit the performance of the expert system.

To provide both flexibility for M1 and ease of development for CGEN, a canonical form was adopted for all rules with simple customizations made for each partition. The canonical form is shown in Figure 10.1 with variables italicized. Groups 1 and 2 form the LHS; Groups 3 and 4 form the RHS. Group 1 and Group 3 are constant for all rules in a given partition and are termed *partition definitions*. Groups 2 and 4 are customized for each training session and the type of knowledge being acquired. Section 10.4 provides more detail on the implementation of the canonical form and all of its variants.

The canonical form was created by examining the rules in each of the knowledge-base partitions in an early version of M1. The condition elements (CEs) related to context control (i.e., specifying the partition to which the rule belonged) were separated from those used to specify a design state. The process was repeated for the right-hand side of each rule. In order to fit all rules into the canonical form, some restrictions were imposed on the design state-related portions of the rules. The first restriction required each CE to be composed of two attribute-value pairs: One pair specifies the name of a variable of interest, and the second pair provides constraints on its value. The second restriction is that no procedure calls are allowed in any CE[1].

The canonical form guided the development of both CGEN and M1. It is natural for implementors to custom craft rules to fit situations [117]. By conforming to standards, however, this practice is reduced. The knowledge-acquisition tool developers, then, do not have constantly changing coding styles in the expert system, thereby easing the task of building the tool.

10.1.2 Rule Dependencies

M1 is expected to track technological change over many years. During this time many hardware designers, who are not necessarily working together, will be adding knowledge to M1. This presents a problem: It must be ensured that newly added knowledge will not inadvertently affect existing, still valid, knowledge. While rule-based programming allows new knowledge to be added easily, ensuring that this knowledge will not interact with existing knowledge is difficult.

A potential source of problems lies with the implied interaction between rules. A rule's RHS will create or modify a set of WMEs, that will, in turn, cause some other rule's LHS to match. In many instances, more than one LHS will match, so that conflict resolution must be used to decide which rule to actually fire. Conflict resolution schemes, such as MEA [47], generally rely on recency, among other things, as a metric in the resolution process. In these schemes, weight increases with recency. If there is more than one rule which can create a WME, then there is a potential for time tags to vary depending upon the rule that fired. Consider that if Rule 1's RHS creates WMEs in the order (B, A), and Rule 2 creates WMEs in the order (A, B), then the behavior of the rule-based system may change depending on whether Rule 1 or Rule 2 fired first. Thus, the writer of rules must be aware of all potential ways in which a WME is created to ensure that the behavior of the expert system is consistent. This can be a significant burden with large knowledge bases.

This problem is felt in the knowledge partition $k_{template}$, where only one of potentially many templates is selected for firing. Recall that rules in knowledge partition $k_{template}$ are formed using a combination of the design state information produced by M1. By definition this combination is unique, thus no two $k_{template}$ rules can be in the conflict set simultaneously, and no conflict resolution is needed. Knowledge can be added to $k_{template}$ *ad infinitum* without side effects. In the other partitions, this is not a problem, since more than one rule may execute and the order of execution is not important.

---

[1]OPS83 allows procedure calls to be made in a CE. While this is a useful feature, it is difficult to utilize from a knowledge-acquisition standpoint because additional control knowledge is encoded that is separate from the control knowledge embodied in the problem solver.

10.2   The Models

Recall that CGEN performs the following three functions: (1) acquire knowledge from the hardware designer, (2) reformulate it into an intermediate representation and generalizes it, and (3) generate executable code. Each function requires an understanding of M1's behavior from a different perspective.

The following set of models of M1 were developed to speed the development of CGEN, and enabled it to perform the mapping process.

Development: The activation of partitions in the knowledge base, which represent M1's problem-solving architecture, are represented in this model. This model was derived from M1's implementation. This model was formed during the development of M1 and provided a firm interface between the developers of M1 and CGEN. This allowed concurrent development of both CGEN and M1.

Rule forms: This set of models captures both the control information and rule forms used in M1's knowledge base, in addition to M1's procedures for connecting nets, retrieving parts from the DB, and so forth.

Code syntax: The syntax for code generated by CGEN is given in this model, which is predicated on OPS83's syntax.

Each model is discussed in the following sections.

10.3   The Development Model

The knowledge acquired by CGEN must be cast into OPS83 and must also be assigned to the proper context. Assignment to the proper context is essential for ensuring that the knowledge is applied at the proper point in the problem-solving process. For example, k_{spec} rules should only be applied during d_{spec}. Each knowledge partition, therefore, is associated with a context (see Section 5.2) corresponding to its design cycle step. Thus, the development model is a map between the conceptual design cycle and its implementation in M1.

The development model provides the following for CGEN:

1. relationship of contexts with each design cycle step,

2. form of each CE associated with each context definition (how a CE should be written to properly match its goal WME), and

3. interactions between contexts.

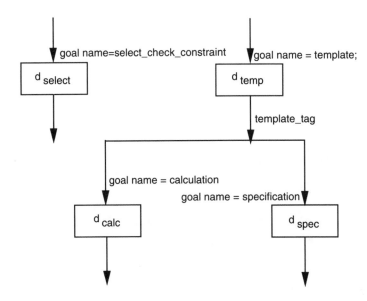

Figure 10.2. A portion of the development model.

Interactions between contexts occur when a context's invocation depends on another context creating the proper goal WMEs. This information is used in the Group 1 portion in the canonical rule's LHS.

The development model is a flow chart. Each box represents a context, and lines interconnecting boxes imply interactions. Near the top of each box is the name and status of the CE(s) controlling invocation of the box. Figure 10.2 illustrates a portion of the model.

The development model allowed CGEN's control structure to be designed. The model, therefore, was used as a specification document, a means of describing the dynamic behavior of M1 to the CGEN developer. When the M1 architecture became stable, i.e., the context definitions and relationships became fixed, the development model was no longer useful as CGEN's representation of M1 also became stable. The development model, however, allowed the concurrent development of CGEN and M1.

10.4   The Rule Form Model

After all inputs to CGEN have been parsed and generalization has been performed, the intermediate form of the acquired knowledge is ready to be op-

```
Generate_Template_LHS
   instantiate proper Group 1 based on rule form model and type of template
   instantiate Group 2 using syntax model

Generate_Template_RHS
   instantiate proper Group 3 based on rule form model and type of template
   for each part in the template
     instantiate Group 4 using rule form model to assert part
   for each connection in the template
     instantiate proper Group 4 using rule form model to assert connection
```

Figure 10.3. Procedure for generating code for partition k_{template}.

```
Generate_Other_Rules
   for each method in intermediate form
     instantiate Group 1 using appropriate rule form model
     instantiate Group 2 using syntax model
     instantiate Group 3 by using rule form model
     instantiate Group 4 by using syntax model
```

Figure 10.4. Procedure for generating code for partitions k_{calc}, k_{spec}, and k_{select}.

erationalized. At this point, the rule form models, and eventually the syntax models, are used by CGEN to generate code. The rule form models are represented as a set of procedures called in sequence to create the necessary context definition for each partition.

All rule form models are based on the canonical rule form. Groups 1 and 3 in the canonical rule are broken into a set of models called context definitions. These models are constant across all training sessions. The Group 2 and Group 4 sections of the canonical rule form vary, depending on the training case, and are filled in the following way. The intermediate representation of the newly acquired knowledge is sorted into two sets. The first set, called LHS information, is used to fill the Group 2 portion of the canonical rule form. The canonical rule's Group 4 information is filled with the second set of information, called RHS information. The procedures used to generate code for each partition using the rule format and syntax models are given in Figures 10.3 and 10.4.

In the following sections, each rule form model is described in detail. A brief description of the syntax models follows in the next section.

10.4.1   Rule Form Representation of k_{template}

The greatest number of rule form variations is for the k_{template} partition. Recall from Section 5.2.3 that there are the following six types of k_{template} rules:

Type AND: Used for an AND node.

If (goal design_cycle_step = template for_part = $\boxed{part}$) and
~(template_tag for_part = $\boxed{part}$ type = 1)

Figure 10.5. Model of Group 1 for Type k_{template} (AND).

Type OR-simple: Used for an OR node, when the successor part is not organized into an array structure and has just one functional unit.

Type OR-functional-unit-specific: Used for an OR node, when the successor part is not organized into an array structure, but has multiple functional units; it shows the connections specific to the functional unit being used.

Type OR-common-connections: Used for an OR node, when the successor part is not organized into an array structure, but has multiple functional units; it shows the connections common to all functional units on the successor part.

Type OR-row-of-array: Used for an OR node, when the successor part is the boundary element on Row 1 of an array structure.

Type OR-column-of-array: Used for an OR node, when the successor part is the boundary element on Column 1 of an array structure.

Each template type has its own model; however, these models differ only in Group 1 information. All rule types share the same Group 2, 3, and 4 information. As part of the design state definition, M1 tells CGEN which context definition to use for the template. (M1 determines the type based on how it failed in the search for structure.)

LHS Models
The Group 1 models are given Figures 10.5 through 10.10. The template part, n_i, and successor part, $S(n_i)$, names are given by the variables *part* and *successor_part*, respectively. CGEN replaces these variables with the names used in the actual template. All fields replaced by CGEN are indicated in the models by $\boxed{\textit{italicized boxed text}}$.

The Group 2 model is common for all the k_{template} rules types. The Group 2 model is the list of preconditions represented as CEs as shown in Figure 8.10. These preconditions are derived from the design state. The CEs are produced directly by the syntax models from the intermediate knowledge representation.

If (goal design_cycle_step = template for_part = [*part*]) and
  (part name = [*successor_part*] predecessor = [*part*]) and
  ~(template_tag for_part = [*part*] type = 2)

Figure 10.6. Model of Group 1 for k_{template} (OR-simple).

If (goal design_cycle_step = template for_part = [*part*]) and
  (part name = [*successor_part*] predecessor = [*part*]) and
  ~(template_tag for_part = [*part*] type = 2a)

Figure 10.7. Model of Group 1 for k_{template} (OR-functional-unit-specific).

If (goal design_cycle_step = template for_part = [*part*]) and
  (part name = [*successor_part*] predecessor = [*part*]) and
  ~(template_tag for_part = [*part*] type = 3) and
  ~(connection pin_of = [*successor_part*])

Figure 10.8. Model of Group 1 for k_{template} (OR-common-connections).

If (goal design_cycle_step = template for_part = [*part*]) and
  (part name = [*successor_part*] predecessor = [*part*] row = 1 col = C) and
  (specification name = ROWS for_part = [*part*] value >= -1) and
  (specification name = COLUMNS for_part = [*part*] value >= -1) and
  ~(template_tag for_part = [*part*] type = 4 col = C)

Figure 10.9. Model of Group 1 for k_{template} (OR-row-of-array).

If (goal design_cycle_step = template for_part = [*part*]) and
  (part name = [*successor_part*] predecessor = [*part*] row = R col = 1) and
  (specification name = ROWS for_part = [*part*] value >= -1) and
  (specification name = COLUMNS for_part = [*part*] value >= -1) and
  ~(template_tag for_part = [*part*] type = 5 row = R)

Figure 10.10. Model of Group 1 for k_{template} (OR-column-of-array).

make (template_tag name = | *template_tag* | for_part = | *part* |
        type = | *type* | row = | *R* | col = | *C* |);

Figure 10.11. Model of Group 3 for template RHS.

instantiate_part (| *new_part* |);

Figure 10.12. Model for asserting parts into a template.

RHS Model

The Group 3 model is similar for all $k_{template}$ rules varieties and is shown in Figure 10.11. The model creates the *template tag*; CGEN fills in the *for_part* field with the name of the template part, generates a unique name for the name field, and fills in the type field based on the type of the template. The col and row fields are filled only for OR-row-of-array and OR-column-of-array templates respectively.

After the Group 3 model is instantiated, the Group 4 information is created. This information comes from the wire list where the parts and connections are specified. Two models are used for this process; Figures 10.12 and 10.13 provide simplified portions of the models for asserting parts and creating connections, respectively. The function used in the model shown in Figure 10.12 gets a part, new_part, from the database. Recall from Section 5.2.3 the functions used in the model shown in Figure 10.13 perform the following operations:

connect_net: This procedure makes a connection between the pins on the parts given in the parameter list.

connect_net_bus: This procedure is used for connecting buses, where the parameters are the same as in the procedure connect_net with the addition of bus_type, which indicates the type of bus being used. CGEN interprets the special bus-expander symbols in the drawings to determine the bus_type.

connect_net (| *partFrom, pinFrom, partTo, pinTo* |);
connect_net_bus (| *partFrom, pinFrom, partTo, pinTo, bus_type* |);

Figure 10.13. Model for creating connections.

If (goal design_cycle_step = imm_calculation for_part = | *part* |) and

(template_tag name = | *template_tag* | for_part = | *part* |)

Figure 10.14. Model of Group 1 for k_{calc}.

(characteristic name = | *char_name* | of = | *successor_part* |

value = | *char_value* |) and

(specification name = | *spec_name* | for_part = | *part* | value = | *spec_value* |) and

(report name = | *report_name* | value = | *report_value* |)

Figure 10.15. A portion of the model of Group 2 for k_{calc}.

10.4.2   Rule Form Representation of k_{calc}

The models for the remaining partitions are relatively simple compared with those of k_{template} since only a single model is needed for each of the rule's groups.

LHS Model

The Group 1 model for k_{calc} rules is shown in Figure 10.14. Each k_{calc} rule is tied to a specific template, and it is necessary to identify that template. The model does this by instantiating values for the template's template_tag and part fields.

Recall that k_{calc} is used to generate and introduce new information into the design state. This is done by executing an expression given by a method. Often, the expression assumes that certain information is available in the design state. An example expression is shown below:

```
CYCLE_TIME = 10000000000 / CLOCK_SPEED.
```

Here, CLOCK_SPEED is assumed to exist. Due to the syntax of rule-based programming languages, any variable used in the RHS of a rule must be declared in the LHS. Thus, the Group 2 portion of k_{calc} rules is composed of variables used in the expression. The necessary variables are instantiated as CEs and are generated using syntax models. The model is shown in Figure 10.15.

RHS Model

The RHS of k_{calc} rules are simple; no Group 3 information is needed. The equations specified in the methods file as either string_calculation or integer_calculation are written directly from CGEN's intermediate representation using the syntax models.

If (goal design_cycle_step = specification for_part = $\boxed{part}$) and

   (part name = $\boxed{part}$ predecessor = $\boxed{predecessor\_part}$) and

   (template_tag name = $\boxed{template\_tag}$ for_part = $\boxed{predecessor\_part}$) and

   ~(specification for_part = $\boxed{part}$ name = $\boxed{spec\_name}$)

Figure 10.16. Model for the first part of Group 1 for k_{spec}.

   ~(specification for_part = $\boxed{part}$ name = $\boxed{neg\_spec}$

             set <> $\boxed{spec\_name\_group}$ value <> DEFAULT[2])

Figure 10.17. Model for the second part of Group 1 for k_{spec}.

10.4.3 Rule Form Representation of k_{spec}

The k_{spec} rules are almost identical to k_{calc} rules; the only significant difference being the Group 1 information.

LHS Model

The k_{spec} Group 1 model has two parts. The first part, shown in Figure 10.16, links the rule to the template tag and identifies to which parts asserted in the template the specification belongs. In the figure, spec_name is the name of the specification being filled. The second part of the model, given in Figure 10.17, creates code to ensure that M1 will not execute this specification rule if any other specification in another group is filled. This model is repeated for all specifications not in the same group as the specification being written, indicated as the variable neg_spec. This group is called spec_name_group in the figure.

   The process for creating the Group 2 model is identical to that for k_{calc} rules.

RHS Model

The RHS for k_{spec} has no Group 3 portion, and the Group 4 information is created exactly as was done for k_{calc}.

10.4.4 Rule Form Model for $k_{\text{select\_rule}}$

The $k_{\text{select\_rule}}$ partition is the most easily modeled partition. Since $k_{\text{select\_rule}}$ knowledge has no dependencies on any other partition, a template tag is not needed. Essentially, the model for this partition consists only of Group 1 and

---

[2]DEFAULT is a value that will always match, such as -1 if the range of values will be greater than 0.

If (goal design_cycle_step = selection_check_constraint

    for_part = | *part* |) and

    (candidate name = | *candidate_part* | is_successor_of = | *part* |) and

    (characteristic name = | *char_name* | of_part = | *candidate_part* |

        value = | *X* |) and

    (specification name = | *spec_name* | for_part = | *part* | value | *OP* | | *X* |)

Figure 10.18. Model of Group 1 information for k_{select_rule}.

(mark candidate as rejected)

Figure 10.19. Model for Group 3 of k_{select_rule}.

Group 3 information. The only variation occurs in the name of the specifications and characteristics used in the rules. Figures 10.18 and 10.19 show the k_{select_rule} models for the LHS and RHS, respectively.

The entries in the model shown in Figure 10.18 perform the following operations. The variable spec_name is the name of the specification being used in the selection evaluation. The variable char_name identifies the characteristic being compared to the specification; the variable candidate_part represents the set of parts that are candidates for selection. Notice in the specification element that the selection comparison test is denoted by the variable OP.

When a selection rule is fired, it causes a candidate to be rejected. The k_{select_rule} Group 3 model in Figure 10.19 shows the action taken when disqualification occurs; the candidate is marked as rejected. There is no Group 4 information in this partition.

10.5 The Syntax Model

The design-state specific portions of the rule form model, Groups 2 and 4, are in CGEN's intermediate knowledge representation. This representation facilitates the analysis of acquired knowledge but not the creation of executable code. The syntax model directs the necessary translation of this form to executable code. The model is composed of two pieces:

Equation generator: This part of the model captures the OPS83 syntax and applies these rules while interpreting the intermediate representation. The executable portion of this model is called when an equation is to be written, for example, in the design specific portion of the RHS of k_{calc}

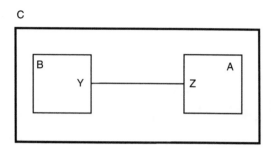

Figure 10.20. Template for the rule generation example.

rules, or when the CEs for $k_{template}$ rules are created from the intermediate representation.

Data structure generator: The data structure declarations used in the implementation of M1 are represented in this portion of the syntax model. These models are used to create segments of Group 4 code.

The data structure models consist of a set of definitions, one for each data structure, that are similar to the rule form models. During execution, CGEN selects the proper definition and fills in the appropriate fields.

10.6   A Rule Generation Example

This section presents a simple example of the generation of rules for the partitions $k_{template}$ and k_{spec}. The example assumes that all the necessary information for rule creation is in the intermediate knowledge representation, and that necessary generalizations have been applied. The template to be acquired is shown in Figure 10.20. A representation of the intermediate forms of information to be used is shown in Figure 10.21.

The first step in the code generation process is creating the $k_{template}$ LHS. M1 has passed the following information to CGEN:

1. Template LHS type : 2

2. Successor Part : A

3. Part : C

Given this information, CGEN selects the $k_{template}$ LHS rule form model 2 for the Group 1 information and fills in the appropriate information, producing the code shown in Figure 10.22.

```
bounding box:    C
successor part: A
support parts:  B
preconditions:  report CLOCK > 200
                report SPEED < 400
connections:    partB,pinY → partA,pinZ
specification:  DELAY = 1,000,000,000 / CLOCK_SPEED + SLEW_RATE
negated spec:   PART_NAME
```

Figure 10.21. Intermediate representation of k_{spec} and $k_{template}$ knowledge.

Rule CGEN$simple_example
  If (goal design_cycle_step = template for_part = $\boxed{C}$) and
    (part name = $\boxed{A}$ predecessor = $\boxed{C}$) and
   ~(template_tag for_part = $\boxed{C}$ type = 2)

Figure 10.22. Template rule Group 1 information.

(report name = $\boxed{CLOCK}$; value > $\boxed{200}$) and
(report name = $\boxed{SPEED}$; value < $\boxed{400}$)

Figure 10.23. Template rule Group 2 information.

make (template_tag for_part = $\boxed{A}$ type = 2 name = g10001a);

Figure 10.24. Template rule Group 3 information.

instantiate_part($\boxed{B}$);
connect_net($\boxed{B, Y, A, Z}$);

Figure 10.25. Template rule Group 4 information.

Rule CGEN$simple_example
If (goal design_cycle_step = template for_part = $\boxed{C}$) and
   (part name = $\boxed{A}$ predecessor = $\boxed{C}$) and
   ~(template_tag for_part = $\boxed{C}$ type = 2) and
   (report name = $\boxed{CLOCK}$; value > $\boxed{200}$) and
   (report name = $\boxed{SPEED}$; value < $\boxed{400}$)
Then
   make (template_tag for_part = $\boxed{A}$ type = 2 name = g10001a);
   instantiate_part($\boxed{B}$);
   connect_net($\boxed{B, Y, A, Z}$);

Figure 10.26. Complete template rule.

Next, the Group 2 information is written. CGEN uses an equation generator syntax model to convert the intermediate form into OPS83 code. The result of this procedure is shown in Figure 10.23.

Once the LHS is complete, the RHS information is generated. The Group 3 information is created using a rule form model to produce the template_tag, as shown in Figure 10.24. The Group 4 information is created by applying the rule form models for part assertion and connections; the result is shown in Figure 10.25. The template rule is now complete and is reproduced in its entirety in Figure 10.26.

CGEN then proceeds to generate the specification rule. CGEN generates Group 1 information by instantiating the rule form model for the LHS of partition k_{spec} and fills the slot for template_tag to produce the rule fragment shown in Figure 10.27. Next, the Group 2 portion of the rule is written, producing the code shown in Figure 10.28. With the completion of the rule's LHS, the RHS can be constructed. The intermediate form of the equation is translated into OPS83 using a syntax model. This process yields the code shown in Figure 10.29. The rule is now complete, and is reproduced in its entirety in Figure 10.30.

10.7 Discussion

The design of M1's knowledge base and the process of acquiring knowledge raises three issues: How can outdated knowledge be supplanted by new knowledge, what types of knowledge cannot be represented, and can multiple domain experts simultaneously deposit their experience in a single knowledge base? These issues are discussed in the following sections.

Rule CGEN$simple_specification
  If (goal design_cycle_step = specification for_part = A) and
    (part name = A predecessor = C) and
    (template_tag name = $g10001a$ for_part = C) and
    ~(specification for_part = A name = $DELAY$ set = S) and
    ~(specification for_part = A name = $PART\_NAME$
        set <> S value <> -1)

Figure 10.27. Specification rule Group 1 information.

    (characteristic name = $SLEW\_RATE$ of_part = C value = X) and
    (report name = $CLOCK\_SPEED$ value = Y)

Figure 10.28. Specification rule Group 2 information.

    make (specification name = $DELAY$ for_part = A
            value = $1000000000 / Y + X$);

Figure 10.29. Specification rule Group 4 information.

Rule CGEN$simple_specification
  If (goal design_cycle_step = specification for_part = A) and
    (part name = A predecessor = C) and
    (template_tag name = $g10001a$ for_part = C) and
    ~(specification for_part = A name = $DELAY$ set = S) and
    ~(specification for_part = A name = $PART\_NAME$
        set <> S value <> -1) and
    (characteristic name = $SLEW\_RATE$ of_part = C value = X) and
    (report name = $CLOCK\_SPEED$ value = Y)
Then
    make (specification name = $DELAY$ for_part = A
            value = $1000000000 / Y + X$);

Figure 10.30. Complete specification rule.

10.7.1 Supplanting Old Knowledge

The development of the knowledge base over time requires that new knowledge should not destructively interfere with existing knowledge. The representation scheme employed by M1 and CGEN ensures that interference does not occur. There is, however, another side to this issue: The knowledge-acquisition tool should allow outdated knowledge to be either supplanted by new knowledge or removed. Facilities for replacing or eliminating existing knowledge are needed in domains where technology is rapidly changing. In these domains new parts and design techniques that better meet specifications should be chosen over older, inferior ones. Often new design techniques will be discovered to utilize parts better (frequently the case when a new microprocessor is introduced), thus invalidating older structures.

When a new part or structure is introduced into the knowledge base, there must be some quantifiable differences between it and existing knowledge. This leads to three cases:

Case 1: The new part or structure performs better for the set of existing criteria.

Case 2: The new part or structure introduces some previously unknown criterion.

Case 3: The old knowledge was incorrect.

For example, in Case 1, a new microprocessor may be faster, and, therefore, better along known criterion, e.g., PROCESSOR_SPEED. In Case 2 the microprocessor may perform some new function, such as virtual memory support, thereby introducing an entirely new metric.

Step d_{select} in the design cycle chooses parts that are superior along known criteria without the need to update the knowledge base each time a new instance of a known part is introduced and, thus, covers Case 1. For Case 2 the design state must be augmented to represent the new feature. This can be done through either the introduction of a new specification for a set of predecessor parts or a new report describing a new feature. If a new specification is added, k_{select_rule} must be updated, and the new specification becomes a criterion for rejecting old parts. In addition, all the old templates that used the predecessor part will need to be regenerated. (See Section 9.4 for more information.)

Through the use of either reports or specifications, old knowledge in partition $k_{template}$ is supplanted through the mechanisms of M1's architecture; the new reports or specifications would not match the old rule's LHS, and, thus, the old rules will not execute. It is possible, however, that both the old and the new specifications will be in the design state, causing both the new and the old rules to appear in the conflict set. Thus, to ensure proper operation, both the old and the new rules need to be rebuilt using CGEN and the new design state.

In Case 3, when the entered knowledge is incorrect, it must be completely removed from the knowledge base. This requires browsing and editing the M1 knowledge base.

10.7.2 Limits of Expression

CGEN restricts both the forms of rules it generates and the types of knowledge a domain expert can describe. CGEN acquires declarative knowledge only; it is not capable of capturing procedural knowledge. Within the scope of declarative knowledge, CGEN does not allow the following types of expressions:

Explicit sequencing: During d_{spec} it is often desirable that specifications being completed via questions to the user be posed in a particular sequence. It is not possible to express sequencing information in specification methods. Significant modifications to the method language and syntax models for k_{spec} would be required to permit sequencing.

Preconditions for calculations: All rules in the k_{calc_now} partition will fire when their associated template is activated. The ability to fire k_{calc_now} rules selectively would be useful in some situations. The method language and syntax model for k_{calc_now} rules would have to be updated to allow the domain expert to express these preconditions.

10.7.3 Multiple Domain Expert Acquisition

CGEN and M1 allow multiple experts to deposit domain knowledge simultaneously. The construction of the knowledge base ensures that there is no interference between knowledge entered by different designers. If properly organized (i.e., all knowledge is compiled into a file shared by all), domain experts can share common knowledge.

To organize knowledge acquisition properly among a group of designers, the interactions between subsystems should be known to all contributing designers. For example, the design of a memory subsystem requires information generated by the processor subsystem, such as data and address bus widths and required access time of the memory. If knowledge about the design of the memory and processor subsystems are entered by different experts, the processor expert must generate the information needed by the memory expert for the design to reach completion. Identifying the interactions between subsystems can be done prior to both designers beginning knowledge acquisition. With proper planning and organization, multiple expert knowledge acquisition is possible. Chapter 12 describes a set of experiments involving the construction of a knowledge base by four experts.

Part IV

Examples, Experiments, and Experiences

11

A Complete Example

This chapter describes the use of M1 and CGEN in designing a 80386-based system. It is assumed that M1 currently has design knowledge for 80386-based systems using an Intel 8251 SIO chip. A domain expert wants to produce a slightly different design using an Intel I8274 SIO chip instead. The complete process that he has to undergo is as follows:

1. Develop a part model for the I8274.

2. Perform synthesis using M1.

3. Get M1 to prompt him for knowledge acquisition for I8274.

4. Use CGEN to teach M1 about designing using the I8274.

5. Rerun M1 to complete the design.

The following sections describe each of these subtasks.

11.1 Developing a Part Model

The first step in adding knowledge about a new part into M1 is to determine its position in the existing functional hierarchy. The functional hierarchy is printed out as an indented list using a database utility program. The relevant portion of the hierarchy printout is given below.

```
. . . .
SIO_0
    68XX_SIO_0
        MC6850
        MC68B50
        HD6850
    80386_SIO_0
        I8251
    8086_SIO_0
        I8251
    . . . .
```

The printout shows the current SIO chips organized based on processor family. Since the I8274 has two SIO functional units and can be used directly with the 80386 processor family, the domain expert decides to model it as having two 80386_SIO_0 links. At this stage, the domain expert may also realize that the I8274 can be used in 8086-based designs too. Anticipating that later someone might want to teach M1 about this usage, he may also add two 8086_SIO_0 links on the I8274 for the same two functional units. Further, anticipating that there might be a second source (i.e., another manufacturer besides Intel) for the I8274 at a later date, he models the chip-name as 8274.

Next, he needs to model the characteristics of the I8274. All relevant design information about the I8274 has to be modeled as characteristics. To determine what information is relevant, the domain expert may look at the part models of the predecessor part, the 80386_SIO_0, and the sibling part (i.e., the successor of the I8274's predecessor part), the I8251. The I8274 must have characteristics that can be used to match the specifications of the 80386_SIO_0 in the part selection design cycle step together with information that any other portion of the design may require, such as the address space used by the I8274. Since the same requirements applied to the development of the I8251 model, the same set of characteristics as the I8251 with different values may be used. The part models of the 80386_SIO_0 and I8251 were given in Figures 5.15 and 5.18. Based on the information in these models, the domain expert develops the model in Figure 11.1. The I8274 does not have any specifications since it is a physical part. The pin related information is obtained directly from the I8274 data sheets.

Note that the domain expert must have sufficient insight into the design when creating part models for an abstract part and its first successor part. It is at this time that he decides the level of detail of the model and the bounds on the design space for that abstract part. In the example, this was done when the models for the 80386_SIO_0 and I8251 were developed. For example, the domain

Name: I8274		Chip name: 8274
Specifications		
spec-name		*group-number*
Characteristics		
char-name		*value*
ADDRESS_BITS		2
ACCESS_TIME		200
Links		
predecessor-name	*edge-type*	*func-unit-number*
80386_SIO_0	OR	1
80386_SIO_0	OR	2
8086_SIO_0	OR	1
8086_SIO_0	OR	2
Pins		
pin-name	*pin-index*	*pin-isa*
D0	0	DATA_BUS
D1	1	DATA_BUS
..	..	..

Figure 11.1. Part model for the I8274.

expert decided that of the numerous timing attributes of the SIO chips, only the ACCESS_TIME was significant for the design process in M1. The domain expert has complete control of what information to include in a part model. The MICON tools neither provide any guidance nor preclude any information. The quality of M1's knowledge base and, thus, indirectly that of the M1-generated designs, depend strongly on these decisions.

11.2   Synthesis Using M1

After the I8274 has been added to the database, the domain expert assumes the role of the M1 user who wants to obtain a 80386-based design with the 8274 SIO chip. A typical session with M1 for this design is shown below. Output produced by M1 is in `typeface`, comments are in *italics* and user input is in bold boxed text . As seen in the trace, M1 repeatedly executes design cycles for abstract parts. Each design cycle is similar to the one explained in detail in Section 5.4. Other issues such as subproblem ordering are explained using in-line comments below.

```
*** M1: Computer System Synthesis Tool ***
Activating SBC_0 design
   Specification
      Total amount of board area < sq. inches > :  32

      Total amount of board cost < nearest dollar > :  5000

     Total amount of power dissipation allowed < mW > :  80000
   Specifications complete
   Selection: AND node - no action
   Part Expansion: AND node - no action
   Structural design: AND node
```
   Top-level template with PROC_0, MEM_0, IO_0, etc.
   shown in Figure 3.2 is invoked
```
   Immediate calculation
Blocking SBC_0 design: waiting for successors to be designed
Activating IO_0 design
   Specification
      Is PIO needed < Y N > :  Y

      Is SIO needed < Y N > :  Y

      Is TIMER needed < Y N > :  N
   Specifications not complete
```
   Specification MAX_ACCESS_TIME is to be filled using report ACCESS_TIME
   which is not yet been generated
```
Blocking IO_0 design: incomplete specifications
Activating MEM_0 design
   Specification
      Is DRAM needed < Y N > :  N

      Is SRAM needed < Y N > :  Y

      Is ROM needed < Y N > :  Y
   Specifications not complete
```
   Specification MAX_ACCESS_TIME is to be filled using report ACCESS_TIME
   which is not yet been generated
```
Blocking MEM_0 design: incomplete specifications
....
Activating PROC_0 design
   Specification
      Processor name :  80386

      Minimum clock speed < Hz > :  20000000
   Specifications complete
   Selection
```
      Rejected 68XX_PROC_0, 8086_PROC_0, etc.
      due to mismatch with specified Processor name
```
      Selected 80386_PROC_0, independent structure
   Part Expansion
```

```
Structural design: OR node
```
Template shown in Figure 3.3 invoked
```
Immediate calculation
Blocking PROC_0: waiting for successors to be designed
Activating 80386_PROC_0 design
   Specification
```
   Specifications are filled by formulation
```
   Specifications complete
   Selection
```
   I80386_16 is rejected due to lesser clock speed
```
      Selected I80386_20, independent structure
   Part Expansion
   Structural design: OR node
```
   Template integrating physical 80386 (I80386_20) to 80386_PROC_0
   is invoked
```
   Immediate calculation
```
   Report ACCESS_TIME is computed based on timing-related
   characteristics of the I80386_20
```
   Delayed calculation
Done 80386_PROC_0 design
Activating 80386_CLK_GEN_0 design
. . . .
Done 80386_CLK_GEN_0 design
Activating MEM_0 design
   Specification
```
   Specification MAX_ACCESS_TIME is now filled using formulation
   since the report ACCESS_TIME now exists in the design state
```
   Specifications complete
   Selection: AND node - no action
   Part expansion: AND node - no action
   Structural design: AND node
   Immediate calculation
Blocking MEM_0 design: waiting for successors to be designed
. . . .
```

11.3 Getting Prompted for Knowledge Acquisition

Recall, the domain expert's motive for running M1 is to get it to prompt for knowledge acquisition for the I8274 chip. Therefore, the expert must input specifications to M1 such that it selects an 8274. One way of doing this is to ask for an 8274 chip explicitly as shown in the M1 trace below. Since M1 does not have any template for mapping the 80386_SIO_0 to the 8274, it will fail in the search for structure, prompt for knowledge acquisition, and halt.

```
    . . . .
Activating 80386_SIO_0 design
   Specification
```
Enter tag for this SIO port : **SIO_1**

Name of SIO chip to use   : **8274**

External interface < RS-232 RS-422 etc. > : **RS-232**

Baud rate < 300 1200 4800 etc. > : **4800**

Baud rate selection switch
                  < FIXED HW_SWITCH > : **HW_SWITCH**

Should this SIO do interrupts < Y N > : **N**

Should interrupts if any be maskable < Y N > : **Y**

Interrupt priority level if any : **0**

Port size < 3 5 9 > : **5**

Port type < DTE DCE > : **DTE**

Connector type < MALE FEMALE > : **MALE**

Connector size < 9 25 > : **25**

```
Specifications complete
Selection
```
I8251 is rejected due to mismatching chip-name
```
      Selected I8274, independent structure
Part Expansion: Using functional unit 2
Structural design
      *** Template not found for integrating
      common connections of 8274 to 80386_SIO_0 ***
```
A suitable template is missing from M1's knowledge base,
initiating the knowledge-acquisition process.
M1 writes out the design state in files D1.DAT for use by CGEN
and file D1.PREVIEW for use by domain expert.
```
Do you want a save-state here < Y N >  :  Y
```
M1 saves the working design in save-state files
allowing M1 to restart at this point so that entire design
does not need to be re-created.
```
  *** M1 execution terminated ***
```

11.4 Knowledge Acquisition Using CGEN

Now that the knowledge-acquisition process has been initiated by M1, the domain expert takes the M1-generated design-state files and goes through a training session in which he uses CGEN to add knowledge related to the I8274 template to M1. The training session includes generating inputs for CGEN – the

```
/ *** Template not found for integrating common connections
      of 8274 to 80386_SIO_0 *** /
Report name = M_INT_COUNT value = -1
Report name = BOARD_AREA value = 32000000
Report name = BOARD_COST value = 500000
Report name = REMAINING_BOARD_AREA value = 1500000
Report name = REMAINING_BOARD_COST value = 460000
Report name = SYSTEM_PROCESSOR value = 80386
Report name = ACCESS_TIME value = 200
Specification name = SIO_TAG value = |SIO_1|
Specification name = CHIP_NAME value = |?|
Specification name = EXT_INTERFACE value = |RS-232|
Specification name = BAUD_RATE value = 4800
Specification name = BAUD_SWITCH value = |HW_SWITCH|
Specification name = INTERRUPTS value = |Y|
Specification name = INTR_MASKABLE value = |Y|
Specification name = INTR_PRIORITY_LEVEL value = 0
Specification name = PORT_SIZE value = 5
Specification name = PORT_TYPE value = |DTE|
Specification name = CONNECTOR_TYPE value = |MALE|
Specification name = CONNECTOR_SIZE value = 25
Specification name = MAX_ACCESS_TIME value = 200
```

Figure 11.2. Design state preview file for template found missing in Section 11.3.

template and methods – and running CGEN to get a new set of rules to be added to M1. Each of these subtasks are described in the sections below for the template not found by M1 in the previous section. The corresponding design state D1.PREVIEW file is given in Figure 11.2. Note that the actual design state has a larger number of variables – only a few variables of each representative category are considered in this section.

11.4.1 Drawing the Template Schematic

The template has to integrate the common connections of the 8274 to the 80386_SIO_0. The only common pins (i.e., pins that are shared between all functional units on a part) on the 8274 are the power, address and data bus, clock, read/write control, and interrupt pins. The template for this is relatively straightforward and is shown in Figure 11.3[1]. The domain expert uses a drawing

---

[1]The INTR_BUS_RESOLVER part is used to connect the interrupt pin of the I8274 to the appropriate interrupt priority level of the PROC_INTR_BUS.

80386_SIO_0

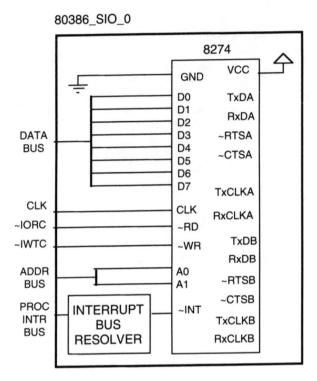

Figure 11.3. Template for connecting common connections of 8274 to 80386_SIO_0.

editor to create this template schematic and subsequently extract the corresponding wire list file WIRE.LIST.

11.4.2 Writing the Methods

A utility program, FILTER, accesses the PREVIEW file and the database and allows the domain expert to create the METHODS file interactively. There are three broad categories of methods that are included with each template. First, the generalization methods relax the range of applicability of the template beyond the design state in the PREVIEW file. The domain expert peruses the PREVIEW file and identifies the overly specific variables. Some of these variables are generalized automatically by $k_{general\_rule}$ in CGEN. A list of these variables is consulted, and variables generalized automatically are deleted from further consideration (the FILTER utility does this automatically). For example, the variables M_INT_COUNT, BOARD_AREA, BOARD_COST, REMAINING_BOARD_AREA, and REMAINING_BOARD_COST are not consid-

```
method_type: integer_generalization
method: ACCESS_TIME = DELETE
/* DELETE removes the pre-condition */

method_type: string_generalization
method: SIO_TAG <> NULL
/* NULL is an empty string, so this will match any string */

method_type: string_generalization
method: CHIP_NAME <> NULL

method_type: string_generalization
method: EXT_INTERFACE <> NULL

method_type: integer_generalization
method: BAUD_RATE > -1

method_type: string_generalization
method: BAUD_SWITCH <> NULL

method_type: string_generalization
method: INTERRUPTS <> NULL

method_type: string_generalization
method: INTR_MASKABLE <> NULL

method_type: integer_generalization
method: INTR_PRIORITY_LEVEL > -1

method_type: integer_generalization
method: PORT_SIZE > 0

method_type: string_generalization
method: PORT_TYPE <> NULL

method_type: integer_generalization
method: MAX_ACCESS_TIME > -1

method_type: integer_generalization
method: CONNECTOR_SIZE > 0

method_type: string_generalization
method: CONNECTOR_TYPE <> NULL
```

Figure 11.4. Example generalization methods.

```
method_type: integer_imm_calculation
method: SIO_ADDRESS_SPACE = 2 ** CHAR_8274_ADDRESS_BITS
```

Figure 11.5. Example calculation method.

ered since they are automatically generalized by CGEN. The domain expert
writes a method for each of the other variables to be generalized. Since this
template is applicable anytime an 8274 is being used for the 80386_SIO_0, all
other variables are deleted. Generalization methods for the example design state
are given in Figure 11.4.

Second, the specification methods indicate how specifications for any abstract
parts used in the template must be computed. Since there are no abstract parts in
the example template, no specification methods are needed. Finally, the calculation methods provide equations for creating reports. In this example, a report
indicating the address space occupied by this particular port is created using
the ADDRESS_BITS characteristic of the I8274. The corresponding method
is shown in Figure 11.5, where the domain expert decided to create the report
SIO_ADDRESS_SPACE in the $d_{\text{calc\_now}}$ step.

11.4.3 Running CGEN

The WIRE.LIST and METHODS files together with the M1-generated design
state file are the inputs to CGEN. A typical session in CGEN for the example template is given below. Output produced by CGEN is in typeface,
comments are in *italics* and domain expert input is in | **bold boxed text** |.

```
*** CGEN: Code Generator for M1 ***
Commands:
     a. Read input files
     b. Create structure-specific super-partition rules
     c. Create part-specific super-partition rules
     d. Exit
Please enter choice: a
 %samepage
Asserting variables
  Made Variable ACCESS_TIME
  ....
  Made Variable CONNECTOR_SIZE
  Made Variable SIO_ADDRESS_SPACE
```
  CGEN reads all variables used in methods and checks
  if they are legal variables in the design state.
  Otherwise, they are treated as constants.

```
Asserting methods
  Made Method integer_generalization ACCESS_TIME
  ....
  Made Method integer_imm_calculation SIO_ADDRESS_SPACE
```
  CGEN reads all methods and checks for legal syntax.
All input files have now been read and converted into intermediate form.
```
Commands:
     a. Read input files
     b. Create structure-specific super-partition rules
     c. Create part-specific super-partition rules
     d. Exit
Please enter choice: [b]
Template part: 8274
Functional unit number: 0
Predecessor part: 80386_SIO_0
```
CGEN confirms the current template being acquired.
```
Part function utilization
  Considering VCC
  ....
  Considering I8274
```
  CGEN checks what functional unit on each part is being utilized
  in the template. User input may be required in ambiguous cases.
```
Using generalization knowledge
  Generalize: M_INT_COUNT
  Ok? : [y]
  ....
  Generalize: REMAINING_BOARD_COST
  Ok? : [y]
```
  CGEN uses $k_{generalize}$ to perform generalizations.
```
Variables not generalized
```
  CGEN warns of any variables not generalized, here no variables are listed.
```
Creating rules
  Created template rule 1
  Created calculation rule 1
```
  CGEN writes out OPS83 rules in RULE file.
```
Commands:
     a. Read input files
     b. Create structure-specific super-partition rules
     c. Create part-specific super-partition rules
     d. Exit
Please enter choice: [d]
*** CGEN execution terminated ***
```

11.5   Continuing with Synthesis

The CGEN-created RULE file is inserted into one of M1's knowledge base files, and the file recompiled and re-linked to get an updated M1. M1 is restarted at the point of failure. The M1 session is given below. After the acquired common connections template is invoked, M1 immediately requires another template for making the connections specific to functional unit 2. Since this template is missing, M1 once again prompts for knowledge acquisition.

```
*** M1: Computer System Synthesis Tool ***
Restoring design from save-state files
```
The example template just acquired is invoked and
common connections on the 8274 are completed.
```
    *** Template not found for integrating functional unit 2
            of 8274 to 80386_SIO_0 ***
```
A suitable template is missing from M1's knowledge base.
As before, this initiates the knowledge-acquisition process.
M1 writes out the design state in files D1.DAT for use by CGEN
and file PREVIEW for use by domain expert.
```
Do you want a save-state here < Y N >  :  [Y]
```
M1 saves the working design in save-state files.
This allows M1 to restart at this point so that entire design
does not need to be re-created.
```
*** M1 execution terminated ***
```

11.6   Another Training Session Using CGEN

The domain expert goes through another training session. The design-state file is the same as in Figure 11.2. The domain expert needs to create a template that integrates functional unit 2 on the 8274 to the 80386_SIO_0. This template must connect the I8274 to an RS232 port interface. The domain expert knows (or can find out by browsing the database) that the database has an abstract part for the RS232 port, so instead of designing an external interface, he can use the existing RS232_PORT_0 part. The completed template is shown in Figure 11.6. (No connections to the boundary of the 80386_SIO_0 are need in this template, since all connections to the 80386_SIO_0 are common to the two functional units on the 8274 and were already included in the template in Figure 11.3.)

Next, the domain expert writes the methods given in Figure 11.7. The generalization methods are the same as for the common connections template, except that the EXT_INTERFACE and PORT_TYPE variables are not generalized since the template is specific to a DTE RS232 port. For each of the abstract parts in the template, methods for generating their specifications must be given.

80386_SIO_0

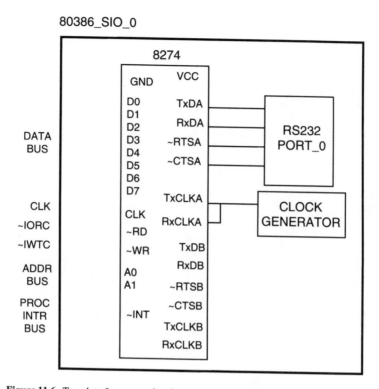

Figure 11.6. Template for connecting functional unit 2 of 8274 to 80386_SIO_0.

For example, the CLOCK_GENERATOR_0 has two specifications – the FRE-QUENCY specification is computed using the BAUD_RATE specification of the 80386_SIO_0, and the FREQ_SWITCH specification is computed using the BAUD_SWITCH specification of the 80386_SIO_0. All specifications are generated using the formulation mechanism. This mechanism is preferred since it minimizes redundant questions to the user. No calculation methods are used in this example.

Next, the WIRE.LIST and METHODS input files, together with the M1-generated design-state file, are run through CGEN. The CGEN session trace is given below.

```
method_type: integer_generalization
method: ACCESS_TIME = DELETE
. . . .

method_type: string_generalization
method: CONNECTOR_TYPE <> NULL

method_type: integer_specification
method: CLOCK_GENERATOR_0_FREQUENCY
        = SPEC_80386_SIO_0_BAUD_RATE * 16

method_type: string_specification
method: CLOCK_GENERATOR_0_FREQ_SWITCH
        = SPEC_80386_SIO_0_BAUD_SWITCH
. . . .

method_type: integer_specification
method: RS232_PORT_0_PORT_SIZE
        = SPEC_80386_SIO_0_PORT_SIZE

method_type: integer_specification
method: RS232_PORT_0_CONN_SIZE
        = SPEC_80386_SIO_0_CONNECTOR_SIZE

method_type: string_specification
method: RS232_PORT_0_CONN_TYPE
        = SPEC_80386_SIO_0_CONNECTOR_TYPE
```

Figure 11.7. Example methods for 8274 functional unit 2 template.

```
*** CGEN: Code Generator for M1 ***
Commands:
      a. Read input files
      b. Create structure-specific super-partition rules
      c. Create part-specific super-partition rules
      d. Exit
Please enter choice: [a]
Asserting variables
  Made Variable ACCESS_TIME
  . . . .
  Made Variable CONNECTOR_SIZE
  Made Variable CLOCK_GENERATOR_0_FREQUENCY
  Made Variable CLOCK_GENERATOR_0_FREQ_SWITCH
```

```
....
Made Variable RS232_PORT_0_PORT_SIZE
Made Variable RS232_PORT_0_CONN_SIZE
Made Variable RS232_PORT_0_CONN_TYPE
```
*CGEN reads all variables used in methods and ascertains
if they are legal variables in the design state.
Otherwise, they are treated as constants.*
```
Asserting methods
Made Method integer_generalization ACCESS_TIME
....
Made Method integer_specification CLOCK_GENERATOR_0_FREQUENCY
Made Method string_specification CLOCK_GENERATOR_0_FREQ_SWITCH
....
Made Method integer_specification RS232_PORT_0_PORT_SIZE
Made Method integer_specification RS232_PORT_0_CONN_SIZE
Made Method string_specification RS232_PORT_0_CONN_TYPE
```
CGEN reads all methods and checks for legal syntax.
All input files have been read and converted into intermediate form
```
Commands:
    a. Read input files
    b. Create structure-specific super-partition rules
    c. Create part-specific super-partition rules
    d. Exit
Please enter choice: [b]
Template part: 8274
Functional unit number: 2
Predecessor part: 80386_SIO_0
```
CGEN confirms the current template being acquired.
```
Part function utilization
Considering part CLOCK_GENERATOR_0
Considering part RS232_PORT_0
....
Considering I8274
```
*CGEN determines which functional unit on each part is being utilized
in the template. User input may be required in ambiguous cases.*
```
Using generalization knowledge
Generalize: M_INT_COUNT
Ok? : [y]
....
Generalize: REMAINING_BOARD_COST
Ok? : [y]
```
*CGEN uses $k_{generalize}$ for generalization, while the user may
override any generalization.*
```
Variables not generalized
```
CGEN warns of any variables not generalized. Here no variables is listed.

```
Creating rules
  Created template rule 1
  Checking for complete specifications on CLOCK_GENERATOR_0
    Specification: FREQUENCY
    Specification: FREQ_SWITCH
  Created specification rule 1
  Created specification rule 2
  . . . .
  Created specification rule 10
  CGEN writes out OPS83 rules in file RULE1.CGEN.
Commands:
      a. Read input files
      b. Create structure-specific super-partition rules
      c. Create part-specific super-partition rules
      d. Exit
Please enter choice: d
*** CGEN execution terminated ***
```

11.7   Completing Synthesis Using M1

M1 is recompiled and reinvoked as before. If all templates required for the design are present in M1's knowledge base, the design process finally terminates as shown in the trace below.

```
  . . . .
  Activating SBC_0 design
    Delayed calculation
  Done SBC_0 design
  Do you want a netlist < Y N > : Y
  With abstract part connections < Y N > : N
    File M1.NETLIST written.
```

The netlist file is the complete logic design for the computer system. Commercial physical design tools may then be used to place and route the netlist, and the design could subsequently be fabricated.

12

CGEN Experimentation

This chapter describes experiments with using CGEN to build M1's knowledge base. The experiments were conducted to verify that CGEN could effectively capture expertise from hardware designers and translate it into an M1-usable form. M1's use of the generated knowledge was verified using a separate set of experiments described in the next chapter. The descriptions here cover both the experimental process and the results. Note that the data presented in this chapter refers to the state of M1 and CGEN during the experimental period.

12.1 Overview

A set of experiments were formulated to accomplish the following:

1. test CGEN's ability to capture design knowledge,

2. test CGEN's ability to generate operational code for M1,

3. validate assumptions about M1's knowledge partition growth rates, and

4. quantify the semantic advantage of using a knowledge-acquisition tool over hand encoding expert knowledge.

177

The experiments run on CGEN also provided an opportunity to examine M1's behavior. The experimental procedure allowed validation of the following assumptions about M1's architecture and knowledge base:

1. ability to perform design synthesis,

2. adequacy of knowledge representation,

3. uniqueness of template preconditions, and

4. ability to support knowledge acquisition.

From the experiments, we concluded:

1. CGEN successfully captures design knowledge and provides an order of magnitude increase in productivity;

2. CGEN correctly compiles expertise;

3. design knowledge grows very rapidly with respect to new parts while architecture knowledge remains constant;

4. CGEN's inputs provide significant semantic abstraction as compared to hand coded rules. Software science metrics indicate that the abstraction level is raised by a factor of 2.

12.2 Experimental Set-Up

The experiments were designed to simulate as closely as possible the conditions under which CGEN was intended to perform in the field. A version of M1 with a minimal knowledge base was used as the baseline system. At the beginning of the experimental process the M1 knowledge base contained

$$K_I^T = k_{\text{select\_func}} + k_{\text{casc}} + k_{\text{arch}}.$$

Therefore, M1 contained no design knowledge about any parts (see Section 8.3). In these experiments, M1 was taught exclusively using CGEN to design with the following microprocessor families: the Motorola 6809, 68008, 68010, and Intel 80386.

A complete single board design based on each processor was obtained from either published designs or our industrial affiliates. One hardware designer, the domain expert, was assigned to each microprocessor; he was responsible for adding knowledge to M1 about all designs based on that microprocessor.

None of the four designers, except one of the authors[1], were involved in the development of either CGEN or M1. Furthermore, the experts were not familiar with AI programming techniques, the OPS83 language, or the implementation of CGEN and M1. The designers received training in M1 and CGEN design philosophy and tool usage, equivalent to the information presented in Chapters 4 and 8 in this book. They used information about parts in the designs and databooks [26, 27, 110, 109, 111] to form the functional hierarchy as indicated in the following section and used CGEN for several training cases as indicated in the subsequent section. The domain experts neither wrote any OPS83 code nor modified the rules created by CGEN in any way. At the end of this process, M1 contained knowledge about synthesizing several designs based on the four microprocessors; the testing of M1's design capability is described in Chapter 13.

12.2.1   Forming the Functional Hierarchy

The main functions in each design were supplied by processor family-specific components with a variety of smaller parts used as support functions. For example, the 6809 design uses 68XX family IO devices. Hence, it was decided to organize the functional hierarchy around processor families. The top level of the hierarchy was a general computer system composed of general subsystems (see Figure 12.1 for the corresponding template); each designer was responsible for building the processor family-specific links in the hierarchy below the general subsystems.

To allow maximal sharing of design knowledge, a set of generic parts were developed. These parts correspond to functions that are independent of processor-specific designs and have a functional boundary that has signals common to all families. A brief description of some of these parts is given below.

Static RAM is a generic SRAM array that can be expanded to fit any size data bus and any SRAM memory size while satisfying a set of timing constraints. Its functional boundary has a variable sized DATA_BUS, ADDRESS_BUS and CHIP_SELECT_BUS (signals used to select various banks of memory). The size of the DATA_BUS and memory size are specifications for this abstract part.

ROM is a generic ROM array similar to the SRAM array above.

Latches provides a generic level-triggered set of latches that can be expanded out to fit any size input and output buses. The size of the input and output buses are specifications, together with other functional and timing specifications, for this abstract part.

---

[1] Birmingham.

RS-232 Port provides an RS-232 interface port to any SIO device. The port is configured to any of 3, 5, or 9 wire RS-232 protocols, performs voltage level conversion, and utilizes a suitable type of connector.

PIO output port provides a general parallel port interface. The port is configured up to eight bits, utilizes any of TTL, schmitt-triggered or optically coupled drivers (or no drivers at all), and any type of connector.

Power up circuit provides the power-up reset synchronization function that is common to all designs.

Interrupt bus resolver provides a general interrupt interface for all IO devices. It can be configured for either a maskable or non-maskable interrupt, at any priority level, with or without an acknowledge line. A different part interfaces the general interrupt bus to the specific interrupts available for each processor.

In addition to these parts, there were other hierarchies for support circuitry such as crystals, resistors, capacitors, and random logic. Several designs also utilized programmable logic arrays (PALs) for random logic functions, mainly as address decoders and wait-state generators. The MICON part model is not targeted to modeling and exploiting interrelationships between functional units inside PALs[2], hence PALs are modeled as a one unit part and linked as successors to all abstract parts that may utilize it in the design (e.g., address decoder, wait-state generator). The mapping is done explicitly using a template; no reasoning about the PAL's size or logic minimization is done in MICON.

12.2.2   The Knowledge-Acquisition Process

After the designers were familiar with their example designs, the knowledge-acquisition process began, which included the following steps:

1. Part models were developed for all abstract and physical parts and were entered into the central database. This included the definitions of processor family buses as functional boundaries of processor family-specific abstract parts.

2. M1 was executed until it failed in the search for structure and requested the addition of knowledge about a specific template.

3. A suitable template was drawn.

4. All methods associated with the template were prepared.

---

[2]This involves using elaborate logic minimization and technology mapping algorithms, a research issue addressed by several other projects, such as [49, 96].

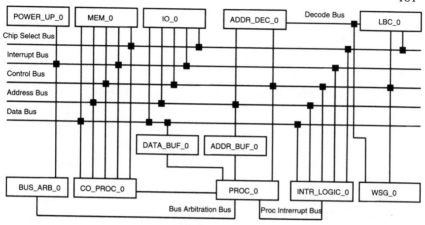

Figure 12.1. Single board computer top level template.

5. A knowledge-acquisition session was conducted using CGEN. (These steps were described in Chapter 11.)

6. Steps 2 through 5 were repeated until M1 successfully completed the design.

Since the functional hierarchy was organized around microprocessor families and each designer was working on different microprocessor-based designs, the designers could independently go through the acquisition process. The designers were, however, strongly influenced by the top-level single board computer template (see Figure 12.1), which was shared by all. Interactions between designers was limited to the use of the generic parts listed in the previous section. The use of generic parts was encouraged since it reduced the total number of templates being added; however, the person entering the template the first time was responsible for making sure that it was generalized sufficiently to be applicable for all designs.

During the acquisition process, each designer was supplied with a copy of M1. Each copy was symbolically linked to a central copy, except for a set of private files into which the designer placed the CGEN-generated rules. When the designer reached a milestone, such as the capture of an entire subsystem, the private file was released to the central version, thereby integrating it with a knowledge base containing knowledge from the other designers. In this manner all designers shared a common "virtual" knowledge base, but individual designers still had a local copy of their own knowledge under their control until it was ready for release. Releases were made as often as was practically possible.

Database Statistics	
Abstract Parts	167
Physical Parts	215
Total Parts	382

Table 12.1. Total part models.

Design	Cases	Total Rules	k_{spec}	k_{select_rule}	$k_{template}$	k_{calc}
M6809	85	343	197	4	89	53
M68008	38	173	102	1	38	32
M68010	19	147	94	0	19	34
I80386	79	256	158	3	80	14
Total	221	919	552	8	226	133

Table 12.2. Number of training cases and rules per design.

12.3 Experimental Results

Data was collected for each training session throughout the knowledge-acquisition process, which lasted around four months. This data is used to support various conclusions about the knowledge-acquisition process in general and CGEN in particular.

12.3.1 Ability to Capture Design Knowledge

The size of the database at the end of the experimental process in terms of part models is given in Table 12.1. The number of training cases and rules for each knowledge partition for each design is given in Table 12.2. The 6809 design has a high number of training cases considering its relative simplicity since it was the first design entered into M1. The first design had to account for the learning curve introduced because M1 had to be taught to design with a large set of abstract parts to build the upper levels of the hierarchy (e.g., PROC_0, MEM_0, WSG_0, ADDR_DEC_0, INTR_LOGIC_0, POWER_UP, etc.) and the generic parts (e.g., SRAM, ROM, PIO port, RS-232 port, latches, resistors, capacitors, NAND gates, etc.). Other designs, therefore, could take advantage of the learning curve absorbed by the 6809 design.

The data shows that CGEN was able to capture a large amount of design knowledge from the four designers in a short period of time. This data provides substantial evidence of CGEN's knowledge capturing capabilities.

Partition	Growth Rate	Std. Dev.
k_{spec}	2.5	4.8
k_{select_rule}	.04	0.3
k_{select_func}	0	0
k_{casc}	0	0
$k_{template}$	1.0	0.2
k_{calc}	0.6	1.8
k_{arch}	0	0
Number of cases	221	—

Table 12.3. Average growth rate per partition in the rules/training case.

12.3.2 M1 Knowledge Partition Growth Rates

The knowledge-acquisition process began with M1's knowledge base containing only k_{casc}, k_{select_func}, and k_{arch}. Table 12.3 shows the average growth rates for all partitions in units of rules per training case. This data was calculated using the following formula for each partition:

$$\text{Growth rate} = \frac{\text{Total number of rules acquired}}{\text{Number of training cases}}$$

From this data, it is clear that knowledge in the k_{spec}, k_{select_rule}, $k_{template}$, and k_{calc} partitions grows rapidly as new parts and design styles are added; knowledge in the k_{casc}, k_{select_func}, and k_{arch} partitions remains fixed.

12.3.3 Generalization of Input Knowledge

The preconditions on the template rules are the design-specific portion of the LHS of the template rules. Initially, all the variables in the design state are preconditions, then some of these preconditions are deleted and some are relaxed based on input methods from the domain expert or knowledge in the $k_{general\_rule}$ partition of CGEN. The number of variables in the design state and the preconditions deleted and relaxed in all the training cases, are tabulated in Table 12.4. It is seen that a high percentage of preconditions are generalized (i.e., deleted or relaxed). This emphasizes the usefulness of the generalization capability provided by CGEN.

Some generalization was done using knowledge present in CGEN's knowledge base. This knowledge was added midway into the knowledge-acquisition process. Data on the size of this partition and its usefulness is provided in Table

	Number/rule
Design State variables (preconditions)	35
Preconditions deleted	22
Preconditions remaining in template	13
Preconditions relaxed from remaining	10
% Preconditions generalized (deleted or relaxed)	91%
Number of cases	221

Table 12.4. Generalization of template preconditions.

Number of CGEN $k_{general\_rule}$ rules	44
Avg. number $k_{general\_rule}$ rules applied per case	28
Avg. number of total preconditions generalized per case	32
% Generalizations made using $k_{general\_rule}$	$\frac{28}{32} = 88\%$
Number of Cases	117

Table 12.5. CGEN generalization rule data (averages).

12.5. It is seen that a high percentage of the preconditions can be generalized using CGEN's knowledge.

One of the assumptions underlying the M1 architecture is the orthogonality of invocation conditions for templates. Over-generalization of preconditions of the template being added can possibly violate this assumption. To test this assumption, the M1 architecture was instrumented to write to a file every time more than one template was included in the conflict set. Every run of M1, including all training runs, contributed to the file. At the end of the experimental period, examination of the file showed the conflict set never contained more than one template rule, thereby confirming the assumption.

12.3.4 Enhancement in Knowledge Acquisition Productivity

CGEN reduces the amount of effort required to encode expertise. This productivity gain results from two factors:

Reduction of learning curve: Programming in any expert system implementation language requires training in AI programming techniques, the specifics of the implementation language, and the particular coding techniques used in the expert system (e.g., the canonical rule formats used in M1). Assimilating all this material requires substantial effort.

Knowledge-acquisition tools provide domain-specific interfaces, thereby hiding implementation detail. Thus, the learning curve for knowledge-acquisition tools is reduced to the time it takes to learn to use the tool.

Automatic code generation: Knowledge-acquisition tools produce code more quickly than humans. Perhaps more importantly, the code is error free and operates properly the first time.

The experimental work supports the productivity increases claims. All 919 rules captured by CGEN were acquired in a four man-month period. This works out to about 11 rules per day (all rules are fully debugged). This provides an order of magnitude increase in the productivity of knowledge engineers based on the generally accepted figure of one rule per day for professional knowledge engineers. In addition, CGEN can be learned in about two days (see Chapter 14) while we estimate it would take about four months to become proficient in OPS83 and the implementation of M1.

12.3.5 Raising the Semantic Abstraction Level

While it is generally accepted that knowledge-acquisition tools provide a significant advantage over programming directly in the expert system's implementation language, there has been no supporting quantitative evidence. To remedy this shortcoming, a set of experiments were devised to provide quantitative indicators of the advantage of using CGEN over programming directly in OPS83. The experiments measured the language level [61] of OPS83 and CGEN's inputs. As described below, the higher the language level of a programming language with respect to a particular algorithm, the higher the abstraction level of the language. The higher the abstraction level of a language, the easier it is to use to encode an algorithm.

The analysis presented here is based on software science. We first review the basics of software science before describing the experimental procedure.

Please note that the construction of an efficient user interface or efficient programming language were not objectives of this research. However, insight into the advantages of knowledge acquisition can be gained through the analysis of CGEN's interface, no matter how baroque it may be.

Software Science

Halstead [61, 46] developed a set of methods for quantitatively measuring various properties of computer programs that he called *software science*. The methods were based on empirical evidence that Halstead collected on a variety of algorithms implemented in different languages. Software science tries to measure the goodness of a programming language for representing an algorithm, although the results can be generalized for indications of programming language applicability across a variety of algorithms.

While software science is controversial, it has been subjected to a number of independent tests and appears to have met a minimum of its claims [46]. For the purposes of this discussion, software science metrics are used as *indicators* of relative abstraction level of CGEN's inputs and OPS83. They are a means of providing some minimal experimental evidence to support claims made about the tool.

A brief review of the basics of software science is provide here, and the interested reader should consult Halstead [61] for more information. The following direct measurements are made for a program to be tested:

n_1: the number of distinct operators in a program,

n_2: the number of distinct operands in a program,

N_1: the total number of operators in a program,

N_2: the total number of operands in a program.

These measures are easily gotten from a parser. The measurement of n_1 counts all operators in the program, including end of statement (EOS) operators. EOS operators take a variety of forms depending on the implementation language; in OPS83 ";" is used, while CGEN employs both <newline> and ";".

The following code fragment:

```
Y = 8 * Z * Y;
```

has the following software science measures:

- $n_1 = 3$ (=, *, ;),

- $n_2 = 3$ (Y, Z, 8),

- $N_1 = 4$, and

- $N_2 = 4$.

Based on the measures described above, two relationships are defined: program vocabulary and program length. Vocabulary is defined as $n = n_1 + n_2$, and length is given by $N = N_1 + N_2$.

Based on the measures given above, Halstead observed the following set of empirical relationships [46]:

Program volume (V): The number of bits needed to represent a program in a given programming language V can be computed using

$$V = N \log_2 n.$$

Language	λ
PL/I	1.53
FORTRAN	1.14
CDC assembler	.88

Table 12.6. Example of λ for some common languages.

Program level (L): The ratio of V to the theoretical minimum program volume V^* for a program. According to software science, V^* is a single operator. For example, multiplication can be implemented as a set of shifts and adds or as a single operator (*) yielding the minimum program for multiplying two numbers as Y = N * M;. Thus, L is an indicator of program efficiency compared to the best possible implementation and is computed using

$$L = (2/n_1)/(n_2/N_2).$$

Language level (λ): The relative abstraction level of language. The higher this number, the more abstract the language. λ is computed using

$$\lambda = L^2 V.$$

Table 12.6 presents some λ values calculated by Halstead [61] for three common languages for some small algorithms.

An underlying assumption in software science measures is the purity of the program, i.e., that the program is free of anything that might skew the basic measures. Halstead [61] identified and classified all possible impurities. Example impurities include the declaration of unused variables or the inclusion of statements having no purpose, such as the following:

```
a = 3; this assignment is unnecessary
a = 4;
```

Impurities must not be included in the program in order to get accurate measures. This assumption is important in analyzing the results of any experiment. In the course of experiments conducted in this work, every attempt was taken to ensure purity of CGEN inputs. A filter program was written to help identify and remove unnecessary variables. With experiments involving many people, however, it is difficult to ensure that all programs are free of impurities. Any impurity not filtered out will be minor and will tend to skew the results against CGEN (by increasing the basic measures) – the most conservative way to tend. CGEN generated OPS83 code was free of impurities.

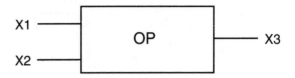

Figure 12.2. Example circuit used by Ostapko.

The basic software science measures are typically gathered by modifying a language parser to produce the values n_1, n_2, N_1, and N_2. Measuring the inputs to CGEN presents a special problem – how is the schematic (template) information counted? Recall, this information is graphically generated by the drawing editor and is converted into a wire list format. Ostapko [100] provides insight to this problem. He has used software science to predict the number of signals necessary to implement a block of combinational logic. In developing his work Ostapko needed to equate circuit schematics to software science measures. The circuit in Figure 12.2 can be represented in the following equivalent program statement:

```
X3 = X1 OP X2;
```

which is easily analyzed using software science by equating the gate to a statement and the input and output signals to variables. This would yield the following:

- $n_1 = 3$ (=, OP, ;)

- $n_2 = 3$ (X3, X1, X2)

- $N_1 = 3$

- $N_2 = 3$.

A problem arises though, since single board computers are built from components with multiple inputs and outputs, not simple combinational gates. The representation used by Ostapko can be easily extended and still be within the bounds of software science by the following translation of form:

```
X3 = X1 OP X2 ==> X3 = OP(X1 X2);
```

For many circuits, however, it is difficult to identify the inputs and outputs, especially if the signals are bidirectional. Consider determining whether the data bus for a microprocessor counts as input or output. We contend the actual determination of direction of a signal is superfluous if the following rules are applied during the analysis of a wire list:

1. Initialize $n_1 = 2$. (The operators ";"and "=" are implicitly used in each wire list statement.)

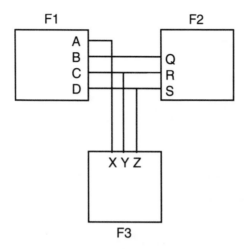

Figure 12.3. Example circuit with ambiguous input and output signals.

2. Increment N_1 by 3 for each part instance used in the design. (Each part implies the operators ";"and "=" and the part type.)

3. Increment n_1 by 1 for each part type. (Each part type represents a new operator.)

4. Increment n_2 by 1 for each signal associated with each part type. (Each signal is a unique variable.)

5. Increment N_2 by 1 each time a signal is used in a connection. (The variable is referenced.)

The example circuit shown in Figure 12.3 provides the following values:

- $n_1 = 5$ (these being ";" "=" F1 F2 F3)

- $n_2 = 10$ (these being A B C D Q R S X Y Z)

- $N_1 = 9$

- $N_2 = 12$.

A parser implementing the rules given above was built to analyze the wire lists.

The remaining CGEN input, the methods, and OPS83 are written as standard code and conform to the software science analysis methods directly.

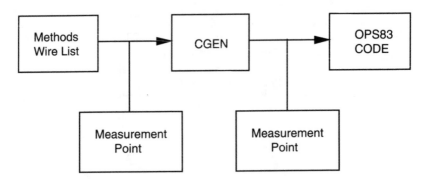

Figure 12.4. Model of a system for determination of λ.

Experiments

Languages with higher λ are better suited for implementing the particular class of algorithms under which the tests were made. Thus, if CGEN's λ is higher than OPS83's λ for a set of inputs, CGEN's input is better than OPS83 for representing hardware design knowledge. The experiments undertaken find measures for λ. In these experiments CGEN is viewed as a black box, as opposed to those experiments described previously. The experimental model of a system is shown in Figure 12.4. The λ for all CGEN inputs and the resulting OPS83 output were calculated for the experimental trials described earlier. The difference in the resulting λ values provides some idea of CGEN's relative abstraction level to OPS83.

After CGEN was run on a training case, a parser was applied to the CGEN input files. The values for each software science measure for each file were added together to determine the measure for the entire input, covering all input generated by the domain expert. The following equation summarizes the process, with the superscript indicating the file contributing the value:

$$\sum_{i \in \{1,2\}, r \in \{n,N\}} r_i^{\text{TOTAL}} = r_i^{\text{METHODS.CGEN}} + r_i^{\text{WIRE.LIST}}.$$

The parser was then applied to the generated OPS83 in the same fashion:

$$\sum_{i \in \{1,2\}, r \in \{n,N\}} r_i^{\text{TOTAL}} = \text{RULES.CGEN}_i.$$

The results of the calculations are given in Table 12.7. Note that due to some data collection problems, the data for roughly half the training cases was invalid, so only 122 are reported here. The data shows CGEN's λ is relatively higher than OPS83's λ. This indicates that CGEN is a higher level programming

SS Metric λ		
Case	λ	Number of cases
CGEN	12.5	122
OPS83	6.4	122

Table 12.7. Experimentally derived λ for OPS83 and CGEN.

language for this domain, providing a more appropriate interface to the domain expert. This result is expected since CGEN's input was designed specifically for this application, while OPS83 is a general-purpose language.

The λ figures corroborate CGEN productivity figures given in Section 12.3.4 that a domain (algorithm)-specific language should require less programming effort than a general-purpose language. In this case, the format of CGEN's input is specifically "tuned" to hardware design. Thus, information can be transferred more efficiently.

13

M1 Experimentation

This chapter describes experiments in which M1 was used to produce complete computer system designs. In these experiments, M1 utilized knowledge captured from hardware designers using CGEN. An indication of M1's design space at the end of the experimental period is given by describing several synthesized designs. Experiments that illustrate M1's design tradeoff capabilities and limitations are also described. After the experimental period, knowledge about an 80386-based workstation design with a cache memory and AT bus interface was also added to M1 using CGEN; data for this design is also presented.

13.1 Design Space

With its knowledge base and database, M1 is able to create an interesting variety of designs. The input requirements used for some of these designs are shown in Table 13.1. Each of the designs represents a point in the large space of designs that can actually be generated. Since knowledge is acquired for each part individually, unique combinations of parts can be configured into a design. The ultimate limitation on the number of parts in the designs that can be produced by M1 comes from

- the size of the processor's memory space,

- the size of the processor's IO space (if applicable), and

- the ceiling on resources (power, cost and board area).

Hence, the actual design space covered by M1 is much larger than that represented by entries in Table 13.1.

Let us consider the data reported in Table 13.1. As expected, the part count, rule firings and run times increase for designs with more functionality (i.e., larger memory, more IO ports). Notice that Requirement Sets 1 and 2, and also Sets 8 and 9, are the same except for the amount of SRAM memory. To build larger memory, M1 used a memory chip of larger density resulting in the same part count. Also, Set 5 has just one more PIO port than Set 4 (similarly for Sets 9 and 10). As the 6821 chip used for the first PIO port actually has two ports on it, M1 uses the second port for Set 5. Hence, the design for Set 5 has only one more part than that for Set 4, the additional part being a connector for the second port.

For each design, M1 generated a wire list detailing the interconnections between the physical parts used in the design. The wire list for the 68008-based design using Requirement Set 5 from Table 13.1 was manually converted to the schematic shown in Figure 13.1. The wire list was complete – in addition to the ICs, other electrical components such as edge connectors, crystals, capacitors and pullup resistors were all present. The functional hierarchy traversed by M1 while synthesizing this design is shown in Figure 13.2. The corresponding design hierarchy is shown in Figure 13.3. Dashed lines in these figures indicate portions of the hierarchy that are not shown to avoid cluttering. Note that the multiple functional units on the 6820 and the 7473 were fully utilized for the PIO and JK flip-flop function, respectively. One of the two functional units on the 8116 was unused, since only one clock generator was required in the design. A PAL20L8 was used for address decoding since the arbitrary one-to-one connection of the chip-select bus necessitated a programmable device. From the M1-generated wire list, the design was placed and routed in one man-day using commercial physical design tools. Given the layout, a local company returned a fabricated PCB in one week. The fabricated board was stuffed with components and tested using a software monitor programmed into the ROM[3]. The board was stuffed, debugged, and made fully operational at the designed clock speed of 8 MHz in one man-day. Thus, a fully operational single board computer was synthesized from input requirements within ten days, which could be reduced further if we had easier access to a PCB fabrication facility.

Other M1-generated designs were verified by manually converting the wire list to a schematic. While creating the schematic, the correctness of the design was checked. Errors found in the design were all due to mistakes in the schematics

---

[3]The software was manually developed separately based on the memory map of the hardware.

		Design Requirements						Results		
Set	Processor name	Amount of SRAM	Amount of ROM	Number of PIO	SIO	Physical part-count	Abstract part-count	Rule firings	Actual run time[1]	Total run time[2]
1	M68008	32 KBytes	4 KBytes	1	0	20	55	2696	250 sec	1552 sec
2	M68008	60 KBytes	4 KBytes	1	0	20	55	2696	257 sec	1591 sec
3	M68008	60 KBytes	4 KBytes	0	1	28	69	3276	309 sec	1949 sec
4	M68008	60 KBytes	4 KBytes	1	1	31	75	3612	354 sec	4000 sec†
5	M68008	60 KBytes	4 KBytes	2	1	32	80	3819	384 sec	2459 sec
6	M6809	32 KBytes	4 KBytes	1	0	17	52	2484	227 sec	1991 sec
7	M6809	32 KBytes	4 KBytes	0	1	25	66	3065	292 sec	2199 sec
8	M6809	32 KBytes	4 KBytes	1	1	27	71	3347	331 sec	4067 sec†
9	M6809	60 KBytes	4 KBytes	1	1	27	71	3347	334 sec	4122 sec†
10	M6809	60 KBytes	4 KBytes	2	1	28	76	3554	361 sec	2277 sec
11	I80386	60 KBytes	8 KBytes	0	1	79	150	6539	965 sec	4580 sec

Table 13.1. Partial requirements of the designs created by M1.

[1]On a Microvax II, UNIX 4.3BSD.

[2]Actual run time plus time spent accessing shared database over the network. Database server runs on another Microvax II, UNIX 4.3BSD.

† The unusually large value for these is due to the sharing of the database with other programs that happened to be running at the same time.

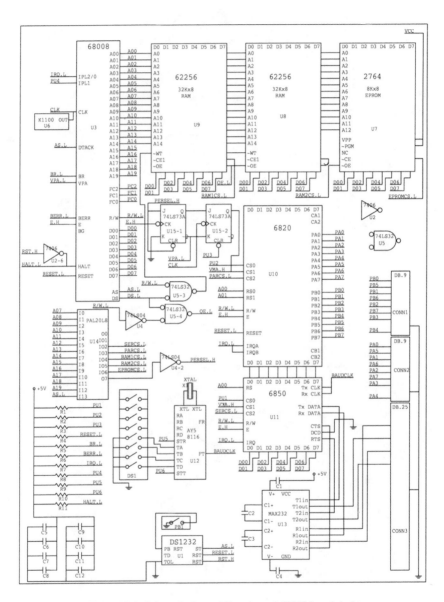

Figure 13.1. Schematic for an M1-generated 68008-based design.

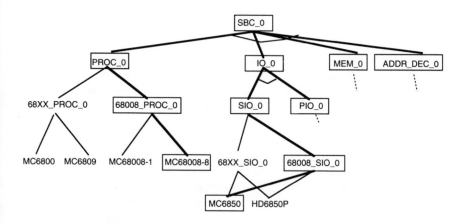

Figure 13.2. Functional hierarchy traversed by M1 for the 68008-based design.

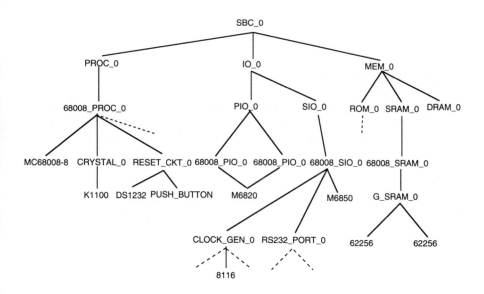

Figure 13.3. Design hierarchy for the 68008-based design.

input to CGEN, which then propagated to M1's knowledge base. Common errors found were missing parts (e.g., pull-up resistors, by-pass capacitors used as support circuitry) and missing connections (e.g., connections shown in schematic not being present in the wire list due to a bug in the schematic editor, or connections missing altogether due to a mistake by the hardware designer). Schematics containing errors were corrected, and new rules were generated, making all designs bug free. Thus, we conclude that CGEN correctly transforms expert knowledge input to it but cannot independently verify the correctness of the input knowledge.

The designs produced by M1 compare favorably to designs produced manually. The designs work at expected clock rates and use no greater number of parts than those generated by a human designer, except in cases where M1's local part selection causes it to make a globally non-optimal choice. In these cases, M1 would be rerun and coerced by the user to select the better chip. For example, if for Requirement Set 11 two SIO ports were required instead of one, M1 would use two I8251 chips (one for each port). But a single I8274 chip, although costlier than one I8251, would be globally better since it has two SIO ports. A user could circumvent this limitation of M1 by explicitly specifying that an 8274 chip be used for the first SIO port. While designing the second SIO port, M1 would use the second functional unit on the 8274 and thus produce a globally better design. This is acceptable as M1's strong point is its rapid prototyping capability – producing comparable results in a small fraction of the time it would take for manual design

13.2   Capabilities and Limitations

While M1's primary goal is to generate a design that satisfies all input requirements quickly, it also attempts to make some tradeoffs in the design process. Some of its capabilities and limitations are described using examples here.

13.2.1   Cost-Area Tradeoff

M1 attempts to meet both the board cost and the board area constraints. In the selection step of the design cycle, the weighted objective function makes an implicit cost-area tradeoff.

An experiment illustrating M1's cost-area tradeoff capability in selecting chips from among three ROM chips was conducted. The three chips had different bit organizations but satisfied all timing constraints. A different number of chips of each type would be used in the design depending upon the amount of ROM memory required by the user. Each choice would incur cost and area expenditures. The cost and area expenses for different amounts of ROM specified for each chip are sketched in Figure 13.4. The figure also indicates the optimal

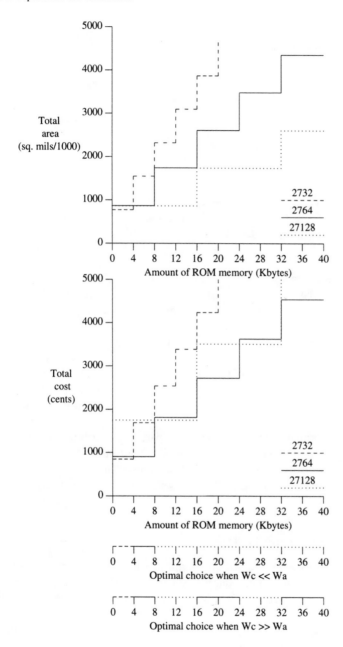

Figure 13.4. Cost and area expense for ROM design space.

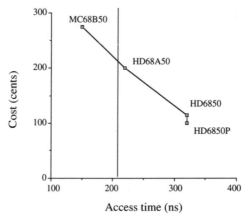

Figure 13.5. Cost and wait-states for SIO design space.

choice for the ROM chip under different conditions, such as when the design is running out of the cost or area resource. M1's selection function biases the choice in favor of smaller consumption of the scarce resource. In experimentation, M1 always selected the chip with the least cost and area expense. For example, for 8K ROM amount, M1 selected the 2764 chip. In cases where different chips resulted in minimum cost and area, M1 correctly biased the selection towards the chip with minimum area (cost), if the design was running out of area (cost) resource. For example, for 20K ROM specification, M1 selected the 27128 when it was running out of area and the 2764 when it was running out of cost.

While this experiment illustrates how M1's part selection function works, it also brings out a limitation of M1. M1 implicitly assumes that the memory array is homogeneous (i.e., made with identical chips). This cuts down some of the design space, and, in some cases, M1 may not be able to obtain the optimal result.

13.2.2 Cost-Performance Tradeoff

Another capability of M1 is maximizing performance while satisfying the global constraint on cost and area. For example, M1 will add wait-states, if needed, to peripherals instead of using costlier chips to meet a global cost constraint. In this experiment, M1 was given a choice of physical parts with different costs and access times (as sketched in Figure 13.5) for the SIO peripheral. A minimum clock speed of 2 MHz, resulting in an access-time constraint of 210 ns on the SIO device, was imposed. With a loose cost constraint, M1 used an MC68B50 as the SIO device. As the cost constraint was made tighter, the MC68B50 became too costly, and M1 added one wait-state on the peripheral (in the failure handling design step); now M1 switched to using the HD6850P since it was the cheapest.

13.2.3 Locally Optimal Designs

A limitation of M1 is that it is a local optimizer. Although the objective selection function considers the global design state, the decision is still made locally and sequentially. A hypothetical pathological case where M1 would overlook a suitable design is given below.

Assume that the ROM design space is populated with the chips shown in Figure 13.4. Assume that there is just one extremely costly SIO chip S that meets timing requirements. Assume that M1 has completed the design except for the ROM and SIO subsystems and has a modest amount of cost and area resources left. Consider the situation when M1 designs the SIO subsystem first. M1 selects and instantiates the chip S and utilizes a large portion of the cost resource. Next, M1 proceeds to design the ROM. It selects three 2764 chips even though they have a larger area than two 27128 chips since the cost resource is scarce. Thus, M1 synthesizes a design without compromising on performance. Now consider the alternate situation, when M1 designs the ROM subsystem first. With modest cost and area left at this stage, M1 does not realize that cost will be a scarce resource later on. Hence, the selection function in M1 selects two 27128 chips for ROM even when they are more expensive than three 2764 chips. Next, M1 proceeds to design the SIO. It may now find that there are not enough cost resources to utilize chip S. M1 has no way of knowing which of its earlier decisions to undo. Using failure recovery knowledge, M1 may ask the user to relax the cost requirement, choose a new memory chip, or add a wait-state on the SIO peripheral so that some cheaper chips instead of chip S can be used. In this case, M1 overlooks the feasible design and compromises on higher cost or lesser performance.

It should be pointed out that such situations may only be hypothetical. In the real-world design space, we may not expect to find singular and skewed chips such as chip S, and M1's selection strategy would be sufficiently effective. Only extended use of M1 in real-world design environments would resolve this issue.

13.3 Other Designs

Since the experimental period, the MICON system has been used to produce several other designs. Of these, an 80386-based workstation design is described here, since it underscores the system's capability of handling large sophisticated designs.

The 80386-based workstation design has a cache, a DMA controller, and an external AT bus interface, in addition to the usual processor, co-processor, memory and IO peripherals. In contrast to the one-level bus structure of previous designs, it has a three-level bus structure to accommodate the 82385 cache controller and address pipelining. Hence, a new top-level template shown in Figure 13.6 was used. The local bus is controlled by the processor, the middle bus by the cache controller, and the system bus by a local bus controller, which supports address pipelining. This template, and several others for different fragments of the design, were added to M1's knowledge base using CGEN. This design is the largest and most complex design entered into M1, and lessons learned from this experience are detailed in the next chapter.

The requirements for the design are shown in Figure 13.7. M1 generated the design in approximately four hours on a Microvax II running 4.3 BSD UNIX. The design had over 200 physical parts, which included over 120 ICs. The M1-generated wire list was manually checked for errors. All errors were traced back to incorrect schematic inputs to CGEN, the schematics were corrected, and CGEN was rerun to generate a new set of rules. The verified M1-generated wire list was manually converted to a set of schematics (which are not included here due to space considerations). The design was placed and routed using commercial physical design tools onto a six layer 10 x 13 inch PCB. A few components such as the clock buffer tree and decoupling capacitors were manually added to the design, since these were tightly coupled to the physical design process. The fabricated board was stuffed and tested using a manually generated software monitor programmed into ROM. The board is running at the designed clock speed of 20 MHz.

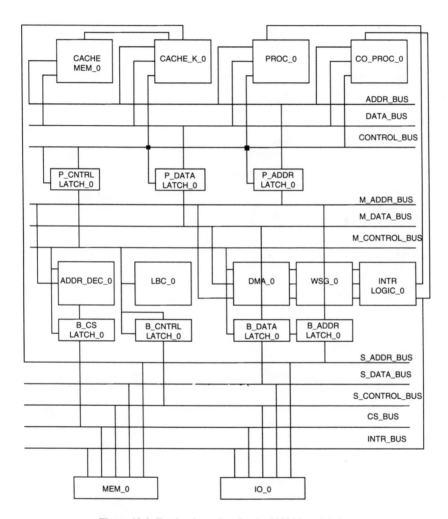

Figure 13.6. Top-level template for the 80386-based design.

Query	User response
Board Area upper bound < sq inches >	100
Board Cost upper bound < dollars >	5000
Board Power Consumption upper bound < milliwatts >	800000
Number of processors in design	1
Number of cards in design	1
Processor name	80386
Minimum processor clock speed < Hz >	17000000
Is Cache Memory needed < Y N >	Y
Is a Co-processor needed < Y N >	Y
Is DMA required < Y N >	Y
Is PIO required < Y N >	N
Is SIO required < Y N >	Y
Is TIMER required on System Bus < Y N >	N
Is KEYBOARD CONTROLLER required < Y N >	Y
How many PIO units are needed	0
How many SIO units are needed	1
How many TIMER units are needed	0
Is DRAM required < Y N >	N
Is SRAM required < Y N >	Y
Is ROM required < Y N >	Y
Number of ROM BYTES needed	64000
Name of ROM chip to use	?
Number of SRAM BYTES needed	1000000
Name of SRAM chip to use	?
Do you want design to be AT compatible < Y N >	Y
How many TIMER are required on the Middle Bus	1
Enter a tag for this SIO port	SIO_1
Name of SIO chip to use	?
External interface < RS-232 RS-422 etc >	RS-232
Baud rate < 300 1200 4800 etc >	4800
Baud rate selection switch < FIXED HW_SWITCH >	HW_SWITCH
Should this SIO do interrupts < Y N >	N
Should interrupts if any be maskable < Y N >	Y
Interrupt priority level if any	0
Port size < 3 5 9 >	5
Port type < DTE DCE >	DTE
Connector type < MALE FEMALE >	MALE
Connector size < 9 25 >	25
Asynchronous mode < Y N >	Y
Synchronous mode < Y N >	N
HDLC_SDLC mode < Y N >	N
Cache organization < DIRECT 2WAY >	DIRECT
Cache size in Kbytes < 32 >	32

Figure 13.7. Requirements input to M1 for the 80386-based workstation design.

14

Experience Using MICON

The MICON system has been distributed to a number of different organizations. We have been able to work with these groups to gain additional insight into the system's usefulness. This information is particularly helpful since it comes from practicing designers who are not part of the development group. These outside users come from the following two groups:

Workshops: MICON is presented as a two-day workshop where participants learn how to use MICON and how to apply it to their design problems. At the end of the workshop the participants are acquainted with all parts of the system and create both a small knowledge base and design.

Industrial designers: The system has been evaluated by several companies. The evaluations consisted of building a proprietary knowledge base and then generating a set of designs.

The following sections further describe our experiences with these groups, but we first start with some general observations.

14.1   General Observations

The MICON system has grown enormously since the end of the experimental period. The number of rules is now over 3,500. This growth has come from incorporating knowledge of several processor families, introducing new subsystems (e.g., caches), and adding new processor families. All the knowledge to date has been acquired through CGEN. It is estimated that MICON now has about 15 man-years of design expertise.

Paralleling the growth of the knowledge base is that of the database that now contains over 600 parts and 750 links. The number of physical parts is 250. Note that there are not as many physical parts as compared to abstract parts, since we have concentrated on adding functionality (i.e., abstract parts) to the design space. If the database were to be used in the real world, the design space for each abstract part would be expanded, and the number of physical parts would be much greater. All the parts have entered the database through ENTRY, although provisions now exist to connect directly to commercial part libraries for pin-related information.

MICON has now produced hundreds of designs. Many of these designs have been for demonstration and testing purposes. Two designs, the 68008 machine and the 80386 machine, have been fabricated; a third design has been extensively simulated. These designs tested the limits of the system and exercised a large portion of the knowledge base. Thus, they were a good set of tests for the system. The successful fabrication or simulation of these designs significantly increased our confidence in MICON's design abilities.

Over the course of building these designs the knowledge base was studied. The predictions of knowledge base growth were confirmed, both in that the overall size of the knowledge base greatly increased and in the size of individual partitions. Partitions k_{select_rule}, k_{spec}, $k_{template}$, and k_{calc} have all experienced substantial expansion, while the k_{arch}, k_{select_func}, and k_{casc} partitions have remained constant. During this period CGEN was used to capture all the rules, and most of the knowledge was entered by hardware designers that were not part of the development group.

As with any experimental system, there were problems with MICON. The most significant complaints about the system fall into the following categories:

User interface: During the construction of the MICON system, the emphasis was mainly on developing functionality and testing its usefulness. The interface has suffered as a result, being rather crude. We have found that in producing large designs, the interface becomes an annoyance to the designers. With a proper interface, the functions afforded by MICON will provide even greater productivity to designers.

Knowledge base maintenance: When building a large knowledge base it is necessary, albeit rarely, to modify a template, usually because of a mistake in creating CGEN's inputs. This requires the user to identify the old rules in the knowledge and remove them. The mechanisms for doing this are very primitive, and the process is time-consuming. Software engineering methods are being used to correct this problem.

Integration with other tools: There are a number of other tools missing from the original MICON system, the most important being schematic generators, field-programmable device programmers, simulators, and test generators. Ad hoc interfaces were established to support the projects where MICON was being used. New capabilities are being added to MICON to support these tools better [65].

Verification of designs: Ensuring the correctness of MICON-generated designs is the responsibility of the domain expert adding knowledge to M1. For ensuring timing correctness, this scheme is inappropriate since it places too much burden on the domain expert. New tools that automatically ensure timing correctness of MICON-generated designs are being developed [59].

Further work on MICON is correcting these problems. Despite the problems, the MICON user community generally considers the system a useful tool, as is discussed in the next section.

14.2   User Experience

Five separate groups of users had the chance to fully explore MICON and to produce designs. The experiences of these groups are summarized here.

14.2.1   Workshops

The MICON system has been presented to about 30 designers at a series of workshops held at Carnegie Mellon University and at a number of industrial sites. The workshops are two days in length, with presentations covering the philosophy of the system, operation of the tools, and instruction on how to cast a design problem into the MICON framework. In addition, there are a set of labs that cover creating a design with M1, entering part models, and using CGEN to build a knowledge base. The labs are oriented toward problem-solving, where the purpose is to combine philosophy with tool usage so that designers are in a position to exploit the system's capabilities fully for their needs on the job.

By the end of the workshop all the attendees were able to create small knowledge bases of about 30 rules to instantiate the SIO_0 branch of the functional hierarchy. Once these knowledge bases were merged with a larger one, all participants were able to generate working designs, though they were relatively simple (equivalent to the 68008-based design described in Chapter 13). That the designers were able to perform all these tasks after a relatively short training period demonstrates the power of the tools and their fit into the normal work practices of hardware designers. This is particularly important, since it is the project's aim to facilitate designers in their daily tasks. For example, there was general agreement that the use of templates mirrors design "reuse" that is common practice in industry; one computer designer mentioned that his company constantly reuses the keyboard controller in all its products because of the design's complexity.

It is interesting to note that some designers appeared to like the blackbox view of MICON, while others wanted more control particularly in part selection. From these comments, it was decided to add a capability to allow designers to approve, or override, M1's part selections.

14.2.2   The 80386SX Design Family

One of the more extensive uses of MICON was to create a family of personal computer boards based on the Intel 80386SX and its associated peripherals [63]. This project took place at a computer manufacturer's engineering site and thus provides a realistic assessment of MICON. This project required that a proprietary knowledge base and database be developed for the following subsystems:

- 80386SX processor (several versions),

- 80387SX coprocessor,

- ROM and DRAM,

- various peripherals, including keyboard, video, hard drive and floppy disk controllers,

- bus interface,

- bus hardware (expansion slots), and

- generic parts such as PALs, buffers, latches, oscillators, fuses, diodes, transistors, capacitors, inductors, and resistors.

Over a three-month period about 1,000 rules were entered into the system. Using this information a baseline design and three variations were created. These designs contained about 250 parts and were complete personal computers. The designs were considered to be nearly production quality[1]. It was estimated that the MICON system saved about six months off a one-year project, thereby doubling productivity.

14.2.3   The 80386-Based Workstation

The 80386-based workstation design described in the previous chapter is the largest and most complex design produced by MICON. An extensive knowledge-acquisition phase was undergone to add knowledge for this design into M1. The design was subsequently fabricated and has resulted in a working board. Lessons learned from this experience are summarized below.

- The domain expert creates designs using a schematic editor and is most at ease in this environment. His progress is hindered by having to go through several MICON tool invocations during the design process. For minimum overhead, the MICON tools must be tied into the schematic editor.

- The M1-generated netlist might have errors due to incorrect inputs to CGEN. Debugging the netlist is tedious and time consuming, especially since, unlike human-generated netlists, it lacks any organization or semantics (e.g., descriptive names for nets). Some mechanism for automatically verifying the netlists is needed. One possibility is patching together a simulation model for the entire design and simulating it using stimuli provided by the designer.

- The M1-generated netlist goes through physical design tools that typically require the designer to place certain key components manually and handroute critical signals. This is extremely difficult to do without a set of schematics that provide some insight into the design. The capability of automatically generating a reasonable set of schematics from the M1-generated netlist is needed. This capability can also help in debugging the netlist. For this design, the schematics were manually produced.

- Debugging the fabricated board is impossible without a set of annotated schematics.

- Mechanisms for browsing the database and the knowledge base are required.

- Some changes need to be made to the M1-generated netlist based on physical design considerations. For example, the clock buffer tree was added

---

[1]Getting the production quality stamp required an extensive qualification process that extended beyond the project's deadline.

to the M1-generated design. Mechanisms for back-annotating designs are needed.

- Support for programmable devices is required.

- Timing correctness is difficult to ensure in a large complex design using the current constraint propagation mechanism.

These lessons highlight some limitations, in both the implementation and the capabilities, of the MICON tools and are topics of ongoing work.

14.2.4 A 6802-Based Design

An interesting case study using MICON was conducted in cooperation with an industrial affiliate. Two hardware designers from the company participated in this study. They went through the complete process of learning about MICON, using the tools to add knowledge about a new design to M1's knowledge base and then producing the complete design. The design had a 6802 microprocessor, one 68681 SIO port at 9600 baud, six 6522 PIO ports, a 8279 keyboard controller, 47K EPROM, 8K EEPROM and 8K RAM. The time spent in various stages of the design process is summarized below.

- 2 days: The MICON workshop.

- 2 days: Teaching MICON about the new 6802-based design; 23 parts (17 physical, 6 abstract) were added; 26 knowledge acquisition sessions were conducted; 141 rules were acquired.

- 4 hours: Running M1 to generate the new design (includes debugging errors in two knowledge-acquisition sessions); the design had 26 parts with 161 nets.

- 1 day: Physical design.

Since the 6802 was a 68XX family microprocessor, substantial leverage was obtained from the shared design knowledge, thus highlighting the design dissemination capability of MICON. The fact that the designers could learn about the system and exploit it to produce a new design[2] within a week highlights the capabilities and maturity of the tools. The short time period underscores the rapid prototyping capability.

---

[2]A member of the MICON project provided guidance occasionally.

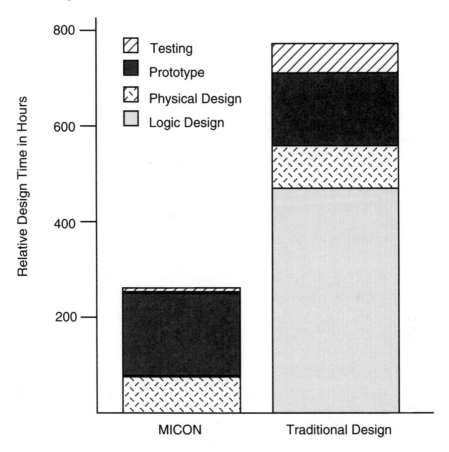

Figure 14.1. Time profile for MICON and traditional methods

14.2.5 Design Time

The experiences with the system have shown that it provides a significant productivity increase. Figure 14.1 depicts the time required to create a prototype using MICON and traditional methods. This figure, based on the accumulated experience with MICON, shows that a MICON-based design methodology reduces design time by a factor of 3.

Part V

Extension to Other Domains

15

Making MICON Domain-Independent

Recall from Chapter 7 that an expert system is composed of a problem solver, which contains the method for reaching a solution, and a knowledge base, which contains the specific knowledge needed to produce a solution. Generally, the problem solver and the knowledge base are kept logically separate; a distinction is made between the knowledge used by each. Such separation is essential for portability, the transfer of an expert system to a new problem area. An important question in expert system research is determining the scope of a system; that is, determining the range of problems to which the problem solver is applicable [11]. In this chapter we describe two experiments in which M1 and CGEN were applied to new problem areas, automated sequencing of tasks in a design environment and mechanical design.

In this chapter we use *application task*[1] to refer to a specific problem to solve, such as designing an 8086-based single board computer. The term *task* refers to a collection of application tasks that can be solved by a given problem-solving method, such as hierarchical design using dynamic subproblem ordering and the design cycle. We use *domain* to restrict the possible applications tasks that the expert system can solve. An example domain is hierarchical design using dynamic task ordering and the design cycle for single board computers. Note, however, that task transcends a single domain. Mechanical design and design

---

[1]The terminology used here is adapted from [11].

215

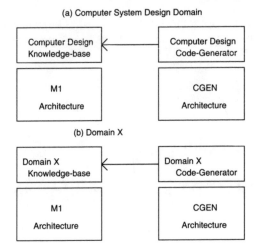

Figure 15.1. Porting M1 and CGEN to new domains.

environments represent two new domains for M1 and CGEN but are the same task. While M1 and CGEN may be applicable to several domains, becoming domain-independent, the tools remain task-specific, and M1's problem-solving method does not change.

15.1 Portable Design Tools

M1 and CGEN were designed and implemented to facilitate extension into new domains with some appropriate modifications. The portability of M1 and CGEN arises from two sources. First, M1's problem-solving technique appears to be applicable to a wide range of engineering design domains. Second, M1 is implemented as a knowledge-based system (KBS) and, when properly engineered, a KBS is inherently portable to new domains. The key to portability stems from the rigid separation of the problem solver from domain knowledge [31]. It is possible to categorize every rule in M1 as belonging either to the problem solver or to the knowledge base. Thus knowledge bases for new domains can simply be plugged into the problem solver. From a pragmatic view, this scheme is successful only if the problem solver has integrated support for creating knowledge bases, which CGEN provides for M1. Figure 15.1 illustrates the principle: In part (a), the system contains a problem solver and a knowledge base specific to computer design design; In part (b), the problem solver remains the same, but the knowledge base for domain *X* is used.

The idea of a domain-independent, task-specific CAD tool is intriguing. Consider that the engines underlying CAD tools, be they problem solvers or algorithms, are usually developed for an application task and technology. For example, printed-circuit board routers cannot be applied to integrated circuit (IC) routing. Essentially, each new application of an existing algorithm requires a new implementation, impeding the development of new tools. A domain-independent tool for the same task, however, could be quickly configured for a new application domain without requiring significant re-coding of the problem solver. A second advantage of a domain-independent synthesis tool is that it provides a consistent framework for studying the design process across many domains. A consistent framework provides a reference point for analyzing design, by concentrating on actions taken during problem solving without regard to application task details. In building a synthesis tool, these advantages of a domain-independent tool must be carefully weighed against the possible disadvantages of lesser performance and extra effort of configuration, as compared to a domain-dependent tool.

The idea of portable problem solvers has been considered by several researchers. The VEXED IC design system [93] has been applied to mechanical engineering problems [76]. A building design system [82] has formed the basis of a domain-independent synthesis shell [81]. The work described in this chapter emphasizes the general applicability of both the problem solver and the integrated automated knowledge-acquisition system not addressed by other researchers.

Throughout the remainder of this chapter the following notation is used:

CGEN$_{CD}$:   The version of CGEN used for computer design.
M1$_{CD}$:   The version of M1 used for computer design.
CGEN$_{DI}$:   The domain-independent version of CGEN.
M1$_{DI}$:   The domain-independent version of M1.
CGEN$_X$:   CGEN$_{DI}$ applied to domain X.
M1$_X$:   M1$_{DI}$ applied to domain X.

15.2   The M1$_{DI}$ and CGEN$_{DI}$ Architectures

The domain-independent versions of M1 and CGEN are abstracted versions of the computer design versions of M1 and CGEN discussed in previous chapters. This section reviews the original architectures of M1$_{CD}$ and CGEN$_{CD}$ and describes how each was abstracted. A general characterization of suitable problems is given at the end of the section.

15.2.1 M1 Architecture

Recall that the M1 problem solver is built on the following elements:

Functional hierarchy is a directed acyclic graph that organizes parts by function by indicating how functionally abstracted parts are related to physical parts. An effect of the functional hierarchy is to break the design of a large system into a set of smaller subproblems, where each subproblem is the design of a part in the functional hierarchy.

Templates represent knowledge of how parts structurally interconnect with each other.

Part models are collections of information about parts, including specifications, characteristics, pins, and links.

Design cycle is the methodology used by $M1_{CD}$ to perform design.

The functional hierarchy appears to be a natural, generally applicable mechanism for organizing components and design subtasks, as many other design systems have employed similar techniques. To be applied to $M1_{DI}$, the definition of the functional hierarchy must be modified slightly in two ways. First, the constituents of the hierarchy do not necessarily have to be parts in the original sense of electronic components but can be any object that is manipulated during the design process. For example, if M1 were applied to software design, the hierarchy could be composed of procedures or functions. The second change is to relax the implied organizational criterion of functionality, thereby allowing any criterion to be used. This provides greater flexibility in forming the hierarchy, which we will henceforth refer to as the *object hierarchy*. Since $M1_{CD}$ does not interpret the meaning of the object hierarchy, these conceptual changes do not affect transforming $M1_{CD}$ to $M1_{DI}$.

A similar argument can be made for part models. Since a part model is used more as an extensible listing of relevant attributes of a part, the model can be easily extended into a new domain and can be used by $M1_{DI}$ without change. To reflect this flexibility, part models are henceforth referred to as *object models*.

Templates and the design cycle require modification for $M1_{DI}$. Templates, design step $d_{template}$, and the part expansion design step, d_{casc}, presuppose that structural knowledge is necessary for the domain. This is not always true; for example, in software design structural knowledge is not used when configuring modules. Steps $d_{template}$ and d_{casc}, however, can be considered forms of design actions for the computer design domain. These actions are to instantiate a part into the design and create connections between parts[2]. In the software design

---

[2]Making part connections is itself a complex action, requiring the interpretation of buses and the application of several consistency checking rules.

domain, design actions might include setting up parameters for procedure or function calls.

The design cycle for M1$_{DI}$ is generalized to the following steps:

Specification (d_{spec}): Same as described previously.

Selection (d_{select}): Same as described previously.

Action (d_{action}): The design actions associated with domain are executed.

Calculation (d_{calc}): Same as described previously.

The M1$_{CD}$ knowledge base supports the design cycle by providing the expertise needed to execute every step for each design situation. The knowledge base is organized into partitions, where each partition corresponds to a design cycle step. For M1$_{CD}$, the partitions are k_{spec}, k_{select}, k_{casc}, $k_{template}$, k_{calc}, and k_{arch}.

To conform with M1$_{DI}$'s design cycle, the new knowledge-base partitions are k_{spec}, k_{select}, k_{action}, k_{calc}, and k_{arch}. The partition k_{action} is defined relative to the actions required for the domain. This impacts CGEN as described in the next section. The differences in the contents of partitions k_{arch} for M1$_{CD}$ and M1$_{DI}$ are minor. The only changes necessary are related to domain-specific data structures. For example, software design does not require netlists, so the code associated with the netlist data structures would be removed; instead some data structure for storing the code to be output (e.g., a parse tree) is needed.

To summarize, the elements of the M1$_{DI}$ architecture are:

- object hierarchy,

- object models,

- design cycle: d_{spec}, d_{select}, d_{action}, d_{calc}, and

- knowledge base: k_{spec}, k_{select}, k_{action}, k_{calc}, k_{arch}.

15.2.2   CGEN Architecture

Recall that the CGEN architecture is built from the following two elements:

Acquisition cycle controls the execution of CGEN by specifying and sequencing the knowledge acquisition subtasks.

Knowledge-base models describe the purpose of each knowledge partition in M1, including the form of rules in each partition so that syntactically and semantically correct code can be created. In addition, these models describe how the design cycle is related to the knowledge acquisition task.

Changes to M1$_{CD}$'s original design cycle, specifically the step d_{action}, have a profound effect on CGEN. CGEN$_{CD}$ was designed to provide a high-level, domain-specific interface for a hardware design expert. The purpose of this interface is to allow the expert to express domain actions without having to write code. For example, templates are described by the domain expert via a schematic drawing, which CGEN$_{CD}$ parses and casts into a form usable by M1$_{CD}$. To allow this high-level interface to work, CGEN must understand how design actions are to be interpreted and translated into M1$_{DI}$'s internal operators and data structures. Therefore, when CGEN$_{DI}$ is applied to a new domain, modifications must be made to allow design actions to be properly interpreted. These modifications apply to both the domain-expert interface and the code generator section of CGEN$_{DI}$. This requires some re-coding of CGEN and modifications to the original expert interface. The removal of step d_{casc} does not have significant impact since it is a special case of d_{action}.

The acquisition cycle, which is partially derived from the interaction between the design cycle and the knowledge base, is left intact. The M1$_{DI}$ design cycle does not fundamentally change its relationship to the knowledge base. In addition, the M1$_{DI}$ knowledge base is not substantially different from the M1$_{DI}$ definition (except as described in the preceding paragraph), thus the CGEN$_{CD}$ knowledge acquisition procedure and its internal representation of acquired knowledge are directly applicable to CGEN$_{DI}$.

15.2.3   Problem Characterization

A set of characteristics of suitable domains for CGEN$_{DI}$ and M1$_{DI}$ is listed below. While this characterization is very loose, it provides an intuitive sense of M1$_{DI}$ and CGEN$_{DI}$'s scope. The characteristics are:

Design object hierarchy: A well-defined hierarchy of the domain's design objects can be constructed through abstraction of each object's function or other relevant criteria.

Complex actions: The design actions may be complex, requiring specific domain knowledge.

Unique invocation condition: The invocation conditions for each set of design actions (corresponding to a template in the computer design domain) must be unique.

Ill-structured domain: An algorithmic solution to the design task does not exist. Furthermore, identifiable and compilable design expertise must be available.

Design constraints: The design space is bounded by a set of well-defined constraints.

Problem-solving approach: The design domain fits the design cycle.

Local object-selection function: It must be possible to select a successor object using some criterion or function evaluated locally at each object in the hierarchy; globally optimal selection and enumerating all satisfactory solutions must not be required.

An example of a design problem not suitable for $M1_{DI}$ and $CGEN_{DI}$ is metal alloy design. In this problem the design objects are metals that do not have a reasonable hierarchical relationship. Furthermore, the design cycle is not appropriate, since the d_{select} step does not have an obvious function.

15.3 Applications

The domain-independent versions of M1 and CGEN were applied to two domains: a mechanical design problem and automated sequencing of tasks in a design environment. This section describes each of these experiments.

15.3.1 Mechanical Design

Several problems in mechanical design involve selecting and integrating a set of primitive components to produce an artifact that satisfies input specifications. An instance of such an application task is the design of a manual window regulator for an automobile. The window regulator is installed between the inner and outer car door panels and raises and lowers the window glass. The CASE system [104] provides an integrated framework of synthesis and analysis tools for this problem; the MICON system was extended to automate the design of a portion of a window regulator.

A window regulator has three main components: a backplate, a sector, and a lift-arm. The lift-arm, shown in Figure 15.2, consists of the following: a power-arm-base segment, a tip-offset segment, a catch-area-tip-offset segment, a catch-area, upper and lower flanges, and a tip segment with a hole. Each of these segments, in turn, is composed of one of five primitive sections shown in Figure 15.3. The corresponding object hierarchy is shown in Figure 15.4. There is a direct analogy between parts and functional abstraction of $M1_{CD}$ and this domain. The design process finds a set of sized primitive sections and integrates them to satisfy a particular functionality.

Corresponding to the nodes in the hierarchy are part models. For example, LIFT_ARM, the lift-arm abstract part, has a specification called LIFT_ARM_-

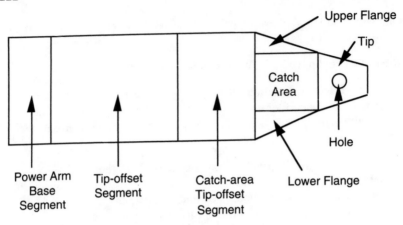

Figure 15.2. Lift-arm of a window-regulator.

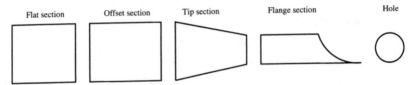

Figure 15.3. Primitive sections in the window-regulator design.

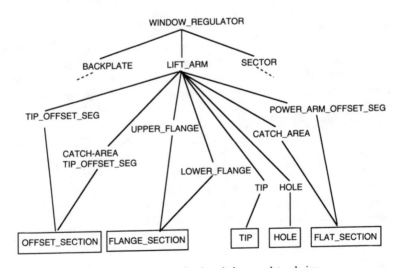

Figure 15.4. Hierarchy for the window-regulator design.

LENGTH; TIP, the tip primitive part, has characteristics OUTER_WIDTH, INNER_WIDTH, and LENGTH.

The M1$_{DI}$ design cycle is the same as described in Section 15.2.1. The step d_{action} instantiates the successor part in the design hierarchy. While M1$_{CD}$ produced an interconnection of pins on parts, the design process here results in the sizing of primitive parts. These sizes are calculated in the d_{calc} step. For example, the outer width of the tip-section is computed using the equation

$$TIP\_OUTER\_WIDTH = 2 * HOLE\_RADIUS + SAFETY\_FACTOR * 2.$$

A special procedure was added to M1$_{DI}$ to print out the characteristics of primitive sections when the design was completed.

The knowledge-acquisition tool CGEN$_{DI}$ in this domain captures parts that must be used and how their size specifications and characteristics are to be computed. The domain-expert interface consists of a list of parts and a set of equations listed in the CGEN$_{DI}$ methods input format.

Both M1$_{DI}$ and CGEN$_{DI}$ were easily extended to this domain. Aside from the output routines, M1 and CGEN were virtually unchanged. The system effectively handled the design of the lift arm of the window regulator. Several lift arm designs were created.

15.3.2 Design Environment

One of the tasks in a design environment is the automated selection and sequencing of design tools to achieve a design goal [113]. Design environments are useful when many tools are needed to accomplish a design task and the procedure for applying the tools is known. Design environments provide an interesting domain for M1$_{DI}$ and CGEN$_{DI}$. The application task was to use M1$_{DI}$ and CGEN$_{DI}$ to automate the sequencing of tools in the MICON system, providing a meta-MICON tool [9].

There are many tasks associated with the MICON environment, such as design synthesis using M1$_{CD}$, database update with the ENTRY program, and knowledge acquisition using CGEN$_{CD}$. These tasks are complex and require tool usage expertise. For example, consider Figure 15.5 which describes the data and control flow during the knowledge acquisition task using CGEN$_{CD}$. Since the inter-relationships shown in the figure are complex, a user of the MICON tool set would benefit from the automation provided by a design environment.

The design objects in this domain consist of design tasks that map into design tools, corresponding to abstract and physical parts, respectively. The design process is to select and invoke one or more design tools appropriate for a design task. The task/tool hierarchy is shown in Figure 15.6. In this case, the hierarchy is organized by abstracting "tasks" as opposed to parts.

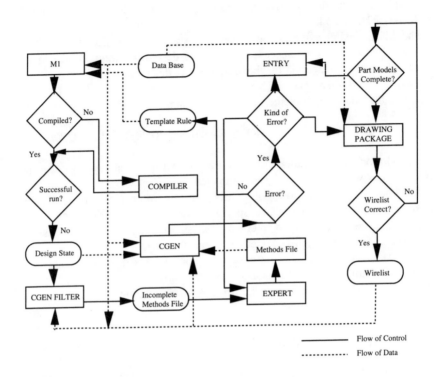

Figure 15.5. Knowledge-acquisition task description.

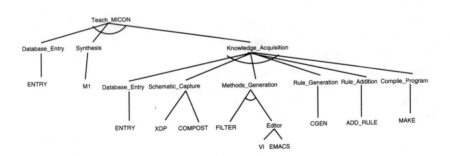

Figure 15.6. MICON tool/task hierarchy.

Corresponding to nodes in hierarchy are task/tool models. For example, the node $CGEN_{CD}$ has characteristic (DOMAIN, Computer-design); the node KNOWLEDGE_ACQUISITION has specifications DOMAIN, SYNTHESIS_-FAILED, DB_SERVER_RUNNING, and so forth.

The $M1_{DI}$ design cycle remains as described in Section 15.2.1. Example design actions for the step d_{action} are given below.

- **Query user:** Ask the user instead of using a tool.

- **Delete file:** Remove file.

- **Create file:** Create file.

- **File exists:** Test existence of file.

- **Process exists:** Test existence of process.

- **Execution error:** Fault occurred during execution.

The knowledge-acquisition task for $CGEN_{DI}$ in this domain consists of capturing tool usage knowledge. For example, as $M1_{DI}$ descends the tool/task hierarchy, it needs to know how to choose between various tools and how to invoke a tool. Tool invocation is a compound operation composed of ensuring inputs exist and are valid, providing the correct command (sequence) to run the tool, and checking that the tool executed properly. This knowledge is acquired by $CGEN_{DI}$, converted into the design actions described above, and integrated into $M1_{DI}$'s knowledge base. The $CGEN_{DI}$ domain expert interface consists of methods and a "fill-in-the-blanks" input form, which is merely a list of tasks/tools to be invoked. The tools are invoked in a sequence that depends upon when the specifications of their predecessor parts are filled, which in turn depends upon the availability of variables used in methods used to compute the value.

Both $M1_{DI}$ and $CGEN_{DI}$ were extended to this domain to form $M1_{DE}$ and $CGEN_{DE}$ tools, respectively [71]. Knowledge about traversing the entire hierarchy shown in Figure 15.6 was added to $M1_{DE}$ using $CGEN_{DE}$. A summary of the knowledge-acquisition sessions is given in Table 15.1. Subsequently, $M1_{DE}$ was used to sequence the tools for several knowledge-acquisition sessions in the computer design domain. A summary of the tool sequencing sessions is given in Table 15.2.

From these experiments, we observe that the $M1_{DI}$ and $CGEN_{DI}$ tool set maps well into the design environment domain. The similarity of tasks between this domain and computer design is interesting to observe.

Training Cases	38
k_{spec} rules	91
k_{select} rules	9
k_{action} rules	38
k_{calc} rules	44
Total rules acquired	182

Table 15.1. Summary of knowledge-acquisition sessions in the design environment domain.

	Number of $M1_{DE}$ rules executed
Any task/tool to successors	50 (average)
BOOT_0 to leaves of hierarchy	1500

Table 15.2. Summary of sequencing sessions in the design environment domain.

15.4 Summary

The M1 and CGEN systems are based on a design paradigm and knowledge representation technique that transcend a single domain. After removing some domain-specific (computer design) features, a domain-independent, task-specific synthesis system has begun to evolve. These tools provide a platform that can be configured for a wide range of problems. Note that when $M1_{DI}$ and $CGEN_{DI}$ are instantiated for a particular application, some minor modifications are required.

16

ASSURE: Automated Design for Dependability

Dependability has long been an important issue for computer systems. While several dependability analysis tools have been produced, no effort has been made to automate the design for dependability. In this chapter we describe AS-SURE, an automated design for dependability advisor in the MICON system[1]. A design for dependability methodology and a formal interface between M1 and ASSURE are presented. ASSURE's operation includes dependability analysis, evaluation of dependability enhancement techniques using predictive estimation, and selection of a dependability technique. Different kinds of knowledge used in designing for dependability are identified, including an algorithmic approach for dependability analysis and a knowledge-based approach for suggesting dependability enhancement techniques. Examples of designs produced using ASSURE as a dependability advisor are provided and show an order of magnitude dependability improvement.

---

[1]This chapter is based on work done by Patrick Edmond and Audrey Brennan and reported in other papers [19, 37]. The reader is encouraged to explore these publications for more information.

16.1   Introduction

Dependability has been defined as *the ability of a system to accomplish the tasks that are expected from it* [77]. Design for dependability is a process that recognizes that the components of the system are not perfect and seeks to minimize the effects of this imperfection [1]. Any area in which a computer failure can have catastrophic results is a candidate for design for dependability. Several techniques for designing dependable electronic systems have been developed and are now routinely used in building systems for real-world applications.

16.1.1   Basic Concepts

The *reliability function* $R(t)$ of a component or system represents the conditional probability that it will operate correctly at time t, given that it is operational at time 0. In a system without repair, the most common reliability function is the exponential: $R(t) = e^{-\lambda t}$ where λ is the failure rate, usually expressed as failures per million hours.

A non-redundant system must have all its components operational for it to function correctly. Such a system's reliability is given by

$$R_{\text{sys}}(t) = \prod_{c=1}^{N} R_c(t).$$

where R_{sys} denotes system reliability, R_c denotes component reliability, and there are N components. If the reliability function is exponential, the system failure rate is simply

$$\lambda(t) = \sum_{i=1}^{N} \lambda_c(t).$$

There are many approaches to design for dependability [114]. Existing parts may be improved or redundancy may be designed into the system in order to reduce the effects of a component failure. The reliability of a redundant system is dependent upon the redundancy structure. Consider the case of triple-modular redundancy with voting (TMR), as illustrated in Figure 16.1. In this scheme, the outputs of three identical serial IO devices (SIOs) are compared by a majority-voting circuit, whose output is whatever is the output of at least two of the three SIOs. This TMR system is operational as long as the voter and at least two SIOs are functional. Thus, its reliability is given by

$$R_v \times (\left(\begin{array}{c} 3 \\ 2 \end{array}\right) (1 - R_s)\, R_s^2 + R_s^3).$$

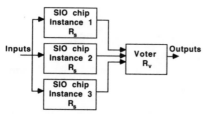

Figure 16.1. Simple triple-modular redundancy with voting.

Some dependability metrics used to compare alternatives are given below.

Mean time to failure (MTTF) is the average period of time for which a system will operate before failing. It is distinct from the mean time between failures (MTBF), which is only meaningful in a system where repair times are also considered. Given the mean time between the occurence of a failure and its repair, the so-called mean time to repair (MTTR), the MTBF is given by[2].

$$MTBF = MTTF + MTTR.$$

In this chapter, we do not model systems with repair.

Mission time (MT) at a given reliability r is the time t_m at the end of which the probability that it is still operational is r, i.e. ,

$$R(t_m) = r \ \Rightarrow \ R(t) \geq r \ \forall \ t \leq t_m.$$

MT is used for systems where continued reliable operation in the absence of repair is vital (e.g., airborne computer systems). If λ is assumed constant, for a non-redundant system, mission time is given by

$$MT(r) = \frac{-\ln r}{\lambda}.$$

Error coverage (EC) is the fraction of errors that are covered (i.e., detected before being propagated through the system). EC is used in applications like financial transaction processing. Calculation of EC is a complex procedure: The various failure modes and their respective probabilities of occurrence must be known [17]. In this work, we consider only single-bit errors for calculating EC and designing error-detection circuitry.

---

[2]This is exact only for non redundant systems but may be only approximate for redundant systems since the repair rate may be altered in the presence of multiple failures.

16.1.2   Motivation

Design for dependability is becoming increasingly critical for computer systems, especially those used in life-critical or revenue-related applications. As computers proliferate into most aspects of society, downtime and errors are becoming increasingly undesirable and even intolerable. Design for dependability broadly consists of two subtasks:

- **Dependability analysis:** Calculation of reliability metrics for different design alternatives.

- **Dependability design:** An iterative procedure, where at each step the designer examines the system, suggests possible modifications, analyzes the new dependability, and evaluates the success of the modifications.

Performing these tasks by hand is unwieldy, complex, and time consuming for realistic designs, especially for redundant systems. Automation can reduce both time and cost for designing for dependability.

16.1.3   CAD for Dependability

A variety of CAD tools have been developed, though mainly for the dependability analysis task. Lambda [39] predicts hard-failure rates for a system. It calculates failure rates based on Mil Handbook 217D [131]. SEC [40] evaluates the MTTF of systems with single error tolerating redundancy, such as error-correcting codes. STARS [25] is a recursive, hierarchically structured, event-driven simulator. It can provide reliability, availability, MTTF, mean uptime and mean downtime evaluations. Mark1 [41] simulates a Markov model of a system, given the model's transition matrix. Mark1 provides availability, MTTF, and state occupancy information. NASA has developed a series of tools for evaluating high reliability systems [122]. Duke University employs a family of Markov modeling tools for evaluating hardware/software systems [52]. Other tools have also been developed at UCLA [83], IBM [55], and several other organizations.

   All the above tools are manually driven analysis tools – no advice as to the design alternatives or reliability techniques that can be applied is given. A larger degree of automation was demonstrated in D0 [53], where Lambda [39] and Advisor [73] (a system design level analysis tool) were integrated into a Reliability Analysis Workbench. However, D0 does not perform synthesis or offer guidance to possible dependability enhancement techniques. To our best knowledge, ASSURE is the first tool that also automates this task.

   In Section 16.2, we describe the design for dependability methodology that forms the basis for ASSURE. A formal model based on the advisor-designer paradigm for handling ASSURE's interaction with M1 is also described. In

Section 16.3, we describe the operation of ASSURE in detail. ASSURE is implemented using a combination of algorithmic and knowledge-based approaches – the implementation is described in Section 16.4. Examples of designs enhanced for dependability using ASSURE are presented in Section 16.5.

16.2 Design for Dependability Methodology

To automate design for dependability, we need a well-defined methodology for the tool to follow. We discuss when ASSURE should be invoked in the overall design process, its overall operation, and its interaction with the synthesis tool M1.

16.2.1 When to Consider Dependability

Usually, dependability analysis is performed only on the completed design, and the dependability engineer's task is rendered considerably more difficult by the lack of flexibility at this stage. Ideally, design for dependability should be integrated from the beginning with the main system design task. However, during the early phases of a design, the dependability expert may lack sufficient information about the system under design to be able to perform a meaningful dependability analysis and evaluate the applicability of various enhancement techniques. When to consider dependability is a tradeoff; the design should be partially completed so that the dependability enhancement task has both sufficient information to evaluate and flexibility to alter decisions relatively easily. In MICON, ASSURE is invoked after M1 has designed the major functionality of the design (e.g., processor, memory, and IO subsystems), but is yet to design supporting logic (e.g., address decoder, wait-state generator).

16.2.2 The Methodology

Design for dependability is an iterative process where one tries to improve the system dependability at each step. This methodology is illustrated in Figure 16.2. First, an initial partial design and a set of user goals (e.g., value for MTTF, MT) and specifications (e.g., system environment, ambient temperature) are given. A dependability analysis is done for the design, and its results are compared to the user's goals. If the goals are met, the process terminates; otherwise dependability enhancement techniques (e.g., package changes, triple modular redundancy, single-error-correcting (SEC) code on memory) are attempted until no more techniques are left or the user's goals are satisfied. This involves choosing a technique from a taxonomy of techniques, applying that technique to the design (i.e., redesigning to incorporate that technique), evaluating the

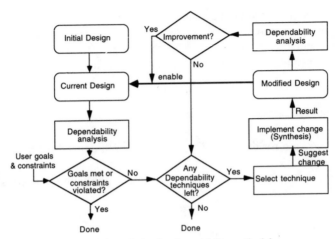

Figure 16.2. A design-for-dependability methodology.

Figure 16.3. Interaction between M1 and ASSURE.

application of the technique after an incremental failure analysis of the design, and, if the evaluation is favorable, accepting the new design as the current design. All these tasks are done by ASSURE, except the redesign task, which involves synthesis and is done by M1.

16.2.3   The Advisor-Designer Paradigm

The paradigm used for interactions between M1 and ASSURE is analogous to the situation of a designer who is inexperienced in design for dependability and who brings the blueprints of a partially completed design to a dependability expert advisor. This expert will examine the design, estimate its dependability, and suggest possible areas for improvement. The designer will go away, attempt to redesign these areas, and return to the expert to announce success or failure. This process will continue either until the dependability goals for the design have been met or until the expert's repertoire of techniques is exhausted. At no point does the expert perform any design function in the sense of altering the blueprints: This is the exclusive domain of the designer. This scheme, with M1 as the designer and ASSURE as the expert, is depicted in Figure 16.3.

This partitioning of tasks between the designer and advisor results in a clean, well-defined interface between M1 and ASSURE. This interface supports the following messages from ASSURE to M1:

- Add design information (attribute-value pairs) to the design-state.

- Change part X to part Y (special case of redesign below, included for efficiency reasons).

- Redesign subsystem A given the specifications $(S_1 = \text{String}_1), ...(S_n = \text{String}_n)$ (causes M1 to undo the previous design for A and redesign A with the new specifications and possibly new design information).

- Finished with recommendations.

- Save design state (for possible rollback at a subsequent step).

- Restore design state (if technique evaluated unfavorably).

M1 responds to ASSURE's suggestions with one of the following messages:

- SUCCESS: M1 was able to carry out the suggestion.

- FAILURE: M1 was unable to carry out the suggestion as it violated some constraint. For example, additional parts required to implement the SEC on memory technique may violate the maximum board area constraint.

- STOP: M1 was unable to carry out the suggestions due to missing design knowledge in its knowledge base. A MICON system user would then use CGEN to add this knowledge to M1 and be able to restart the system at this stage. ASSURE merely saves its state and exits on receiving this message.

In the implementation, M1 and ASSURE run as separate processes that communicate by passing messages using UNIX interprocess communication mechanisms.

In addition to aiding in system development, the decoupling of ASSURE and M1 by a well-defined interface provides a general framework for interfacing experts in other domains (e.g., testability, maintainability) to a synthesis module. Other advisor tools will need to be built to examine the suitability of the interface. Also, the multiple-advisor case requires a scheme for resolving possibly competing or conflicting advice. One possible scheme is a simple central controller that prioritizes the advice from each advisor before forwarding it to the designer; such a scheme was found to be effective in the wire-routing domain [69]. This issue is not addressed in this chapter.

```
module [SBC_0:
  1, [PROC_0:
1, [68XX_PROC_0:
     1, SN74LS00D,
     1, HD6809P];
  1, [SIO_0:
1, [68XX_SIO_0:
     1, HD6850P,
  ...
```

Figure 16.4. An example module description file for LAMBDA.

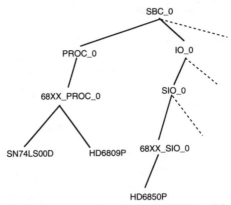

Figure 16.5. Design hierarchy for the 6809-based design.

16.3   ASSURE: Operation

The implementation of each of the subtasks in the design for dependability methodology for ASSURE is described next.

16.3.1   Dependability Analysis

i

The type of dependability analysis is a function of whether the system has any redundant structures or not. For non-redundant systems, ASSURE uses the hierarchical reliability analysis tool LAMBDA [39]. ASSURE creates the following inputs to LAMBDA:

- a hierarchical list of parts in the design (see Figure 16.4 for an example; the corresponding design hierarchy is shown in Figure 16.5),

```
partspecs [
/* Format:
Name, Type, Cost, Quality Factor, Complexity (#gates/#bits)
        #Functions, #Pins, Technology, Integration Scale,
        Hermeticity, Process Maturity (1 for mature),
        Junction Temperature (if 0, use next two values),
        Junction to Ambient Temp Thermal Constant,
        Operating Power Dissipation, Failure Rate (0,if not fixed);
 */
HD6809P,IC,2.0,35,3000,1,40,NMOS,LSI,NH,1,0,100,1.0,0.0;

TMS27C128_20JL,IC,17.57,35,131072,1,28,NMOS,PROM,NH,1,0,0,0.21,0.0;

HD6850P,IC,1.0,35,580,1,24,NMOS,MSI,NH,1,0,120,0.525,0.0 ;
...]
```

Figure 16.6. A parts specification file for LAMBDA.

```
exec (LAMBDA.MOD) ; /* Execute the module specification file */
exec (LAMBDA.PARTS) ; /* Execute the parts specification file  */

temp [] = 30 ; /* Temperature inside cabinet */
env [] = gb ; /* Ground benign environment */
...
lambda [SBC_0] ; /* Perform analysis on SBC_0 module
...
```

Figure 16.7. An example command file for LAMBDA.

- relevant parameters of the parts (extracted from the database, see Figure 16.6 for an example), and

- environmental parameters (e.g., temperature, see Figure 16.7 for an example).

LAMBDA predicts the hard failure rate of a system from component failure rates calculated using Mil-Std-217E [131]. ASSURE parses the results file (see Figure 16.8 for an example) to obtain the failure data for each part.

For redundant systems, the system reliability is given by

$$R_{\text{system}}(t) = \prod_{i=1}^{N} R_{\text{subsys}}(t),$$

where R_{subsys} denotes a subsystem's reliability. The reliability of each subsystem with redundancy must be calculated individually based on the particular redun-

```
Quantity ) Module   Lambda - single module  % Lambda - all module copies
-------------------------------------------------------------------------
   1) SBC_0                    84.0534              100.000
     1) PROC_0                 72.3488               86.075
       1) 68XX_PROC_0          72.3488              100.000
         1) NAND21_0            0.1163                0.161
         6) RESISTOR_0          0.0159                0.132
         1) 6809_CLOCK_0        0.2696                0.373
           1) CAPACITOR_0       0.0848               31.453
...
**** MTTF:  11897.2 hrs.  ****
...
                    Partname summary statistics :

....... Part Name ......... Components    Net Lambda  % System Lambda
HD6809P....................     1.0         71.8672          85.50
TMS27C128_20J..............     1.0          2.5980           3.09
HD6850P....................     1.0          2.5282           3.01
8116.......................     1.0          1.8888           2.25
...
```

Figure 16.8. An example LAMBDA output file with absolute and relative failure rates.

dancy structure employed. ASSURE recognizes certain reliability structures and evaluates their reliability at each time ordinate; multiplying these reliability values gives system reliability as a function of time. ASSURE calculates MTTF (equal to the area beneath the system reliability curve) using adaptive trapezoidal numerical integration from $t = 0$ to $t = t'$, where $R_{system}(t') < \epsilon$, an arbitrarily small value[3]. ASSURE calculates MT (t_m for a minimum reliability r) by doing a binary search over the system reliability curve. Successive evaluations of system reliability are done at different values of time t until one which is within ϵ of r is found; this t is t_m.

16.3.2 Dependability Enhancement Techniques

A taxonomy of design for dependability techniques is given in Table 16.1. In ASSURE, these are divided into two classes:

- **Fault avoidance (fault intolerance)** attempts to increase reliability by a variety of means, including changing the packaging (e.g., from plastic to ceramic), quality levels of parts (e.g., from commercial to military), and environmental conditions for the design (e.g., from airborne to computer room). ASSURE uses information about physical parts in the MICON

---

[3]Currently defined as 10^{-20}.

Fault Avoidance	Component packaging/quality changes
	Component integration level changes
	Environmental modification
Fault Detection	Duplication
	Error detection codes (parity, M-of-N)
	Consistency and capability checking
	Time domain detection (watchdog timers, timeouts)
Static (Masking) Redundancy	N-modular redundancy with voting (NMR)
	Error correction codes (e.g., Hamming, SEC/DED)
	Interwoven logic
	Coded-state machines
Dynamic Redundancy	Reconfiguration (duplication, NMR)
	Standby sparing
	Graceful degradation

Table 16.1. A taxonomy of techniques for dependable design.

database to determine the parts to which these techniques are applicable.

- **Fault tolerance** attempts to add redundancy to detect or mask the effects of faults by a variety of means including fault detection, static or masking redundancy, and dynamic redundancy. ASSURE's repertoire of this class of techniques currently[4] includes:

  - error detection codes (parity),
  - triple-modular redundancy, and
  - error correction codes (Hamming, SEC/DED).

  These techniques are applicable to larger subsystems (e.g., processor, serial IO, RAM array, etc.) and require significant changes to the design. ASSURE uses information about abstract parts (subsystems) in the MICON database to determine the applicable fault tolerant techniques.

16.3.3 Selecting a Technique

Fault avoidance techniques have a relatively low cost with high dependability paybacks and do not change the design significantly (unlike fault tolerant techniques). Hence, ASSURE always prefers fault avoidance techniques over fault tolerant techniques. Also, before evaluating a new design derived by applying a fault tolerant technique, ASSURE attempts to apply fault avoidance to new

---

[4]Several other techniques exist and can be added using the procedure described in Section 16.4.

parts introduced to the design by the fault tolerant techniques. In this way, it obviates rejecting a fault tolerance technique merely because it added parts, whose failure rate could be easily reduced using fault avoidance.

Some designers favor selecting a technique that improves the part with the maximum failure rate until the increase in dependability is too small. This approach was shown to be unsuitable for fault avoidance techniques [19]. With this selection criterion, the MTTF improvement curve was non-monotonic – hence one could not stop attempting another technique just because the previous technique resulted in an improvement below the threshold; detecting a point of diminishing returns on the curve was not sufficient for terminating the search. ASSURE's selection criterion is based on a cost function that evaluates the goodness of the change and thus requires monotonic ordering of the gain of each potential technique. The costs for all techniques applicable to all subsystems are evaluated simultaneously, and the best technique is selected; this requires more computational effort but obviates the non-monotonicity problem. The cost function is also used to evaluate the improvement due to an actual design change.

Cost Function

Since ASSURE can have multiple goals (e.g., increase MTTF to at least 100,000 hours while maximizing error detection coverage), and as a technique can influence several metrics (e.g., single-error-correcting code - SEC - on memory increases MTTF and EC), the cost function must consider the improvement with regard to several metrics. The cost function is simply the weighted sum of the fractional changes in each of the metrics (MTTF, MT, and EC), divided by the weighted sum of the fractional changes in monetary and board-area costs. Since the change has not been implemented, ASSURE uses predictive estimator functions to compute each of the parameters in the function; these are detailed in the next section.

For each candidate technique, the cost function is computed, and the technique with the largest value is selected. The cost function for a design change must exceed an empirically derived threshold for that change to be accepted (otherwise they are deemed to be too expensive, in terms of cost or board-area, or have too small a dependability payoff). Since ASSURE uses a greedy approach to selecting the next technique, it can fall into locally optimal but globally suboptimal solution states. This happens only when the application of one technique influences another. For example, applying SEC on ROM and SRAM requires additional hardware that is shared between ROM and SRAM; the additional hardware may cause the individual techniques of applying SEC on ROM and applying SEC on SRAM to evaluate unfavorably; however, applying both techniques together may still be a good idea.

Predictive Estimation

For fault avoidance techniques, the cost-function parameters (change in MTTF, MT, board-area, cost) can be directly evaluated using information in the database. However, for fault tolerant techniques, the new parts that would be added to the design are embedded as design knowledge in the synthesis program M1; AS-SURE does not know *a priori* about these parts; only after M1 has applied the technique can the parameters be evaluated. Hence, ASSURE uses predictive functions that estimate the parameters for a technique applied to a particular subsystem.

Such an approximation is possible because meaningful bounds can be established even before actual synthesis takes place. For example, we know that the application of TMR to an SIO subsystem (see Figure 16.1) will involve the addition of at least a voter and two more copies of the SIO. ASSURE can therefore access the parts database to find the cost of the SIO and the minimum cost and area of the voter chip; these attributes, together with component failure rate λ, can be plugged into equations that are derived from theoretical expressions for reliability. For this example, neglecting any additional logic required, the changes in cost and area will be given by

$$\triangle_{\text{cost}} = 2 \times (\text{Cost of SIO}) + (\text{Minimum Cost of Voter}), \text{and}$$
$$\triangle_{\text{area}} = 2 \times (\text{Area of SIO}) + (\text{Minimum Area of Voter}).$$

If $R_v \gg R_s$ and $R_s = e^{-\lambda t}$, then

$$\frac{R_{\text{TMR}}}{R_{\text{basic}}} = \frac{3e^{-2\lambda t} - 2e^{-3\lambda t}}{e^{-\lambda t}} \ ; \ \frac{\text{MTTF}_{\text{TMR}}}{\text{MTTF}_{\text{basic}}} = \frac{5/6\lambda}{1/\lambda} = \frac{5}{6}.$$

These equations are needed for each reliability technique applicable to each subsystem. ASSURE reads these equations from an external file, making it easy to add equations to account for new techniques on new subsystems.

16.3.4   Suggesting and Implementing Changes

After the technique and the subsystem to which it is to be applied are selected, ASSURE asks M1 to redesign the subsystem with a new set of specifications. To formulate the suggestion to M1, ASSURE essentially maps the (technique, subsystem) tuple to a (subsystem, set of new specifications) tuple. For example, to implement TMR on the SIO subsystem, ASSURE asks M1 to redesign the SIO subsystem with specification RELIABILITY_TECHNIQUE = TMR. This causes M1 to remove the previous SIO design and redesign it using a template that uses three SIO chips and a voter (similar to Figure 16.1). Note that ASSURE only formulates the suggestion for the change, while M1 actually implements the change; a clean well-defined partition is maintained. For each new (part, applicable dependability technique) pair, knowledge for formulating suggestions is added to ASSURE and template knowledge is added to M1 using CGEN.

16.4   ASSURE: Implementation

ASSURE is implemented as a knowledge-based system (KBS) in OPS83, with several algorithmic routines in C. Like any well-engineered KBS, ASSURE consists of two distinct elements – a knowledge base (KB) and a problem-solving architecture that exploits the knowledge base. The architecture is based on the methodology detailed in Sections 16.2 and 16.3 and essentially activates a KB partition for each step in the flow chart in Figure 16.2. The KB is divided into disjoint partitions, each for a distinct purpose:

- **Architecture:** Directly supports the problem-solving architecture: How to sequence subtasks, how to invoke LAMBDA, how to interact with M1.

- **Predictive estimation:** Includes the equations used to estimate parameters for the cost function used in selecting the next dependability technique to attempt.

- **Dependability analysis:** Includes how dependability of redundant systems can be calculated.

- **Suggestion formulation:** Indicates what design information and specifications should be given to M1 in order to implement a particular dependability technique for a particular subsystem.

Other knowledge used in design for dependability (in addition to knowledge in ASSURE's knowledge base) is listed below:

- **Design knowledge:** Actually implements a particular dependability technique for a particular part and is stored as templates in M1's knowledge base.

- **Component information:** Is stored as attributes of parts in the parts database.

- **Applicable dependability technique knowledge:** Indicates the applicable dependability techniques for each part and is stored as a special attribute in the part database. This allows ASSURE to have a general structure for all techniques; new techniques can be easily added to the parts database (in a manner similar to other parts information).

The representation, anticipated growth, and means of acquisition for all these partitions are given in Table 16.2. For example, if we need to add the TMR technique for the SIO subsystem for the 68XX family, knowledge would be added in the following manner:

Tool	Partition	Representation	Growth rate	Knowledge Acquisition
ASSURE	Architecture	OPS83 rules	None	Coding
	Predictive Estimation	Reverse-Polish expressions	Moderate	Expression writing
	Dependability Analysis	C function	Small	Coding
	Suggestions Formulation	OPS83 rules	Moderate	Coding
M1	Design	OPS83 rules	Moderate	Automated using CGEN
Database	Component Information	DB records	Large	DB entry tool
	Applicable Technique	DB records	Moderate	DB entry tool

Table 16.2. Knowledge partitions for design for dependability.

1. The voter chip would be added to the database if it is not already present. This adds knowledge to the Component Information partition.

2. An attribute would be added to the 68XX family SIO subsystem in the database, indicating that TMR is an applicable dependability enhancement technique.

3. Suggestion formulation knowledge would be added to ASSURE that indicates that the technique can be implemented simply by asking M1 to re-design the SIO subsystem with specification RELIABILITY_TECHNIQUE = TMR.

4. A reverse-polish expression for estimating dependability improvement and cost/area changes for this technique would be added to a file read by ASSURE.

5. A designer would teach M1 to use TMR on a 68XX class SIO using CGEN (as described previously in Part III).

Only Step 3 involves writing code, which we plan to automate using a tool like CGEN in the future. In this manner, a new dependability enhancement technique can be easily added to ASSURE's repertoire.

16.5   Experimental Results

ASSURE's design space currently includes applying parity and SEC to memory and TMR to IO and processor subsystems of 6809- and 68008-based designs. Several designs using ASSURE and M1 have been produced. A trace for a 6809-based computer system is described here. ASSURE is triggered automatically by M1 after M1 has designed the processor, memory, and IO subsystems. ASSURE interacts directly with the user by prompting him for environmental parameters and dependability goals as indicated below.

```
***   ASSURE: Design-for-Dependability Module   ***
What is the expected ambient operating temperature?
   (Enter ? for a default of 30 degrees C) :  25
What is the expected environment?
              Computer Room : 0
              Factory Floor : 1
      Ground Transportation : 2
          Naval Application : 3
      Aerospace Application : 4
   (Enter 0-4 or ? for default of Computer Room) :  0
Do you wish to specify a design goal [y/n] ?
   (Default: Maximize System Mean Time to Failure ):  y
Please choose one of the following:
   Enter explicit lower bounds for goals : 0
                         Maximize goals : 1
   Enter (0-1):  0
Enter relative weights for goals (0 to ignore goal)
   Weight of Mean Time to Failure goal :  1
   Input desired Mean Time to Failure (in thousand hours) :  150
   Weight of Mission Time goal :  0
   Weight of Error Coverage goal (single-bit errors) :  0
Please indicate a weight value (0-10) for the following costs
   Increase in total monetary cost :  1
   Increase in total area :  1
Do you wish to specify a maximum part quality level?
   (Default is Commercial quality parts) [y/n] : y
Please choose an appropriate quality level
              Commercial Commodity : 0
      Burned-in Commmercial Commodity : 1
                      Military Spec : 2
            Burned-in Military Spec : 3
   (Enter 0-3 or ? for default Commercial Commodity) :  1
Would you like to specify a Mil217 quality factor [y/n]
   (Default uses quality factors predefined in Mil217) :  n
```

The user has the option to specify a minimum value for goals (e.g., MTTF or at least 10,000 hours, error coverage of at least 90%) or to ask that some metric be maximized. Environment options include computer rooms, factory floors, ground transportation, and naval and aerospace applications. Part quality limits the space ASSURE searches and can be expanded to burned-in commercial, military, and burned-in military. User can also input relative weights on monetary cost and area that would be used in the cost function.

After gathering these specifications, ASSURE reads M1's current design state and accesses the MICON database for relevant part information. It writes input files for LAMBDA, executes LAMBDA, and parses the results for subsequent analysis as shown below.

```
Design state read OK
Accessing database
  No ceramic version found for part: MAX232
  Ceramic part found: HD6850
  Ceramic part found: HD6821
  Ceramic part found: HD6809P
  Ceramic part found: SN7400J
  ...
  Writing input files for LAMBDA analysis
  Running LAMBDA analysis
  Parsing LAMBDA results
  Top level MTTF returned : 11897 hours
  Initial costs: area = 6 sq. inches
                 cost = $27.52
```

ASSURE goes through several iterations of making suggestions to M1 and evaluating design modifications. It continually attempts to meet the design goal of increasing the MTTF beyond the given value until it has exhausted its repertoire of techniques or the goal is satisfied. The complete trace is shown below.

```
Fault Avoidance Techniques
  Sending suggestion to M1: Change part HD6809P to HD6809[5]
  M1 returns SUCCESS
  Current MTTF : 74057.7 hours
  Sending suggestion to M1: Change part HD6850 to MC6850
  M1 returns SUCCESS
  Current MTTF : 89214.8 hours
  Sending suggestion to M1: Change part HD6821 to MC6821
  M1 returns SUCCESS
  Current MTTF : 98870.0 hours
  Package change on SN7400J rejected
```

---

[5] Actual message uses unique integers and database record pointers for efficiency.

```
(Evaluation: 0.06 -- too low)
Fault Tolerant Techniques
  Predictive evaluation for TMR on 68XX_SIO_0
          Metric : monetary cost
          Metric : area
          Metric : MTTF
  ...
  Predictive evaluation for SEC/DED on 68XX_ROM_0
          Metric : monetary cost
          Metric : area
          Metric : MTTF
Selected SEC/DED on 68XX_ROM_0
Sending suggestion to M1:
      Add (ROM_SEC_CODE_BITS, 13) to design-state
M1 returns SUCCESS
Sending suggestion to M1:
      Add (ROM_SEC_CODE_WORDS, 13) to design-state
M1 returns SUCCESS
Sending suggestions to M1:
      Redesign MEM_SUPPORT_0 given specifications
      (SUPPORT_TYPE = SEC), (ON_ROM=Y)
M1 returns SUCCESS
Design state read OK
Running LAMBDA analysis on 68XX_ROM_0
  ...
Technique accepted
Current MTTF : 135123.0 hours
  ...
Current MTTF : 151538.0 hours
Goal satisfied
Create design space curves? [y/n] :  y
Create MTTF plot? [y/n] :  y
Create Mission Time plot? [y/n] :  n
Create Error Coverage plot? [y/n] :  n
Create cost plot? [y/n] :  y
Create area plot? [y/n] :  y
Create evaluation plot? [y/n] :  n
ASSURE terminating, handing back control to M1 ....
Sending suggestion to M1: Done with recommendations
```

At first, in the fault avoidance phase, ASSURE changes packages on several chips until it recognizes a point of diminishing returns (after the 6821 package upgrade). ASSURE next turns to fault-tolerant techniques. Adding SEC code on ROM and SRAM are selected in turn, since the cost function for these evaluates

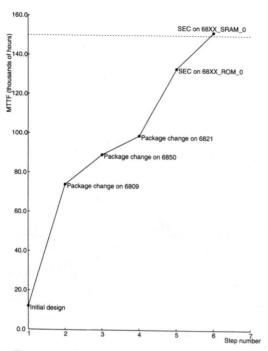

Figure 16.9. MTTF improvement for a 6809-based design.

more favorably than that for other techniques (e.g., TMR on IO devices). As MTTF is beyond the user-specified goal at this step, no further techniques are considered. It then automatically graphs the design space explored; the plot for MTTF is shown in Figure 16.9. Other plots for changes in MT, cost, and area with each design modification are also produced. The cost and area plots show small increases for package changes followed by large increases when SEC is added. Figure 16.10 shows the schematic for the modified design with the SEC circuitry highlighted in the box.

Results from another run of ASSURE that produced a more populated design space for the 6809-based design are shown in Figure 16.11. ASSURE explored a larger space as the goal was maximizing MTTF. Solid lines in this plot indicate techniques that were accepted as they were favorably evaluated. Dotted lines indicate techniques that, though indicated to be favorable by the predictive estimation functions, were found not to be an improvement. For example, adding TMR on the 6821 introduces new parts to the design whose additional failure rate offsets the advantage of using the technique; hence this technique is rejected.

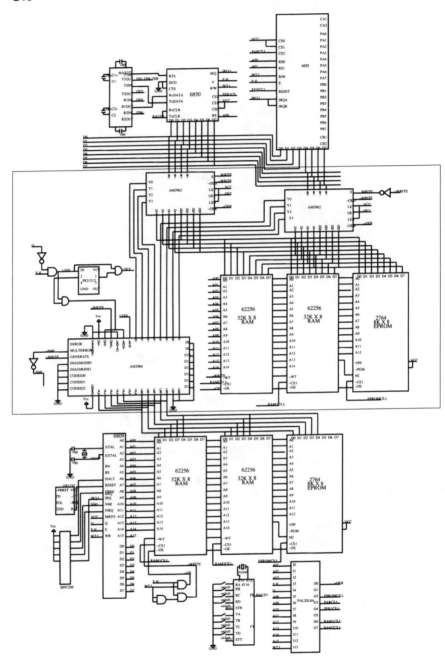

Figure 16.10. Schematic for a 6809-based design with SEC on memory.

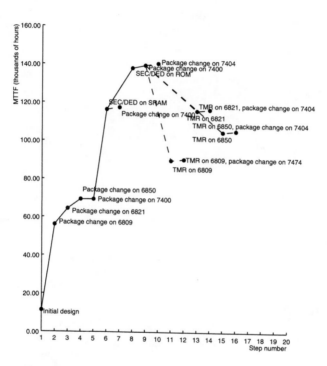

Figure 16.11. Exploring design space for a 6809-based design.

A

The MICON and DEMETER Design Models

Design models are used to categorize the information and identify the subtasks in the overall design process. These models provide the formalism for automated design tools and provide an underlying organization for a design environment in which several designers (human or otherwise) can classify design information and work cooperatively and possibly concurrently on the design problem. Design models used in CAD tools have been reported in [93, 121, 20].

A design model for a domain is formulated after a detailed study of the design process in that domain. The DEMETER project [53, 113] studied the process of designing large digital systems and developed the DEMETER Design Model (DDM). The DDM forms the basis of developing an automated digital system design environment. Since the early phases of MICON are rooted within the DEMETER project, the MICON Design Model (MDM) is based on the same concepts as the DDM. In fact, the MDM can be considered a refinement or evolution of the DDM. In this appendix, we describe the relationships between these two design models.

The first section describes the DDM. In the second section, we abstract some detail from the MDM, which was described in Part II, and show how it is a refinement of the DDM.

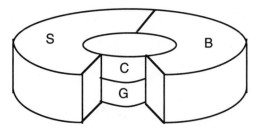

Figure A.1. Objects in the DEMETER design model.

A.1 The DEMETER Design Model

The DEMETER model classifies design information into object categories and identifies the design subtasks that utilize and create these objects. The description of objects and processes given below is adapted from [113].

A.1.1 The Objects

There are four kinds of objects as described below:

Behavior: Describes what the system is supposed to do. It details the functionality of the system and of all of its parts.

Structure: Describes the system as a set of interconnected parts. Depending upon the level of detail, the structure of a digital system can be logical or physical. Information on geometry is included in structure since it is impossible to separate the two. Geometry has a limited role at the higher levels of digital design.

Constraints: Design variables that limit the design space, establishing *a priori* that some solutions would not be acceptable or practical. They express requirements that need to be satisfied by the design.

Goals: Define the goodness of the design. Goals are different from constraints in that they are more flexible – a designer can temporarily ignore a goal, or can bias toward one particular goal at any time during the design process (e.g., favor reliability over performance).

The four objects are all inter-related, as shown in Figure A.1[1]. The fact that all objects influence one another is indicated by each object being adjacent to the other three.

---

[1]The goals and constraints are shown in opposite order from sketch in [113] since we believe this is more clear.

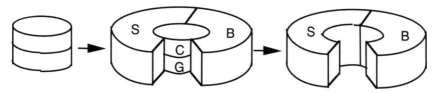

Figure A.2. The design process in the DEMETER design model.

A.1.2   The Process

Given constraints and goals, the design process builds a corresponding structure and behavior. The DDM provides a description of this process, as schematically indicated in Figure A.2. In the initial phase, only the constraints and goals of the design are available. In the middle phase, all four parameters are present and actively being worked on. The final phase shows that only structure and behavior are left after the design is completed. Note that the DDM does not concentrate on the various subtasks during design; it just provides a general description of the overall design process.

A.1.3   The Hierarchy

DDM recognizes that design typically proceeds along several hierarchically-related levels. The DEMETER report identified several levels for a general digital system design task. The objects at each of these levels are represented as cylinders as shown in Figure A.3. The cylinders at lower levels have larger diameters to reflect the greater amount of detail. The cylinders touch to indicate communication of information between levels. The flow of the design process is from top to bottom, i.e., from the rough description of the product to the precisely detailed representation at the lowest level.

A.2   The MICON Design Model

The MDM has been described in detail in Part II of the book. Here, we have abstracted the MDM and presented it in the same style as the DDM above.

A.2.1   The Objects

In addition to categorizing information, objects in MICON also have a corresponding representation utilized by the MICON tools. For example, in addition to classifying some design information as behavior or function, one also needs to represent it either as Boolean equations, state transition tables, or an algorithm

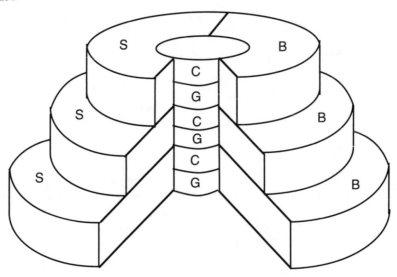

Figure A.3. Multiple levels in the DEMETER design model.

written in a hardware description language. The representation for structure is straightforward as a set of connections between pins on parts. However, for representing behavior, using a language with well-defined semantics would result in an explosion of detail. Hence, behavior is represented loosely as a set of parts with the functionality of the part being implicit in its name. Also, a set of general attribute-value pairs (termed characteristics) associated with each part detail its behavior. Thus, MDM can model the behavior of arbitrarily complex parts with only as much detail as required for the design task. For example, if the design task requires selection based broadly on processor family and not the detailed instruction set, then only the processor family information is associated with the processor parts. Constraints or specifications are also represented as general attribute-value pairs.

Objects in the MDM are described below:

Structure: Describes the system as a set of interconnected parts as in DDM.

Characteristics: Describe the behavior of a part, including abstract parts which in turn may include several other parts. This information is local to each part and details its functioning irrespective of how it is being used in the design.

Reports: Describe the behavior of a set of parts. This information details the functioning of the parts as configured in the current design. Local reports are local to an abstract part, while reports are global across the design.

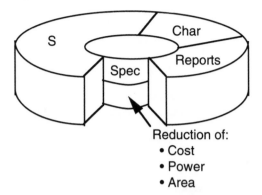

Reduction of:
• Cost
• Power
• Area

Figure A.4. Objects in the MICON design model.

Specifications: Requirements that need to be satisfied by the design of an abstract part. They are like constraints in DDM and limit the design space.

In MDM, the goals are implicit – the reduction of cost, power, and area of the design. Specifications always need to be satisfied, while the design process tries to minimize the cost, power, and area. The emphasis on one goal or another is done automatically by the penalty function used in part selection (see Section 4.2.1).

Figure A.4 depicts the objects and their influence on one another in a manner similar to the DDM. Note that the adjacency requirement is only loosely maintained in the figure due to limited dimensionality of the drawing; there are interactions between structure and reports even though they don't touch in the figure.

By requiring that specifications must be satisfied and doing away with the notion of goals that are attempted to be met, the MDM does not directly capture the tradeoff process in design. Consider the case where part A at level i has a specification or constraint of having delay less than 10 ns. Further, assume A is composed of B and C in series.

- In DDM, the constraint at level $i + 1$ is that the sum of the delay of B and C must be less than 10 ns. At first, this could result in the goal for B and C's design to have a delay of, say, 5 ns each. In designing B and C, an attempt would be made to keep the delay less than 5 ns. Note that since the goal is a flexible target, not meeting it is not sufficient cause for reporting failure. However, if the overall constraint is violated, the goals for B and C would be modified accordingly (i.e., a tradeoff between delays of the two parts would be made). The design would be redesigned until the constraint is met (or the goal at the level i would be listed as violated).

- In MDM, the specification for A is translated to specifications for B and C to have delay less than 5 ns each. If either of these specifications are violated, failure handling needs to redo the reasoning about the overall constraint and respecify both B and C for redesign.

While the MDM scheme loses some information by not maintaining distinct goals and constraints and requires additional reasoning in some cases, it was chosen since it is simpler.

A.2.2 The Process

DDM merely defined the overall design process and did not elaborate on how the design was done. The MDM divides the design process (at one level) into a sequence of subtasks. Each of these subtasks are depicted symbolically in Figure A.5 and described below.

Specification step: Generates the specifications for a level.

Part selection step: Selects the parts for implementing the design. The selection is such that the characteristics of the parts satisfy the specifications while the implicit goals are maximized.

Structural design step: Builds the structure around the selected parts to satisfy the specifications.

Calculation step: Analyzes the design fragment and generates relevant reports to describe its behavior.

Each of these steps is done by a problem solver, which may be a human designer, an algorithm, or a knowledge-based tool. In MICON, the problem solver is the synthesis tool M1. The type of knowledge M1 uses for each subtask is also shown in Figure A.5.

A.2.3 The Hierarchy

Like DDM, MDM recognizes that design typically proceeds along several levels of abstraction. In fact, MDM assumes that these levels can be predefined into a functional hierarchy and gets maximum leverage from this organization by repeating the same design process (detailed above) at each level. In addition to abstraction, the functional hierarchy is based on problem decomposition, which is depicted symbolically by dividing the block representing behavior into several smaller blocks. A simple functional hierarchy and the corresponding symbolic MDM objects are shown in Figure A.6.

At any stage in the design process, there might be several subproblems to be addressed at different levels in the hierarchy. The DDM did not address the

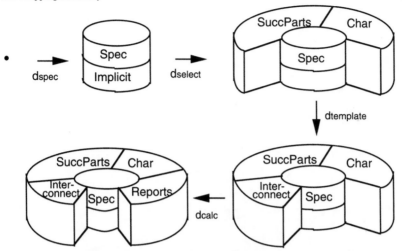

Figure A.5. The design process in the MICON design model.

MICON Design Model	DEMETER Design Model
Specifications	Constraints
Parts and Characteristics	Behavior
Reports	Behavior
Pins and interconnections	Structure
Implicitly minimize area, cost and power	Goals

Table A.1. Mapping of objects between the design models.

issue of ordering these subproblems. In MDM, there is a notion of completeness of specifications; any subproblem with complete set of specifications can be addressed.

A.3 Mapping Summary

In summary, the MDM is an evolution and refinement of the DDM. Table A.1 lists the corresponding objects in each model. Table A.2 lists each subtask in MDM and what it accomplishes in the DDM.

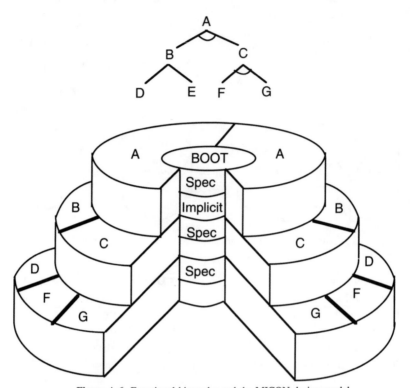

Figure A.6. Functional hierarchy and the MICON design model.

MICON Design Model	DEMETER Design Model
Specification	Create C_i
Translation	$C_{i-1} \rightarrow C_i$
Formulation	$C_{i-1}, B \rightarrow C_i$
Part selection	Create B_i
Structural synthesis	Create S_i
Part expansion	Create S_i
Templates	Create S_i
Support circuitry	Create B_i
Calculation	Create B_i
Subproblem ordering	–

Table A.2. Mapping of processes between the design models.

B

Rule-Base Programming

Rules, a knowledge-representation technique, are of the general form

> if <set of preconditions>,
>
> then <set of actions>.

The left hand side (LHS) describes the preconditions for which the rules should be activated, or fired; the right hand side (RHS) contains a set of actions to perform when the preconditions are satisfied, or matched. The rules are stored in rule memory, sometimes called long-term memory. Data in a rule-based system is represented via working memory elements (WMEs) and kept in the working memory (WM), sometimes called short-term memory. WMEs are sets of attribute value (AV) pairs and are analogous to records in conventional languages, except that they are tagged with their relative creation time. The rule LHS patterns are composed of a set of condition elements (CE). Each CE is written relative to WMEs; each CE specifies the values a particular set of WMEs should have to activate the rule. In other words, the CEs on the LHS form a pattern for a set of WMEs to match. A simple model of the components of a rule-based system are given in Figure B.1.

During an *inference cycle* the entire contents of working memory, the WMEs, are matched to the LHS of every rule. The rules whose LHS are completely satisfied form the *conflict set*. Actually, the members of the conflict set are called rule *instances* since it is possible for a rule's LHS to match in more than one way, causing it to appear in the conflict set as multiple instances. If more than

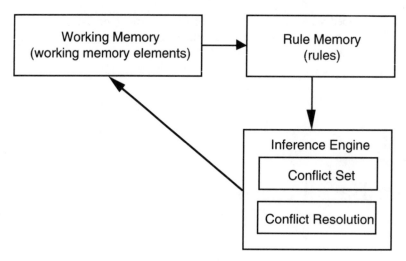

Figure B.1. The basic components of a rule-based system.

one instance appears in the conflict set, a conflict resolution strategy is applied to select a single instance to fire. MEA [48, 23], a commonly used strategy for the OPS5 and OPS83 languages[1], relies on several factors:

Refraction: The same instance will not fire more than once.

Recency: The more recent the WME element matching a CE, the higher the score for that instance.

Specificity: The more CEs an LHS contains, the higher the score for that instance.

MEA is well-suited to depth-first search but has some important side effects that were described in Section 10.1.2.

When a rule instance is fired, its RHS actions are applied to working memory. Typically this will cause modifications to working memory, which will create new WME, which will create a new conflict set, causing another rule to fire. This process continues until no LHS patterns are matched.

Since it is possible for any rule to fire at any time, some means to control the execution of the program is necessary. Contexts [23] are a common means of partitioning a rule-based program. When a context is activated, only the rules in that context can be matched. A rough analogy can be made to procedures in traditional languages, where problem solving at one level consists of deciding on the correct procedures to call, and at a lower level the individual procedures

---

[1]OPS83, however, allows the programmer to generate a custom conflict resolution strategy [48].

can be developed without consideration of other portions of the program. In OPS programs operating under MEA, contexts are defined by the first CE to appear in the LHS. Typically, a goal WME is used to indicate the name of the active context. Goals are manipulated by the problem solver to achieve the behavior required.

A convenient feature of contexts is that they facilitate incremental knowledge acquisition by limiting the interactions between rules. Since a rule can only affect those rules in its context, the scope of influence is substantially diminished. Without contexts, automated knowledge acquisition would be much more difficult to implement due to unintended interactions [117].

Bibliography

[1] A. L. Hopkins, Jr. Fault-tolerant system design: Broad brush and fine print. *Computer*, 13(3), March 1980.

[2] T. Arciszewski, M. Mustafa, and W. Ziarko. A methodology of design knowledge acquisition for use in learning expert systems. *International Journal of Man-Machine Studies*, 26, January 1987.

[3] N. Balram, W. P. Birmingham, S. Brady, D. P. Siewiorek, and R. Tremain. The MICON system for single board computer design. In *Proceedings of 1st Conference on Application of AI to Engineering Problems*. Computational Mechanics, April 1986.

[4] M. R. Barbacci and D. P. Siewiorek. Automated exploration of the design space for register transfer level systems. In *Proceedings of the 1st Annual International Symposium on Computer Architecture*, December 1973.

[5] A. Barr and E. A. Feigenbaum. *The Handbook of Artificial Intelligence, Volume I*. W. Kaufmann, Inc., 1981.

[6] C. G. Bell, J. C. Mudge, and J. E. McNamara. *Computer Engineering: A DEC view of hardware systems design*. Digital Press, 1978.

[7] W. P. Birmingham. MICON: A knowledge-based single board computer designer. Technical Report CMUCAD-83-21, ECE Department, Carnegie Mellon University, November 1983. Master's thesis.

[8]   W. P. Birmingham. Automated knowledge acquisition for a hierarchical synthesis system. Technical Report EDRC-02-07-88, EDRC, Carnegie Mellon University, 1988. PhD thesis. Also CMUCAD-88-25.

[9]   W. P. Birmingham, A. Kapoor, D. P. Siewiorek, and N. Vidovic. The design of an integrated environment for the automated synthesis of small computer systems. In *Proceedings of the Hawaii International Conference on System Sciences - 22*. IEEE Computer Society, January 1989.

[10] W. P. Birmingham and J. Kim. DAS/Logic: A rule-based logic design assistant. In *The Second Conference on AI Applications*. IEEE Computer Society, December 1985.

[11] W. P. Birmingham and G. Klinker. Building knowledge-acquisition tools. Technical Report CSE-TR-44-90, Electrical Engineering and Computer Science, University of Michigan, 1990.

[12] W. P. Birmingham and D. P. Siewiorek. MICON: A knowledge-based single board computer designer. In *Proceedings of the 21st Design Automation Conference*. IEEE Computer Society and ACM-SIGDA, IEEE Computer Society, 1984.

[13] W. P. Birmingham and D. P. Siewiorek. Single board computer synthesis. In Michael D. Rychener, editor, *Expert Systems for Engineering Design*. Academic Press, 1988.

[14] W. P. Birmingham and D. P. Siewiorek. Capturing designer expertise – the CGEN system. In *26th ACM/IEEE Design Automation Conference Proceedings*. IEEE Computer Society and ACM-SIGA, 1989.

[15] J. Boose. Personal construct theory and the transfer of human expertise. In *Proceedings of the 4th National Conference on Artificial Intelligence*. Austin, Texas, 1984.

[16] J. H. Boose and J. M. Bradshaw. Experise transfer and complex problems: Using AQUINAS as a knowledge-acquisition workbench for knowledge-based systems. *International Journal of Man-Machine Studies*, 26(1), January 1987.

[17] D. C. Bossen and M. Y. Hsiao. Model for transient and permanent error detection and fault-isolation coverage. *IBM Journal of Research and Development*, 26(1), 1982.

[18] R. K. Brayton, G. D. Hactel, C. T. McMullen, and A. Sangiovanni-Vincentelli. *ESPRESSO-IIC: Logic Minimization Algorithms for VLSI Synthesis*. Kluwer Academic Publishers, 1984.

[19] A. A. Brennan. Automatic synthesis for reliability. Technical Report CMUCAD-88-3, ECE Department, Carnegie Mellon University, January 1988. Master's thesis.

[20] F. D. Brewer and D. D. Gajski. An expert-system paradigm for design. In *Proceedings of the 23rd Design Automation Conference*. IEEE Computer Society, 1986.

[21] F. D. Brewer and D. D. Gajski. Knowledge-based control in micro-architecture design. In *Proceedings of the 24th Design Automation Conference*. IEEE Computer Society, 1987.

[22] David C. Brown and B. Chandrasekaran. Knowledge and control for a mechanical design expert system. *Computer*, 19(7), July 1986.

[23] L. Brownston, R. Farrell, E. Kant, and N. Martin. *Programming Expert Systems in OPS5*. Addison-Wesley, 1985.

[24] Y. E. Cho. A subjective review of compaction. In *Proceedings of the 22nd Design Automation Conference*. IEEE Computer Society and ACM-SIGDA, 1985.

[25] E. Clune and E. Czeck. *STARS Simulator Manual*. ECE Department, Carnegie Mellon University, 1987.

[26] Intel Corporation. *Intel Microprocessor and Peripheral Handbook, Volume I*, 1987.

[27] Intel Corporation. *Intel Microprocessor and Peripheral Handbook, Volume II*, 1987.

[28] A. Daga. Failure handling in the MICON system. Master's thesis, EECS Department, CSE Division, University of Michigan, December 1989.

[29] A. Daga and W. P. Birmingham. Failure recovery in the MICON system. In *Proceedings of the 27th Design Automation Conference*. IEEE Computer Society and ACM-SIGDA, 1990.

[30] J. A. Darringer, W. H. Joyner, Jr., C. L. Berman, and L. Trevillyan. Logic synthesis through local transformations. *IBM Journal of Research and Development*, 25(4), July 1981.

[31] R. Davis. Interactive transfer of expertise: Acquisition of new inference rules. In B. Webber and N. Nilson, editors, *Readings in Artificial Intelligence*. Tioga, 1981.

[32] R. Dechter and J. Pearl. Network-based heuristics for constraint-satisfaction problems. *Artificial Intelligence*, 34, 1987.

[33] R. Dechter and J. Pearl. Tree clustering for constraint networks. *Artificial Intelligence*, 38, 1989.

[34] T. G. Dietterich. Learning and inductive inference. In P.R. Cohen and E.A. Feigenbaum, editors, *The Handbook of Artificial Intelligence*. Morgan Kaufmann, 1982.

[35] S. W. Director, A. C. Parker, D. P. Siewiorek, and D. E. Thomas. A design methodology and computer aids for digital VLSI systems. *IEEE Transactions on Circuits and Systems*, CAS-28(7), 1981.

[36] A. E. Dunlop. Slip: Symbolic layout of integrated circuits with compaction. *Computer-Aided Design*, November 1978.

[37] P. Edmond, A. P. Gupta, D. P. Siewiorek, and A. A. Brennan. ASSURE: Automated design for dependability. In *Proceedings of the 27th Design Automation Conference*. IEEE Computer Society and ACM-SIGDA, 1990.

[38] E.J. McCluskey, Jr. Minimization of boolean functions. *Bell Systems Technical Journal*, 35(6), 1956.

[39] S. A. Elkind. *Lambda: A MIL-217D System Failure Rate Analysis Program User's Manual*. ECE Department, Carnegie Mellon University, 1983.

[40] S. A. Elkind. *SEC Version 3.3 User's Manual*. ECE Department, Carnegie Mellon University, 1983.

[41] S. A. Elkind. *MARK1 Markov Model Simulator User's Manual*. ECE Department, Carnegie Mellon University, 1986.

[42] L. Eshelman, D. Ehret, J. McDermott, and M. Tan. Mole: a tenacious knowledge-acquisition tool. *International Journal of Man-Machine Studies*, 26, January 1987.

[43] E.A. Feigenbaum. Knowledge engineering: the applied side of artificial intelligence. *Annals of the New York Academy of Sciences*, 246, 1984.

[44] R. Fikes, P. Hart, and N. Nilsson. Learning and executing generalized robot plans. *Artificial Intelligence*, 3(4), 1972.

[45] R. Fikes and N. Nilsson. Strips: A new approach to the application of theorem proving to problem solving. *Artificial Intelligence*, 2, 1971.

[46] A. Fitzsimmons and T. Love. A review and evaluation of software science. *Computing Surveys*, 10(1), March 1978.

[47] C. L. Forgy. OPS5 User's manual. Technical Report CMU-CS-81-135, Department of Computer Science, Carnegie Mellon University, 1981.

[48] C. L. Forgy. The ops83 report. Technical Report CMU-CS-84-133, Carnegie Mellon University Deparment of Computer Science, May 1984.

[49] R. J. Francis, J. Rose, and K. Chung. Chortle: A technology mapping program for lookup table-based field programmable gate arrays. In *Proceedings of the 27th Design Automation Conference*. IEEE Computer Society and ACM-SIGDA, 1990.

[50] D. Gajski, editor. *Silicon Compilation*. Addison-Wesley, 1988.

[51] D. D. Gajski and R. H. Kuhn. Guest editors' introduction: New VLSI tools. *Computer*, 16(12), December 1983.

[52] R. Giest and K. Trivedi. Ultra high reliability prediction for fault tolerant computer systems. *IEEE Transactions on Computers*, C-32, December 1983.

[53] D. Giuse, D. P. Siewiorek, and W. P. Birmingham. DEMETER: A design methodology and environment. In *ICCD*. IEEE Computer Society, October 1983. Also tech report CMUCAD-83-14.

[54] P. Goel. An implicit enumeration algorithm to generate test for combinational logic circuits. *IEEE Transaction on Computers*, 30(3), 1981.

[55] A. Goyal, W. C. Carter, E. de Souza e Silva, S. S. Lavenberg, and K. S. Trivedi. The system availability estimator. In *FTCS-16 Digest of Papers*, 1986.

[56] D. Gregory, K. Barlett, A. de Geus, and G. Hachtel. SOCRATES: A system for automatically synthesizing and optimizing combinational logic. In *Proceedings of the 23rd Design Automation Conference*. IEEE Computer Society, 1986.

[57] T. Gruber and P. Cohen. Design for acquisition: principles of knowledge system design to facilitate knowledge acquisition. Technical Report COINS Tech. Rep. 86-21, Experimental Knowledge Systems Laboratory, Computer and Information Science Department, University of Massachusetts at Amherst, 1986.

[58] A. P. Gupta. A hierarchical problem solving architecture for design synthesis of single board computers. Technical Report CMUCAD-88-5, ECE Department, Carnegie Mellon University, February 1988. Master's thesis.

[59] A. P. Gupta. Timing verification in system-level synthesis. PhD thesis proposal, May 1990.

[60] A. P. Gupta and D. P. Siewiorek. M1: A small computer system synthesis tool. In *6th IEEE Conference on AI Applications Proceedings*, 1990.

[61] M. H. Halstead. *Elements of Software Science*. Elsevier North-Holland, 1977.

[62] R. Harjani, R. Rutenbar, and L. R. Carley. A prototype for knowledge-based analog circuit synthesis. In *Proceedings of the 24th Design Automation Conference*. IEEE Computer Society, 1987.

[63] D. Haworth. Private communication. 1989.

[64] D. Haworth. ADEFT: automated design for testability. Master's thesis, EECS Department, CSE Division, University of Michigan, August 1991.

[65] D. Haworth and W. P. Birmingham. ADEFT: automated design for testability. In *University programs in computer aided engineering, design, and manufacturing.* , College of Engineering, University of Michigan, August 1990.

[66] F. Hayes-Roth, D. A. Waterman, and D. B. Lenat. *Building Expert Systems*. Addison-Wesley, 1983.

[67] Production Systems Technology Incorporated. *OPS/83 User's Manual and Report Version 2.2*, 1986.

[68] Dave Johannsen. Bristel blocks: A silicon compiler. In *Proceedings of the 16th Design Automation Conference*. IEEE and ACM-SIGDA, June 1979.

[69] R. Joobbani and D. P. Siewiorek. Weaver: A knowledge-based routing expert. In *Proceedings of the 22nd Design Automation Conference*, 1985.

[70] G. Kahn, S. Nowlan, and J. McDermott. More: an intelligent knowledge acquisition tool. In *Proceedings of 9th International Conference on Artificial Intelligence*. Los Angeles, California, 1985.

[71] A. Kapoor. The design of an integrated environment for the automated synthesis of small computer systems. Master's thesis, ECE Department., Carnegie Mellon University, March 1990.

[72] K. Keutzer. Dagon: Technology binding and local optimization by DAG matching. In *Proceedings of the 24th Design Automation Conference.* IEEE Computer Society, 1987.

[73] V. Kini and D. P. Siewiorek. Automatic generation of symbolic reliability functions for processor-memory switch structures. *IEEE Transactions on Computers*, C-31, August 1982.

[74] G. Klinker, J. Bentolila, S. Genetet, M. Grimes, and J. McDermott. KNACK – report-driven knowledge acquisition. *International Journal of Man-Machine Studies*, 26, January 1987.

[75] T. J. Kowalski. *An Artificial Intelligence Approach to VLSI Design.* Kluwer Academic Press, 1985.

[76] N. A. Langrana, T. M. Mitchell, and N. Ramachandran. Progress toward a knowledge-based aid for mechanical design. In *Symposium on Integrated and Intelligent Manufacturing.* ASME, 1986.

[77] J. C. Laprie and A. Costes. Dependability: A unifying concept for reliable computing. In *FTCS-12 Digest of Papers*, 1982.

[78] C. Y. Lee. An algorithm for path connections and its application. *IRE Transactions on Electronic Computers*, EC-10(3), 1961.

[79] D. Lenat, M. Prakash, and M. Shepard. Cyc: Using common sense knowledge to overcome brittleness and knowledge acquisition bottle-necks. *AI Magazine*, 6(4), April 1986.

[80] Y-L. S. Lin and D. D. Gajski. LES: a layout expert system. In *Proceedings of the 24th Design Automation Conference.* IEEE Computer Society, 1987.

[81] M. L. Maher and P. Longinos. Development of an expert system shell for engineering design. *International Journal of AI for Engineering*, Summer 1987.

[82] M.L. Maher and S.J. Fenves. HI-RISE : An expert system for the preliminary structural design of high rise buildings. In John S. Gero, editor, *Knowledge Engineering in Computer-Aided Design*, 1984.

[83] S. V. Makam, A. Avizienis, and G. Grusas. ARIES 82 Users' guide. Technical report, University of California, Aug. 1982.

[84] S. Marcus. Introduction. In S. Marcus, editor, *Automating Knowledge Acquisition for Expert Systems.* Kluwer Academic Publishers, 1988.

[85] S. Marcus. Salt: A knowledge-acquisition tool for propose-and-revise systems. In S. Marcus, editor, *Automating Knowledge Acquisition for Expert Systems*. Kluwer Academic Publishers, August 1988.

[86] S. Marcus, J. Stout, and J. McDermott. VT: An expert elevator designer that uses knowledge-based backtracking. *AI Magazine*, Summer 1988.

[87] J. McDermott. Domain knowledge and the design process. In *Proceedings of the 18th Design Automation Conference*. IEEE Computer Society, 1981.

[88] J. McDermott. R1: A rule-based configurer of computer systems. *Artificial Intelligence*, 19(2), 1982.

[89] J. McDermott. Preliminary steps toward a taxonomy of problem-solving methods. In S. Marcus, editor, *Automating Knowledge Acquisition for Expert Systems*. Kluwer Academic Publishers, August 1988.

[90] M. C. McFarland, A. C. Parker, and R. Camposano. Tutorial on high-level synthesis. In *Proceedings of the 25th Design Automation Conference*. IEEE Computer Society, 1988.

[91] T. McWilliams and L. Widdoes Jr. SCALD: Structured computer-aided logic design. In *Proceedings of the 15th Design Automation Conference*. IEEE Computer Society and ACM-SIGDA, 1978.

[92] T. M. Mitchell, S. Mahadevan, and L. Steinberg. Leap: A learning apprentice for VLSI design. In *Proceedings of IJCAI-85*. Morgan Kaufmann Publishers, 1985.

[93] T. M. Mitchell, L. I. Steinberg, and J. S. Shulman. A knowledge-based approach to design. *IEEE Transactions on Pattern Analysis and Machine Intelligence*, PAMI-7(5), September 1985.

[94] S. Mittal, C. L. Dym, and M. Morjaria. PRIDE: An expert system for the design of paper handling systems. *IEEE Computer*, 19(7), July 1986.

[95] S. Mittal and F. Frayman. Towards a generic model of configuration tasks. In *Proceedings of IJCAI-89*. Morgan Kaufmann Publishers, 1989.

[96] R. Murgai, Y. Nishizaki, N. Shenoy, R. K. Brayton, and A. Sangiovanni-Vincentelli. Logic synthesis for programmable gate arrays. In *Proceedings of the 27th Design Automation Conference*. IEEE Computer Society and ACM-SIGDA, 1990.

[97] K. S. Murray and B. W. Porter. Developing a tool for knowledge integration: Initial results. In *Proceedings from the 3rd AAAI Knowledge Acquisition for Knowledge-Based Systems Workshop*. AAAI, 1988.

[98] M. Musen. *Automated Generation of Model-Based Knowledge Acquisition Tools*. Pitman, 1989.

[99] M. A. Musen, L. M. Fagan, D. M. Combs, and E. H. Shortliffe. Use of domain model to drive an interactive knowledge-editing tool. *International Journal of Man-Machine Studies*, 26(1), January 1987.

[100] D. L. Ostapko. On deriving a relation between circuits and input/output by analyzing an equivalent program. *SIGPLAN Notices*, June 1974.

[101] N. Park and A. C. Parker. SEHWA: A software package for synthesis of pipelines from behavioral specifications. *IEEE Transactions on Computer-Aided Design*, CAD-7(3), 1988.

[102] A. C. Parker, J. T. Pizarro, and M. Mlinar. Maha: A program for datapath synthesis. In *Proceedings of the 23rd Design Automation Conference*. IEEE Computer Society, 1986.

[103] B. T. Preas and P. G. Karger. Automatic placement: A review of current techniques. In *Proceedings of the 23rd Design Automation Conference*. IEEE Computer Society and ACM-SIGDA, 1986.

[104] J. Rehg, A. Elfes, S. Talukdar, R. Woodbury, M. Eisenberger, and R. Edahl. *Expert Systems for Engineering Design*, chapter Design System Integration in CASE. Academic Press, 1988.

[105] J. P. Roth. Diagnosis of automata failures: A calculus and a method. *IBM Journal of Research and Development*, Oct. 1966.

[106] F. Rubin. The lee path connection algorithm. *IEEE Trans. on Computers*, c-23(9), 1974.

[107] D. G. Schweikert and B. W.Kernighan. A proper model for the partitioning of electrical circuits. In *Proceedings of the 9th Design Automation Conference*. IEEE Computer Society and ACM-SIGDA, 1972.

[108] C. Sechen. The Timberwolf macro/custom cell placement and chip-planning program. Technical report, Unversity of California, Berkeley, 1985.

[109] Motorola Semiconductors. *Motorola Microprocessor Data Manual*, 1981.

[110] Motorola Semiconductors. Mc68008 data sheet, 1985.

[111] Motorola Semiconductors. Mc68010 data sheet, 1985.

[112] M. L. G. Shaw and B. R. Gaines. Techniques for knowledge acquisition and transfer. *International Journal of Man-Machine Studies*, 27(3), 1987.

[113] D. P. Siewiorek, D. Giuse, W. P. Birmingham, M. Hirsch, V. Rao, and G. York. DEMETER project: Phase 1 (1984). Technical Report CMUCAD-84-35, ECE Dept., Carnegie Mellon University, 1984.

[114] D. P. Siewiorek and R. Swarz. *The Theory and Practice of Reliable System Design*. Digital Press, 1982.

[115] H. A. Simon. *The Sciences of the Artificial*. The MIT Press, 1969.

[116] E. Snow. *Automation of Module Set Independent Register-Transfer Level Design*. PhD thesis, ECE Department, Carnegie Mellon University, 1978.

[117] E. Soloway, J. Bachant, and K. Jensen. Assessing the maintainability of XCON-RIME: Coping with the problems of a VERY large rule-base. In *Proceedings of AAAI-87*. Morgan Kaufmann Publishers, 1987.

[118] J. R. Southard. Macpitts: An approach to silicon compilation. *IEEE Computer*, 16(12), December 1983.

[119] R. M. Stallman and G. J. Sussman. Forward reasoning and dependency-directed backtracking in a system for computer-aided circuit analysis. *Artificial Intelligence*, 9, 1977.

[120] M. Stefik. Planning with constraints (MOLGEN: Part I). *Artificial Intelligence*, 16, 1981.

[121] L. I. Steinberg. Design as refinement plus constraint propagation: The VEXED experience. In *Proceedings of AAAI-87*. Morgan Kaufmann Publishers, 1987.

[122] J. J. Stiffler, L. A. Bryant, and L. J. Guccione. CARE III final report. Technical report, Raytheon Co., November 1979.

[123] G. J. Sussman. Electrical design : A problem for artificial intelligence research. In *Proceedings of the International Joint Conference on Artificial Intelligence*, 1980.

[124] G. J. Sussman and J. Steele. Constraints: A language for expressing almost-hierarchical descriptions. *Artificial Intelligence*, 14, 1980.

[125] S. A. Szygenda. TEGAS2- anatomy of a general purpose test generation and simulation system for digital logic. In *Proceedings of the 9th Design Automation Conference*, 1972.

[126] D. E. Thomas, C. Y. Hitchcock III, T. J. Kowalski, J. V. Rajan, and R. A. Walker. Automatic data path synthesis. *IEEE Computer*, 16(12), December 1983.

[127] D. E. Thomas, E. M. Dirkes, R. A. Walker, J. V. Rajan, J. A. Nestor, and R. L. Blackburn. The system architect's workbench. In *Proceedings of the 25th Design Automation Conference*. IEEE Computer Society, 1988.

[128] C. Tong. Toward an engineering science of knowledge-based design. *International Journal of AI for Engineering*, 2(3), July 1987.

[129] L. Trevillyan. An overview of logic synthesis systems. In *24th Design Automation Conference*. IEEE Computer Society and ACM-SIGDA, 1987.

[130] Chia-Jeng Tseng and Daniel P. Siewiorek. Facet : A procedure for the automated synthesis of digital systems. In *Proceedings of the 20th Design Automation Conference*. IEEE and ACM-SIGDA, IEEE Computer Society, 1983.

[131] U.S. Department of Defense, Rome Air Development Center, NY. *Military Standardization Handbook: Reliability Prediction of Electronic Equipment*, MIL-HDBK-217D edition, 1982.

[132] A. van de Brug, J. Bachant, and J. McDermott. The taming of R1. *IEEE Expert*, 1(3), 1986.

[133] R. A. Walker and D. E. Thomas. A model of design representation and synthesis. In *Proceedings of the 22nd Design Automation Conference*. IEEE Computer Society and ACM-SIGDA, 1985.

[134] C. Westphal and K. McGraw. Special issue on knowledge acquisition. *ACM SIGART*, (108), April 1989.

Index